TRUE FAMILY AND WORLD PEACE

Reverend and Mrs. Sun Myung Moon

Distributed by:
HSA Publications
4 West 43rd Street, New York, NY 10036
www.hsabooks.com

ISBN: 1-931166-01-3

Reverend and Mrs. Sun Myung Moon

TRUE FAMILY AND WORLD PEACE

Section 1
The Proclamation of True Parents

Section 2
The Proclamation of the Completed Testament Age

Section 3
True Family

Foreword

The following collection of major speeches was given by Reverend Dr. Sun Myung Moon and Dr. Hak Ja Han Moon, worldwide religious leaders and torch bearers of world peace, during their numerous public speaking tours since 1990.

Since being called by God at the age of 16, Reverend Moon has been totally dedicated to the establishment of God's Kingdom. His lifetime motto for education has been: "Love God, Love People, Love the Nation," and his lifetime mottos for practicing this ideal have been: "Live for the sake of others" and "Love your enemy."

As the founders of the Family Federation for World Peace and Unification, Reverend and Mrs. Moon's scope has always been inter-religious, interdenominational and interracial. Thus during his lifetime, they already have followers throughout 185 nations in the world. Although they are spiritual leaders, their activities for the fulfillment of world peace transcend the religious arena to cover the fields of academia, the arts, sports, mass media, technology, business, the environment and philosophical thought as well.

Overriding and guiding all these endeavors, however, is Reverend Moon's prayer life. Whether he is on the mountaintop or on the ocean, he prays day and night. He prays to comfort the lamenting heart of God, who lost His children due to the fall of Adam and Eve. He also prays to love all human beings who, having lost their original Parent, wander like the prodigal son. Through his communication with Jesus and other saints and sages in the spirit world, he discovered that God is in tears, pain and suffering. Therefore, his lifelong mission has been to bring God back to His original throne of honor and glory.

Reverend and Mrs. Moon are also a couple who embody God's Word. As long as Reverend Moon has one person to speak to, he totally invests himself to convey God's heart and truth, sleeping only a few hours a day. He has spoken approximately 7,000 times to the public, and his words have been published in 330 volumes. He has traveled extensively throughout the world, including Russia and even North Korea.

Reverend Moon selected landmark speeches delivered over the past ten years, for this book. The overall theme is "World Peace Through Ideal Families."

In this year of 2001, with Reverend Moon having just turned 81, he is about to embark upon a speaking tour of all 50 states. We publish this book in order to share God's message with all Americans. May it enable all of us, from new friend to longtime follower, to better understand His providence and will for America at this time.

Dr. Chang Shik Yang
Continental Director of North America
The Family Federation for World Peace and Unification

The Proclamation of True Parents

Unification of the World and the Responsibility of Humankind

Mrs. Hak Ja Han Moon President, Women's Federation for World Peace
This address was given on April 10, 1992 at the founding rally of the Women's
Federation for World Peace, Seoul, Korea.

9/17/04

Distinguished guests, representatives of the Women's Federation for World Peace from seventy countries, women leaders and members of the Women's Federation for Peace in Asia: Let me first express my deep gratitude that such a tremendous crowd has gathered today for this grand occasion: the establishment of the Women's Federation for World Peace and the Seoul Rally of the Women's Federation for Peace in Asia. By your presence, you bring many blessings to our Federation's future, and inspire us to multiply our determination to achieve world peace.

This may be the first time that women have taken the initiative by bringing so many women together in one place. I am certain that from this day forward, women around the world will come to understand their noble role which has been ordained by God, and that a road will be opened for us to build an ideal world filled with peace, happiness and freedom. To mark this occasion, I would like to speak to you on the topic, "Unification of the World and the Responsibility of Humankind."

I want to deliver a declaration centered on the teachings of Reverend Moon, which are based on the heart of God that transcends past, present and future. My words today are a declaration before heaven and earth, with history as my witness. The words I am about to speak may seem unfamiliar to some of you, but they deal with the secrets of heaven that all women today need to understand.

History Began in a Diseased State

9/18/04

We live in a diseased world whose destruction is inevitable. Every day we hear the ugly sounds of its final death rattle. We can trace the origin of this disease to the original human ancestors, who lost their position in paradise. Our original ancestors contracted a serious disease. In religious terms, this event is referred to as the human fall. Thus history began in a diseased state. This disease and Satan have been the focus of human history.

The tragedy of human history was that it originated with Satan, the lord of evil, who stood in contra position to God's ideal of creation. The marriage of Adam and Eve resulted in the children of evil. Inevitably, humankind inherited Satan's love, Satan's life and Satan's lineage. The human reproductive organs, by which husband and wife are intended to join together in virtue, were originally intended to be temples of true love, true life and the true lineage. Love should be an experience in which a husband and wife join in a virtuous union

---

3

to procreate children who will carry on the lineage. The center of life is love, and the human lineage is transmitted by means of the love and life of a husband and wife. The linkage of love, life and lineage is what gives history its continuity.

After the fall, the human race has been held captive by satanic love, satanic life and a satanic lineage. Adam and Eve were in their youth when they sowed the seeds of false love, false life and the false lineage. Thus, when the Last Days come, we can expect the increase of moral decadence among young people to arise as a global phenomenon. In fact, we live in just such a time now.

Satan used fallen love as a condition to create a den of sin in which an eternal blow could be struck against God's ideal of true love. The relaxation of standards concerning sexual behavior, the increasing moral decadence of young people, the plague of drug addiction, and the decline of family structure and traditional values has turned this world into an earthly hell. Thus, it has become impossible to find a true man, true woman, true brothers and sisters, a true husband and wife or true parents anywhere. Until now, there could be no hope of creating a true society, true nation or true world.

Mankind Must Engraft onto God and True Parents 9/21/09

The world must understand that Satan exists and that he has brought about this reality we face today. With this knowledge, we can find the cause of the disease and uncover the origin of the human fall. We must reveal to the world that Satan, Adam and Eve formed a trinity of evil, and that it is up to us to restore the trinity of God, Adam and Eve that is in accordance with the ideal of creation.

For this issue to be resolved, someone must testify to the fact that Satan committed sin and clearly explain the fundamental truths concerning the sin committed by the original human ancestors. God and Satan have always known the details about the fall. There were many things that Adam did not understand, however, because he was still young at the time. In the Last Days, the restored and completed Adam will come and make all this information known. He will reveal the sins committed by Satan throughout the course of history. When he comes, it will be possible to expel Satan from this world. For the first time, humankind will be able to make a fundamental change in direction toward a world of hope, peace, happiness and freedom.

In order for humankind to make a total break from the false love, false life and false lineage that derive from Satan as their parent, it is necessary that we be grafted onto the true olive tree. That is, all people need to be grafted onto God and True Parents in order to recover true love, true life and the true lineage. This will make it possible for us to build heaven on earth as well as in the spiritual world. This, in fact, is the final purpose of God's providence of salvation, restoration and recreation.

Thus, the reappearance of the True Parents is an event of the greatest historic importance. The True Parents represent the conclusion and final fruit of human history. The True Parents embody the completed form of human cultural history. They signify the victory of religion and philosophy within history. Prior to the emergence of True Parents, however, there must be a period of restoration through indemnity, that is, a period of recreation.

God's Providential History of Restoration

9/22/04

I would like to speak for a while about this historical period, based on the biblical record, to illustrate the difficulties. By understanding this, we can understand how important it is that we fulfill our responsibility today.

In the record of the Old Testament, history was a course of indemnification, eye for eye, tooth for tooth and life for life. The responsibility of the fall passed from Eve to Adam, with Satan at the center. As seen from the standpoint of Eve after she had received the seed of false life, the fall occurred when Satan took over God's position as Eve's father and became one with her to bear Adam. In the course of the fall, Eve placed the archangel in the position of her father and Adam in the position of her son. Consequently, women, who in the course of the history of restoration through indemnity have come to stand in the position of Eve, have had to risk their lives, if necessary, in order to assure that God's will is passed on to the next generation.

When we study the historical record in the Bible, we come across a number of events that seem to defy explanation. God's original intention in His creation was that Eve would become one with God, her Father, and with God's son, Adam. As a result of the fall, however, she became one with Satan and Adam, the false son. Immediately after the fall, God began working through the family of Adam in order to undo what had been done, that is, to accomplish restoration through indemnity by the reverse course. He worked with Adam's family, because even the fall had not deprived the members of this family of the element of eternity with which they had been endowed at their creation.

Cain, the first fruit of the love by which Satan took Eve, was conceded to the side of Satan, and Abel, who was born as the second fruit of the love with her husband Adam, was placed on the side of heaven. This was the beginning of the history of the struggle between good and evil aimed at fundamental restoration through indemnity.

It was necessary in history that the second son be blessed so that the second son realm of heaven could restore and claim the birthright of the first son held by Satan. For example, Cain and Abel made offerings to God simultaneously, but God received only the offering of Abel, the second son, while refusing the offering of Cain. The reason for this was that the second son on heaven's side should restore the birthright from the first son.

Had Cain made his offering through Abel, an orderly path could have been established from God to Adam and to the archangel, and restoration could have been accomplished. Because Cain killed Abel, however, heaven established Seth and extended the providence to his descendants.

Cain and Abel were brothers who had been born into this world. Because of their failure to accomplish God's will in their position outside their mother's womb, God's next dispensation had to be carried out within the maternal womb.

Thus, when Rebecca asked God why it was that Esau and Jacob fought within her womb, God said to her: "Two nations are in your womb, . . . the older shall serve the younger." (Genesis 25:23) From that time, Rebecca came to take greater care of the second son, Jacob.

Jacob, as the second son, had to restore through indemnity the birthright of his brother Esau. For this to be successful, Rebecca needed to fulfill her responsibility in the position of Eve.

The blow struck at the firstborn of Egypt during the course of the Israelites' Exodus from Egypt and Jacob's switching of his hands over Joseph's sons Manasseh and Ephraim at the time of their blessing (Genesis 48) all contained the hidden will of heaven to bring about a reversal of the realms of first and second born.

God's Providence to Send the Messiah

In her fall, Eve deceived God, her Father, and Adam, who was in the position of her son. To restore this, Rebecca stood on the side of heaven and deceived the father Isaac and her son Esau so that Jacob could receive Isaac's blessing. Jacob purchased the birthright of the firstborn, and initiated the lineage of the Israelites on the foundation of a victory won through the cooperation of a mother and her son. He conditionally claimed the first-son realm and the second-son realm for the side of heaven, and established the foundation of victory for the Israelite nation that was to descend from him.

Jacob, however, was more than forty years old at the time that he took full control over the birthright of the firstborn. Thus, the realm of the human age prior to forty was still left without the condition of having won victory over Satan. Once again, therefore, a dispensation was carried out for the purpose of gaining victory in the womb. Tamar, the daughter-in-law of Judah, had in her womb the twin sons Zerah and Perez. Although Perez was the younger, he pushed his brother Zerah aside in order to be born first. In fact, the name "Perez" is derived from this event. (Genesis 38)

At the beginning of history, the lineage of Satan was planted in the maternal womb. With Tamar, the womb was restored to the side of God. The side of heaven took control over the first-son realm and the second-son realm so that God's original lineage could be established. It was in this way that the tribe of Judah came to form the foundation on which the Messiah would later be born.

As a woman, Tamar placed herself in the position of having deceived father and son; she denied her father-in-law and his sons, in order to separate the position of Eve from Satan. As a result of Tamar's separation of the womb from Satan, a basic tradition was established whereby God's children could be conceived and given birth without Satan's invasion. It was then up to the Israelites and Judaism to carry on this standard of victory in the womb until such time that the Messiah could be sent as the True Parents. Because Satan had already been able to establish his nations in the world, the sending of the Messiah had to wait until such time that the Israelites could establish a national base sufficient for indemnifying the other nations of the world.

God waited nearly 2,000 years until there was a sufficient national foundation, and a woman who could stand in the position of Eve, for Him to carry out His providence. This finally took place through Mary, the mother of Jesus. When Adam and Eve committed the fall, they were already engaged to be married at a later date. In the same way, Mary and Joseph were betrothed to each other centered on God. As with Rebecca and Tamar, Mary was a revolutionary woman called by God to take part in the process of recreating Adam.

Mary risked her life to form an absolute unity with God, and placed herself in the position of having deceived father and son in order to accomplish the history of restoration through indemnity. It was in this manner that Jesus was conceived. During the time that Jesus was in Mary's womb, Satan could make no invasion in terms of his lineage. Jesus was born of the womb of a victorious woman as the first fruit of the first love who could be claimed only by God. It was the first time in history that a child was born as God's only begotten son.

Even among the saints, there exists no one else whose birth followed such a process for making a separation from the satanic lineage. Thus, we refer to Jesus as a saint among saints. This was the reason that the Christian cultural sphere was able to spread throughout the world. Finally, in our century, God has worked to use the victory of the Second World War and the Christian cultural sphere to accomplish the unification of the world.

The Pioneering Road of the True Parents   7/24/06

The Second World War had a particular significance in the context of God's providence. In this war, the results that the fall had on the brothers Cain and Abel, who were born of Eve, was manifested on a global scale. Thus, the island nation of Britain stood in the position of Eve. The United States, a nation historically "given birth" by Britain, stood in the position of Abel. France stood in the position of Cain holding the birthright of the firstborn. These three countries formed an alliance led by the United States. On the other side, the satanic Eve country Japan, the satanic Adam country Germany, and the satanic archangelic country Italy formed the Axis Powers. It was God's plan to establish a unified world on the basis of the total victory of the Allied Powers, who had been placed on the side of heaven.

God's fervent hope for the post-war world was that God and the True Parents, who are the Adam who brings true love, could form a central point around which humankind could make a quick separation from the false seed inherited from the false parent. Humanity could then make a new beginning by connecting to the True Parents' original true love, true life and true lineage. In this way, the world would inherit the seed of true love.

Opposition from Christianity, however, forced the True Parents into the wilderness. As a result, the course of indemnity built up through the 4,000-year history of Israel was lost. It became necessary for the True Parents to go a single-generation, forty-year course of indemnification in order to bring God's will to completion.

The Lord of the Second Advent comes as the third Adam. He brings with him the contents of the secrets of heaven and completes a course of indemnification of the satanic side on the level of individual, family, nation and world. He makes total indemnity for Adam's misdeed and the mission that Jesus left uncompleted.

In this way, the third Adam must take the fall committed by the first Adam on the family level, and restore it through indemnity on the worldwide level. He then must complete the victory by restoring the entire world through indemnity.

The Lord of the Second Advent Fulfills the Highest Victory   9/25/06

The Reverend Sun Myung Moon, founder of the Unification Church, and I, his wife, Hak Ja Han Moon, standing in the position of the True Parents, have borne upon ourselves all the historical conditions of invasion from the satanic side. In a state of unity with God, we have walked the course of worldwide indemnity so that all of humanity may be liberated from their bondage. In contrast with Jesus, the True Parents are given the historic calling to climb over the Hill of Calvary without succumbing to physical death. It has been the fate of the True Parents to go this pioneering course.

Two thousand years ago, the mind-body split of the world could have been bound together in unity if only Judaism, in the position of Abel, and the nation of Israel, in the position of Cain, had become one for the purpose of attending Jesus. On this foundation, and centering on Jesus' true love, the Israelites could have been grafted onto the true lineage and been reborn as the nation holding the birthright on a worldwide level.

The Israelites took great pride in the knowledge that they were God's chosen people, but they failed, at least at that time, to comprehend the will of God for worldwide salvation centering on Jesus the Messiah. They only believed that when the Messiah came the whole world would bow down to the Kingdom of Israel. They did not realize that God's Will was not to limit salvation to the individual, family or national levels, but to bring it to the entire world. Today, Christianity faces a similar situation.

For the entire period of his 33-year life on earth, Jesus invested every last ounce of his energy into the mission for national restoration. Finally, he was forced to leave it unaccomplished. In order to complete this mission, God, in the twentieth century, has established the United States, which has become the central Christian nation, in the position of a second Israel. The United States and Christianity are called at the time of the Second Advent to stand in the positions of Cain and Abel, respectively, in order to re-indemnify the failure of the first Israel, that is, the nation of Israel and Judaism of Jesus' time. It is up to the United States and Christianity now to accomplish restoration through indemnity and complete the work of unification.

As a result of Jesus' death on the cross, not only was the mission that should have been accomplished during the time of Jesus left uncompleted, but also the nation of Israel itself was lost. For this reason, the Christian Church sought to establish itself as a spiritual nation during the course of its history.

In the time of the Second Advent, it is necessary to re-indemnify the failures of Israel. To do this, the Messiah of the Second Advent must be able to achieve victory at the highest point in the world.

The biblical record of Jesus' trial and crucifixion contains references to three criminals: the two thieves who were crucified along with Jesus on his left and right, and the notorious prisoner Barabbas. These three represent three ideologies that came into being as a result of Israel's failure on earth. At the time of the Second Coming, the three paradigms can be identified as Christianity in the position of the thief on the right, communism in the position of the thief on the left and Islam in the position of Barabbas.

As he now achieves his Second Advent, Jesus is responsible for binding the left and right together to give them a common direction and then add the Islamic realm as well. He should make restoration through indemnity so that all things are resolved in a common direction. He comes with the crucially important mission to have all humanity, now speeding toward hell, turn 180 degrees toward heaven.

Jesus of the Second Advent, who has come in the position of the True Parents of humankind, has devoted immeasurable effort to gather together the entire spirit world and realign the nations of this world, centering on Christianity, so that God's foundation of victory can be reformulated on a worldwide level.

World Peace Centered on the True Parents

Centered on Christianity, however, Britain, the United States and France opposed the True Parents. Therefore, heaven had the Unification Church prepared to take the place of Christianity. Through the Unification Church, it became possible for the True Parents to pass over the mountain of tribulation. Here, they were opposed not only by the communist world standing on the satanic side, but also the Christian countries and the entire world. Finally, now, they have come to the point where the side of heaven can claim and welcome the satanic side. Today, Korea, Japan, the United States and Germany now emerge in the world as countries able to receive True Parents. God has been able to carry out His history of indemnity centering on these countries.

In the context of the worldwide dispensation of the True Parents, Korea has been placed in the position of the Adam country, Japan in the position of the Eve country, the United States in the position of the Abel country and Germany in the position of the Cain country. Japan was once an enemy country of the True Parents, the United States and Japan were once enemies, and Germany was once an enemy of the United States.

True Parents, in order to fulfill what Christianity in the United States failed to accomplish after the Second World War, have fostered cooperation among these four countries at the center of the providence and walked a 21-year course of re-indemnification. Through their success, they have established the realm of victory.

The Unification Church, which has victoriously crossed over the Hill of Calvary on the individual, family, national, world and cosmic levels, has given the United States a new sense of direction. It has given new hope to Christianity, and is resolving the issues related to the communist and Islamic worlds.

On the Korean peninsula, the Jacob and Esau of the twentieth century confront each other in the form of the two Koreas. The True Parents working with true love in this conflict, with Kim Il Sung in the position of the false parent, have restored through indemnity the realm of the victorious parent. Through this process, Korea is established as the third Israel that has accomplished history's ultimate victory and becomes the chosen nation of the new unified world.

Korea, as the third Israel, is the base from which the True Parents and their children are able to accomplish their fervent hope for a unified world of peace. It holds a central position for building heaven on earth and in the spirit world.

It should be understood that, from the providential standpoint, the great prosperity experienced by Korea, Japan, the United States and Germany in the post-war period has been due to the fact that these countries received God's blessing, with Korea as Adam, Japan as Eve, the United States as Abel and Germany as Cain.

The Age of Women

In the Garden of Eden at the time the fall was committed, the archangel was with Adam and Eve. In this age, when the seed planted then on the level of the individual is bearing its fruit on the worldwide level, the Adam country of Korea has as its neighbor the Eve country of Japan and three archangel countries—the United States, China and Russia—who vie for advantages on the Korean peninsula. With the protection of God, however, these countries are developing an alliance among themselves centered on Korea. Though Jesus was not able in his time to bring about a unification of the nations of Asia, today we are seeing the fulfillment of the will of God on a worldwide level.

Similarly, the significance of the coming of the Asian-Pacific cultural sphere is that a worldly sphere of material and spirit, such as what Jesus sought to accomplish in his time, is now being constructed in Asia. In other words, the countries of Asia must now establish a unified world centered on the True Parents.

Now is the time to attend the True Father, who has established the victorious tradition in world history, and the True Mother, the global representative of women who has gained victory as the representative woman in history. By doing so, we must establish not only a true concept of manhood, but also the true concept of what it means to be a mother, a wife and a daughter, in the context of a new society, nation and world, and become forerunners in inheriting the tradition of the True Parents and harvesting the victory.

We women have the mission to give proper guidance to men who lead lives of moral decadence and disorder so that the tragedy of the destruction of Adam and Eve may be resolved within the context of history.

Beloved women members, today's rally is being held by the Women's Federation for Peace in Asia for the important purpose of establishing the Women's Federation for World Peace. In the age of women that is now dawning, our members must embrace our husbands and properly educate our children so that we may be a model movement for practicing true love throughout the world. We must gain the active cooperation of our husbands and children for the development of the Women's Federation for World Peace.

Our women's movement is not for women alone. First, a movement of true love for our husbands and children must bear fruit in ideal families. The ideal families formed in this manner will come together to form ideal nations and an ideal world. For this reason, the Women's Federation for World Peace must someday develop into a Family Federation for World Peace.

For the sake of world peace, we women must take the lead in government, finance, culture and society. The basic values we should uphold in this federation of women are found in Headwing philosophy and Godism. These values are what unite left and right and overcome atheistic materialism. They are certain to be the guiding ideas of the world of the 21st century.

As women, let us remember our forbearers, Rebecca, Tamar and Mary, who fulfilled major responsibilities in the history of God's salvation providence. Let us inherit the strength of will by which these historic women overcame life-threatening dangers and difficulties. Let us establish our families as homes for true parents, true husbands and wives and true children, so that we may join in the holy cause of changing this world of evil into a heavenly world. Let us march forward toward a world of peace centered on the True Parents, who are the center of true love.

I pray God's blessing may be upon you, your families and this beautiful world.

Thank you.

Women Who Will Take the Leading Role in the Ideal World

Mrs. Hak Ja Han Moon, President, Women's Federation for World Peace
This address was given on June 10, 1992 at the first Nationwide Rally of the Women's Federation for World Peace, Seoul, Korea.

Distinguished guests and members of the Women's Federation for World Peace:

I am very honored that I can share my beliefs about world peace with such a tremendous gathering of women leaders from every level of society. The title of my address today is "Women Who Will Take the Leading Role in the Ideal World."

We are now entering the pivotal age for the creation of one world. The time in which we are living is the age where humanity has started to go beyond the barriers of ideology and language, the differences between cultures and the conflicts between races.

It is the cherished desire of humankind for all war, oppression and exploitation to be banished forever from this world, leaving only the promised future of true freedom, peace and prosperity.

All the while, my husband, the Reverend Sun Myung Moon, has advocated the ideology of Godism and has overcome strong opposition and persecution from those individuals who have relied on strength alone. In the past he played the deciding role in opening the door to leave behind the age of the Cold War. Today in this historical age of transition where conciliation and cooperation are sought, I am presenting Godism to be the great principle and basis upon which we can build the eternal world of peace. I would like to stress again that the Headwing ideology of Godism proclaimed by Reverend Moon must be the principle followed by all women who will pioneer the future world.

To Possess God's Love

Originally God created an object of love in order to feel joy. Where does the heart of a sculptor, who is willing to invest his youth and work unceasingly day and night in order to create one masterpiece, come from? Doesn't it resemble the heart of God who created an object of love in order to feel joy?

If we look at the world, we can see that everything has an inherent duality. Minerals, plants, animals and people all exist in pairs. Do you know why everything exists in pairs? It is to be able to interact with each other. In the world of minerals, there is the action between the positive ions and the negative ions. If there is no common point between atoms, they will not join together. God also is unable to hand down His system if the reciprocal elements are not right. However, on the opposite side, if the reciprocal elements are right, then even God cannot prevent them from becoming one. Even though it is on a low level, the action in the world of minerals can become the ideal model of the love of creation.

So it is inevitable that centered on true love, God's heart and an individual's heart, the whole of creation and even animals will be able to communicate together. The problem is that you have not had such a relationship. If you go into the land of ideals, then the whole of creation is harmonious. In the land full of love and joy, if I laugh, then the whole of creation, including God, laughs in harmony.

Ladies and gentlemen! All of you have loving husbands and loving wives, don't you? How much do you love your spouse? If somebody offered you a billion won or ten billion won for your wife, would you sell her? Is there a wife who would exchange a truly loving husband, if she were offered heaven and earth? What it all comes down to is that man was born for woman, and woman was born for man. It is all because of true love, which always exists for others. God created woman and man as the harmonious yin and yang, so that they could realize the ideal of love. We can only find the unified true love through true man and woman. God and an individual as well become one through true love.

Marriage is such that, after a man and a woman join together horizontally through absolute true love, they try to possess God's vertical, absolute true love. The absolute God set up true love in the highest position as the center of absolute true value. When a true man, a true woman, and God become completely united, centered on true love, then they will find the solution to all problems concerning our view of the universe, our view of life and our view of God.

The Path of Sacrifice

God's true love is such that, though He loves and loves again or gives and gives again, He forgets what He has done. If some kind of memory about what you have given remains, then love cannot be eternal. Because love is an eternal action, you should not remember what you have given. Love continues to flow because you give and give and forget what you have been given.

Thus the path of true love is not to receive something; it is the path of sacrificing and living for others. That is why when God Himself created an object of true love, God stood in the position of living for others. He wanted to invest and invest again, one hundred percent of everything He had. The reason why God wanted to invest Himself completely is that He wanted His object of love to be better than Himself. The creator of the heavens and the earth, our heavenly Father God, the original central existence, has this kind of heart. Thus the act of living for others, which is contained within true love, means that you give one hundred percent or even one thousand percent until there is a vacuum. In the earth's atmosphere, when a low pressure system forms, then a high pressure system starts circulating automatically. It is the same with love. When you create an absolute low pressure or vacuum of love, then God's love starts circulating. Living absolutely for others is like creating a typhoon which unleashes tremendous power.

My dear members of the Women's Federation for World Peace! There is an old saying, "Women are weak, but mothers are strong." A woman by herself may be weak, but if a woman as a mother assumes the position of being the subject of love, or as a wife or a daughter, if she performs the role of being the center of love, then she will be the strongest of all.

The reason for this is that if a woman as a mother, wife or daughter assumes the position of being the subject of love and if she gives one hundred percent to her object, then God's love will come to fill up the vacuum that is left after she has given everything. That is when the power of God's love starts working. So even though she is a woman, if she resembles God and assumes the position of being the subject of love, then a tremendous force will be let loose and the power of that love will give life to the family, it will give life to the nation, and it will give life to the world. As an example, the fact that Yu Kwan Sun, a young girl of sixteen, caused such a great surge in the Korean Independence Movement, was a miracle which occurred out of her burning, sacrificial patriotic heart to save the nation.

Centered on True Love

God stands in the position of being the subject of love living completely for His children, humanity. Through continuing the action of His original nature, which is to give and give again, He can exist for eternity. In this way, the way of true love, the logic of eternal life, is established.

If God's companion of true love, humanity, had matured according to God's will and inherited God's absolute, unchanging love, then the world would have seen a history of absolute unity, and there would not have been a history of war, bloodshed and misery. If your mind and body become one centered on true love, then each of you will become God's companion of love and will come to be in the position of God's eternal object. Not only that, you will come to inherit the eternal love of God.

Contained within the inheritance of love is the right to inherit, the right to live together with God and the right to participate in what God does. Even though a woman may have been born to a lowly family and did not graduate from elementary school, if she becomes the wife of the president and they become a loving couple, then what belongs to the husband belongs to the wife. She can be together with her husband day and night; she also has the right to participate in what her husband does.

Because true love contains the three great attributes of inheritance, living together and participation, if you stand in the position of being one with God's absolute, unchanging true love, then you can go to where God is and you have the right to be together with Him and participate in anything and everything He does. Because humankind fell, God's heart came to be full of grief. There are those who have experienced God's sorrowful heart. Such people, as they walk along, will stop and burst into tears because they feel God's grief so deeply.

Even in the fallen world today, there are many cases of a mother feeling intuitively that something has happened to her child, and sometimes, even while she is sleeping, she wakes up calling her child's name. A mother's love is like this.

If we can come to absorb in our mind and body one hundred percent of God's love, which wants to live for others for eternity, then the root of God's true love will form in our hearts and we will be able to communicate with God freely and feel everything He does; then our body will automatically act in unison with our mind. Centering on true love in the world of the mind, the body was created to be the body of unison. So you must know today that we have to recover God's true original love in order to bring back the unified world of our mind and body.

According to the principle of "unison" which arises from true love, when a person becomes one centered on true love, and enters the realm of communal oneness, then we can say that God's love is my love, God's life is my life, God's blood is my blood and God's creation is my creation. Accordingly, the mother and father who embrace the universe in their hearts will have their names entered in the family register of the Kingdom of Heaven.

Is love first or is life first? Love is first. A person has life because of love, and conception takes place centered on the ideal of love. So the essence of a person's life is love. Therefore, it is a heavenly law that life, which has its essence in love, must be "a life for others." Thus we can say that from the moment a person is born, he was born for his mate.

If we say that I was born only for myself, or that everyone else was born for me, then the concept of love cannot be established. The starting point of love is when you sacrifice yourself and live for another person. The person who lives for his family can initiate family love, and a person who sacrifices himself for his friend can initiate friend's love.

If you sacrifice for others, it may seem as though you will lose everything, but actually the opposite is true. Not only do you become the subject of love and master of everything, you go to a higher level.

It is a principle that love is such that the more it sacrifices for others, the higher the level that love becomes. If you sacrifice for some bigger purpose, you will not be absorbed by it; rather, you will stand in the central position of it, and a new and higher level will be realized. Christianity has become a religion of resurrection because it teaches people to sacrifice themselves for others. The sinless Jesus went to meet his death on the cross, praying, "Not as I will, but as You will," fervently asking God to forgive the ignorance and sin of the Roman soldiers who were piercing him with spears.

Jesus' life was a model life showing how to sacrifice and live for others. It should have become the base and central ideology of Christianity in making the new history of resurrection. If you sacrifice your life for others, then you will come to have a higher level of life.

God Always Protects

It is precisely through true love that the base to occupy hell is formed. If you come to possess true love, then all pain and suffering will resurrect in that true love and become joy. In other words, true love, which is part of the original nature of a person, transcends any individual desire for power, knowledge or wealth.

Seen in this light, God's strategy to save humankind throughout human history, and the strategy of Satan, who has tried to prevent God from doing so, have been completely opposite. It has been God's strategy to be hit and then take, while Satan always strikes first to take, but loses.

Look at the First, Second and Third (war of ideology) World Wars. The side that struck first perished. God does not recover what has been stolen from Him by killing the people on Satan's side and taking back what is His. God, as the master of the universe, has the power to strike and take back what is His at will; however, He does not do this. Rather He lets His side be struck first.

Parents cause their unfilial child to repent by continuing to sacrifice for him or her. In order for God to set up the great highway of heavenly law, He went to Satan and taught him that when the master comes, he should do this or do that. But history shows us that the master who went to teach was beaten. But what happened after he was beaten? He could receive everything with compensation added. Confucius, also, received a lot of persecution and

Jesus died being accused of rebellion against the Roman Empire. But as history passes, the names of the saints remain. Who became a saint in their own lifetime? Even though they died wretched deaths in their own lifetimes, as the different ages of history pass they gradually go up to a higher level.

God does not ask compensation to be paid for only ten or twenty years. The longer the time that passes, the more God recovers until finally the whole world is completely recovered. Patiently waiting for thousands of years, God has calculated the compensation to be received. It is like putting money in the bank: over the years the interest keeps accumulating until one day you have more than enough money to buy the bank. God is a being who bides His time and uses the strategy of being hit first and taking back later.

If you are persecuted by the evil world, then heaven will help you and let you jump over all these hardships. God has let my husband and me experience this kind of thing many times. Being persecuted is another way to inherit the possessions of the enemy. God always protects those He loves in such a way. The reason why God cannot kill a person He wants to punish is because He knows that the individual has parents, a wife or children who still love him. Because God also has gone through the valley of tears, when He feels the heart of the person's parents, wife or children, He cannot strike that person.

Meet God and Self

If you truly come to feel God's heart, how can you settle accounts with your enemy? On the contrary, what you should do is mobilize people to help your enemy. Wanting to embrace your enemy and to become one centered on love means that you will come to stand in front of the gates of the Kingdom of Heaven. There, the heavens and the earth will be moved and God, also, will start to cry. God will say, "You resemble me!" and He will be so joyful. Because God is like this, we can come to understand the words "Love your enemy." That kind of power is not caused by knowledge, money or authority. It is caused only by true love.

Therefore, just as you live for your lovely children and parents, you have to go beyond the feeling that North Korea is your enemy and you have to desire unification with sacrificial true love in your hearts.

The unification of North and South Korea, which we desire so much, is only possible with the spirit of sacrificial true love, through which we can love even our enemies. Just as parents take care of their children, or just as brothers and sisters love each other, we should treat the pain of our brothers and sisters in North Korea as "my" pain, and we should meet together and work so that we can be unified again under the unchangeable true love of God.

The point of intersection where, centering on true love, Adam and Eve can meet God and settle, can only be at the angle of ninety degrees, where vertical and horizontal meet. This is the official point that causes true love to settle.

God is the parent of vertical true love; Adam and Eve should have been the parents of horizontal true love. We should have been born inheriting the love, the life and the blood lineage of these two types of parental love; then my mind becomes the vertical "me" and my body becomes the horizontal "me." When my vertical "me" and my horizontal "me" become unified at the point of ninety degrees, then a person can become the companion of true love of the eternal God.

God has true love, true life and true blood lineage. Because we originated from God, we also should have true love, true life and true blood lineage. Centering on the true love of God, an individual was born to be one body with God. Just as God's mind and body, centering on true love, are naturally united, the mind and body of all humankind also should have been naturally united through true love.

However, fallen humankind inherited Satan's love, life and blood lineage. The body is the front line for Satan and the mind is the front line for God; both continually struggle against each other. The love that an individual has today does not center on an individual's mind, but on his body. Our bodies became Satan's dance hall. Our body is the past to which Satan's anchor is attached. The mind is in the position of being a plus representing heaven, but the body has become another plus and is toying with the mind. It is our duty to rectify this situation within our own lifetime. God knows this, so He made religion as the repair shop. This is why religion teaches us to deny the body through fasting, sacrifice and service. Religion teaches the mind to over come the body. In order for the desires of the body to be weakened so that the body follows the mind, we need to live a life of faith through which the mind conveys good habits to the body for at least three to five years. Religion tells us: do not rest; pray constantly.

God stands only in the vertical position, so He can only be active through the mind. Satan is active in all directions. He can be active in each one of the 360 degrees, so fallen humankind is bound to fall prey to Satan's activity.

Because the mind is in the vertical position, it is one. Because the vertical base is not the horizontal base, the mind cannot enter the horizontal base. Because it is easy for the mind to be dragged along by the body, the mind in the vertical position has to lead a life of devotion and prayer, through which it can receive three or four times more strength. Then it can dominate the body freely and lead the body along the right way for three to five years, creating good habits. There is no method to repair the body other than the union of the vertical and horizontal. Unless humankind goes through the door of a religion that teaches people to lead such a life, humanity cannot go back to its original position. The road of philosophy, knowledge or conscience alone is not enough. The vertical mind and the horizontal body have to become one.

What is the cause of the fall of man, which led to an individual's mind and body not becoming one with God's ideal? The Bible tells us that it is because man ate of the fruit of the tree of knowledge of good and evil. However, what part of the body did Adam and Eve cover after they had eaten of the fruit? They should have covered their mouths and hands, but they covered their lower parts; after that, they married, centering on Satan. This is the origin of how Satan's evil blood lineage multiplied.

However, the origin of true love, true life and the true blood lineage for a person are the sexual organs of love. Because of the fall, the organs of love, which should have been the most holy place, became the most abominable place, destroying the way of heaven. The organs of love became the headquarters of evil. And from here they sowed the seeds of false love, false life and the false blood lineage.

The ancestors of man, Adam and Eve, fell when they were teenagers and still not mature. Historically, the evil blood lineage of humankind started because Adam and Eve had sown the seeds of evil. Thus, when the time of the Last Days comes, the youth all over the world will destroy the ethics of love as Adam and Eve did, and the tide of corruption will flow throughout the world.

When we see these phenomena, we must know that the age of Satan's dominion has arrived. It is at this very time that the day of judgment, when God rules with His rod of iron, has arrived.

History teaches us that any city or country that ignored God and engaged in wantonness was destroyed. Sodom and Gomorrah were destroyed by fire and brimstone; Rome was destroyed because the people became morally decadent and did not keep their chastity.

Look at America, Europe and Japan, the advanced nations of the world. Who is able to stop free sex, which is rampant everywhere? This world is becoming cosmopolitan and is full of corrupt love and drug abuse. This is the method by which the body is being dragged to its death. It is not the path our mind wants; it is crying out in despair.

All the people who were called to lead humanity back to the embrace of God failed. Somebody must appear who can lead the people of the world out of the fallen environment to the road of truth.

We can compare fallen man who came to stand on Satan's side to a wild olive shoot. From among fallen men, God has separated the wild olive shoots. Those wild olive shoots that are in the sphere of religion belong to God. God can dominate these wild olive shoots freely. He has prepared everything so that when the Lord returns, he will be able to cut down the trees in one stroke and graft them onto him. In this way the wild olive shoots become the true olive tree, returning back to their original state. That is why the people who already believe in a religion must find the original true father. This is because they were not born with the original seed of life from the true father. They were unable to fulfill God's ideal and connect with God's blood lineage centering on the original true love; therefore, the Messiah has to come.

Do You Know Who the Messiah Is?

The Messiah is the person who has come with the tremendous responsibility of coming as the True Parent, pulling out and throwing away the roots of all those born from the false parents and restoring them to their original state. He has the responsibility to banish Satan, liberate humanity and build the Kingdom of Heaven on earth and thus be welcomed by all.

If you become sons and daughters who can inherit God's love, God's life and God's blood lineage and also inherit True Parents' love, True Parents' life and True Parents' blood lineage, then, like God, your mind and body will not fight, and you will become the true unified origin of world peace. The point where the mind and body become unified will be the starting point for the eternal world of peace.

My dear members of the Women's Federation for World Peace! Let us all fulfill our duty as servants with the heart of parents. Let us shed our sweat for the earth, our tears for humankind and our blood for heaven. And let us liberate our Parent, the Lord and Creator of the universe, from His grief—and in order to build one world of peace, let us march forward along the road of salvation bearing the cross.

Please do not forget that, even though our destination may be in the world, our starting point must begin when our mind and body become one, centering on true love. Each of us must remember that not until my family becomes the place of eternal happiness and true love will our hope for the ideal country, the ideal world and the ideal Kingdom of Heaven on earth bear fruit.

In the not too distant future, our Women's Federation for World Peace will be joined by all people in the world and will become a Family Federation for World Peace; then we will build a world of true love in which all races will live for each other for eternity.

Let us determine to rise up and take the lead to complete this historical mission. I pray that God's blessing may be upon you and your families.

Thank you very much.

The Central Role of Women in the Ideal World

Mrs. Hak Ja Han Moon, President, Women's Federation for World Peace
This address was given on July 6, 1992 at the Rally for Leaders of the Women's
Federation for World Peace, Seoul, Korea.

My fellow co-workers and women members! I am very happy and honored to stand before you as President of the Women's Federation for World Peace today. Let me express my deep appreciation to all of you members and supporters who prepared this rally today. Today, I would like to speak to you on the subject of "The Central Role of Women in the Ideal World."

If someone asked you whether our world today is good or evil, what would you answer? Without a doubt, you would answer that it is evil. But it is not just the world of this age that is evil; we cannot help but say that all the ages of the past and all the nations and the world were evil. Therefore, our world has been one in which sin continues to grow more than good deeds, war more than peace, immorality more than righteousness, hatred more than love, and division and discord more than unification and harmony.

No one wants this kind of evil world. Therefore, we cannot help but investigate how we can establish an ideal world of true love overflowing with peace, freedom and happiness and clear up this world of evil. What all individuals and leaders of the family, tribe, race, nation and world desire as well must be the establishment of a world overflowing with freedom and happiness. Since the beginning of human history, for thousands of years, humanity has been struggling toward this kind of ideal and dream, but we have not yet established the ideal world we desire.

Today, I would like to reveal to you the fundamental cause of these problems. In addition, I intend to present the solution which will make it possible to realize the ideal world which people have desired so much. This is not content that comes from human speculation or wisdom. As you already know, my husband, the Reverend Sun Myung Moon, has devoted his entire life to solving these problems. During the time I have lived supporting my husband, I have been moved and inspired beyond words by his teachings and by his life of love for God and humanity.

Be Fruitful, Multiply and Fill the Earth

If a wife, as she lives supporting her husband, gains deep insights into the truth and is continuously moved and inspired by his life and character, this is an occurrence that should be revealed to the world. Why? Because the fundamental reason for this world becoming an evil world where sexual license, criminal activity, conflicts and corruption are rampant is the breakdown and disharmony in the basic relationship between husband, wife and children.

At present, over five billion people are living on the earth, but if we look at it in another way, only two people are living here. We could say that a man and a woman, a husband and a wife, only two people, are living here. Countless numbers of people are living together and there are all kinds of relationships and problems, but at the core of all of those problems are the problems and relationships between two people, a man and a woman. When we look at things in this light, it becomes important for us to investigate the way of heaven that man and woman were to go when God created the first ancestors.

In Genesis it is recorded that after God had created the heavens and the earth, He created the ancestors of humankind: a man, Adam, and a woman, Eve. At the same time that He gave them the three great blessings, He gave them a portion of responsibility. The three great blessings were: "Be fruitful and multiply; fill the earth and subdue it; and have dominion over the fish of the sea, over the birds of the air, and over every living thing...." But to the man and woman He also gave the responsibility: "... but of the tree of the knowledge of good and evil you shall not eat...."

This teaches us the purpose for which God created the universe and humanity, and also shows us the basis for life. The blessing to be fruitful means that all people born on the earth must grow to be people of perfected character. The second blessing of life, to multiply, means that, as a man and a woman with a perfected character, they must establish the bond of husband and wife, give birth to children, and raise them. God's purpose of creation is, as a husband and wife fulfill their duty as father and mother leading a family, they should construct a far more comfortable, prosperous world and establish the Kingdom of Heaven on earth.

This purpose of creation was to be realized if the first ancestors had obeyed God's commandment, "...but of the tree of the knowledge of good and evil you shall not eat...." But before the first ancestors, Adam and Eve, were perfect, while they were still immature, they did not keep God's commandment; because of Satan, they fell, and all humanity became the recipients of an evil blood lineage.

Due to the Immoral Fall of the Original Human Ancestors, Humankind Has Lost the Purpose of Creation

Ladies! What is the fruit of the tree of knowledge of good and evil that God told the original ancestors, Adam and Eve, not to eat? It is not the real fruit of a tree. It is a way of expressing the husband and wife love relationship that the first ancestors were to have in the future. Due to the temptation of a third being, while still in an imperfect state, the first man and woman entered into an immoral sexual relationship. Actually, in the Garden of Eden, the third party besides Adam and Eve was the archangel. In the Bible it is revealed that Lucifer was the archangel who tempted Eve and committed an immoral sexual sin. This was the fall of man, the original sin which planted the root of sin in the world.

Man committed the sexual sin before his Father God, the Lord and Master of heaven and earth, and the first ancestors had children out of this immoral love; the world of evil was realized. In other words, they married centered on Satan, and by planting false love, false life and a false lineage they became ancestors of evil.

As human society expanded from the individual, family, tribe, race and nation to the world level, due to this immoral relationship between man and woman, the root of the evil blood lineage was established everywhere, at all times, and this world became hell on earth: it became a false world filled with sin, war and fear. The fallen ancestors, Adam and Eve, should have established the position of True Parents as the eternal good ancestors of humanity, but they fell and became false parents, leaving a blood lineage of evil.

This is the first cause of all the tragedy and misery of humankind. What could be more tragic or cause greater indignation than becoming the descendants of false parents and all humankind losing their True Parents? And how great must be the suffering and sorrow of God, the Father of humanity, whose purpose of creation, to establish the true ancestors of humankind and to multiply people of goodness, was stolen by the blood lineage of sin through the immoral fall of the first human ancestors.

Just as the cause of a disease must be discovered and treated in order to save a person suffering from it, in order to liberate human society from the suffering of such sin and misery, the fundamental cause of this sin and misery must be revealed and corrected. The fundamental cause is the fall of the human ancestors, the original sin. Accordingly, unless the cause of the disease called original sin is eliminated, we cannot pull up the root of misery and sin from the world. No matter how many great men, heroes, scholars, politicians or philosophers appear and try to straighten out the world through the reform of the laws and systems or through the education of moral principles, unless the original sin and the content of the fall is clarified, it will be impossible. All remedies will prove useless. That is because the original root of sin and misery is still alive, and it will continue to sprout buds.

The Role of Religion: The Salvation of Humankind from Evil

Religion teaches the fact that man fell, it reveals the contents of the fall, and directly and indirectly shows God's providence through which He seeks to save man completely from sin. Therefore, all religions are the most active prescriptions for saving the sinful world. Religion is the fount of all education or teachings. The teachings of the four great saints, Confucius, Buddha, Jesus and Mohammed, and the teachings of the founders of other religions transcended their ages and locations and have preserved the conscience and morals of humanity, and have been the generative powers of cultural development. Accordingly, all religions seeking to liquidate the world of evil and to establish the ideal world which God and people desire are co-workers and collaborators.

Among them, the scriptures through which God most directly revealed His providence of salvation is the Bible. Through the Bible we can know that the ancestors of humanity, Adam and Eve, committed the original sin and became false parents, and that God's work in the providence of salvation is to restore the lost purpose of creation. The main point of the message of the Bible is that in order to give rebirth to all, the Messiah or the True Parents must come in place of Adam and Eve who became false parents. Adam should have become the true father, and Eve should have become the true mother; that was the purpose of the original creation. In order to restore the purpose of creation back to its original state, God cannot help but carry out the providence for the recreation of Adam.

That is the main point of the providence of preparing the chosen nation of Israel and having Jesus born there. From the time Adam and Eve fell and humanity multiplied with its blood lineage centered on Satan, God immediately began working to separate the blood lineages of goodness and evil. From Adam's family, God separated the second son, Abel, who was in a position to relate to God, and the first son, Cain, who was in a position to relate to Satan. He sought to restore the order of the creation to its original state by having Cain yield to Abel of his own accord. Through Cain's murder of Abel, the history of struggle to separate good and evil was extended for a long time.

The Mission of Jesus who Came as the True Father

After Noah, Abraham and Isaac, Jacob through the help of his mother, was able to make his elder twin, Esau, yield of his own accord. Jacob took a decisive role in the establishment of the chosen people of Israel. Jacob's son, Judah, had twins Perez and Zerah through his daughter-in-law, Tamar. Perez struggled with Zerah inside Tamar's womb and pushed Zerah aside, who was supposed to be born first. Instead, Perez was born first as the elder brother. The battle of the first and second born is the battle of good and evil. Thus, when the younger brother won over the elder brother while still in the womb and was born as the first son, this achieved restoration within the womb.

Jesus Christ, who came as the Messiah forty generations later, was born from the lineage of Perez, because of this restoration within the womb. Conceiving and giving birth to Jesus was an act of extraordinary devotion and risk in which Jesus' mother, Mary, put her life on the line. Because God's providence of salvation is the providence of restoration, God had to carry out a providence to cut the blood lineage of sin. This sin has been transmitted from generation to generation because the ancestors, Adam and Eve, had an immoral sexual relationship due to the temptation of Lucifer, the archangel, who became Satan.

This course from Cain and Abel until Jesus was born is the history of the chosen nation of Israel. Due to the fall, Adam fell to the position of a false father. Accordingly, following the course of restoration of the struggle to separate good and evil, Jesus came as the true father of humanity, that is, as the good second ancestor of humankind. Because of that, Jesus had to restore as his complement a woman in the position of Eve, and they had to become a couple, have children and take dominion over creation. This was the purpose for which Jesus came as the Messiah.

Thus Jesus came as the Messiah to restore the three great blessings which God gave to Adam and Eve: be fruitful, multiply and have dominion over all the creation. However, Jesus, who came as their father and Messiah, was crucified by mankind. What an incredibly unfilial act! What a horrendous sin! Jesus who died on the cross promised that he would come again to the earth, that he would come as a bridegroom, and that all people on the earth should prepare themselves as brides and be ready. In Revelation chapter 19, it is recorded that Jesus returns to the earth and holds the Marriage of the Lamb. This refers to the restoration of the position of the true couple and the True Parents.

The Messiah Reveals the Path of the True Parents, the True Couple and the True Children

Members and women co-workers! How can we straighten out this society in which all kinds of sexual sin, immorality and corruption are destroying our families? It will bring a destruction like Sodom and Gomorrah's upon itself. The fire of judgment has already begun to fall. The frightening disease, AIDS, is a warning from heaven against the chaos of sexual immorality.

Jesus said he would come again in the Last Days of this evil world. The returning Jesus will come as True Father of humankind. He will show the way of the True Children, the True Couple, and the way of the True Parents which all men and women must go. Only in this way can the problem of sexual corruption, the original sin, be fundamentally solved. This will be the true gospel which will save humankind from the world of sin.

The mission of the Messiah, the Savior, is to teach the way to end the tangled history of sin created when humanity lost the way of the True Parents, the True Couple and the True Children.

Today, in this place, I proclaim to the whole world that my husband, the Reverend Sun Myung Moon, has devoted his entire life to pioneering this path of the Messiah, the True Parents. As you well know, my husband Reverend Moon has revealed the purpose of the creation of God, and through examining the original sin committed by the first ancestors he has pioneered the future of humanity despite the brutal opposition and persecution of this evil world.

According to the Divine Principle, the teaching of my husband, each major religion is awaiting the return of its founder in some form: the Maitreya, the True Man, the new Confucius and the return of Jesus will be fulfilled by the return of one Messiah, the return of the True Parent of humankind. All religions will be united into one. That Messiah, the True Parent who comes, will not be the same Jesus who died 2,000 years ago, as some Christians believe, nor will he come on the clouds in the air; rather, a new person who has inherited the mission of Jesus is to be born on the earth. The country in which that person is born is the nation of Korea; however surprising it may be, the fact is that the Messiah, who is the True Parent of humankind, comes as a Korean.

Unification Is the Key to World Peace

When will the Messiah who is coming in this way appear? According to the Divine Principle, the Last Days are the time when this evil world comes to an end, and the Messiah is to return. Briefly, the Last Days are from the end of the First World War to the year 2000— a period of about eighty years. During this period the Lord of the Second Advent, who is the True Parent of humankind, is to be born in our land of Korea. This is the worldwide historical age of transition when the Lord of the Second Advent is building the ideal out of the world filled with sin, war and struggle.

Therefore, this era is an age of great chaos with the confrontation and struggle between goodness and evil occurring in the mutual relationships of all parts of the world: the individual, family, tribe, race, nation and the world.

The Realization of World Peace Through the Power of Women

Women leaders! What I am telling you today is not only for the Unification Church members who are following my husband. Now leaders from every level of society, in more than 160 nations, and many thousands of young people, are following this teaching and shedding sweat to build a new unified world overflowing with freedom and peace. Already Korea is being looked to by many people from all over the world as the country to which the True Parents of humankind have come, and the number of foreigners who are visiting Korea to learn the Korean language, culture and customs is rapidly increasing.

Our Women's Federation for World Peace has the fundamental remedy to save our families which are threatened by the present-day reality of the degeneration of sexual morality, the proliferation of drugs and all sorts of wantonness and sexual corruption. This is a worldwide women's organization which was founded last April 10, in Seoul Olympic Stadium with 150,000 Korean women, including representatives from 72 countries. We cannot wait any longer to save the society of tomorrow, which is rotting with all kinds of immorality and corruption, and the fallen social climate where men have oppressed women.

Finally, we must endeavor to learn and practice the duty of the True Parents, the true spouse and the true child. Through the organization of the Family Federation for World Peace, we must make sure that immorality and corruption will not be able to set foot anywhere in this world. In this way, humankind must cleanse the evil blood lineage and suffering which was caused by the original sin of fornication committed in the Garden of Eden, which has lasted until today, and quickly prepare to meet the new world.

Until now everyone has been helpless to stop the wantonness and immorality which has been destroying humankind. But now a new truth which can completely solve these problems has appeared in Korea in the very age in which we are living. This truth which was revealed by the True Parents will be the light that will bring about the unification of North and South Korea and build a world of peace and happiness. Let us learn this new truth and rise up and become women soldiers who will end this world of sin, which has caused us to suffer since the beginning of history. Let us build a unified world overflowing with freedom, peace and happiness.

Let us go the way of the True Mother. Let us go the way of the true wife. Let us go the way of the true daughter.

Thank you very much.

The Reappearance of the True Parents and the Ideal Family

Reverend Sun Myung Moon, President, Federation for World Peace
This address was given on July 6, 1992 at the rally for leaders of the Women's
Federation for World Peace, Seoul, Korea.

President Hak Ja Han Moon, distinguished guests, and women leaders: Today, I received much comfort through the words of President Han. As I went along this single road following the order of heaven, my life has been one of extraordinary suffering. The road establishing the way of heaven is a straight road, and it allows for no compromise. This road does not allow one to worry about honor or human dignity. It was a lonely road on which one can live only for God's will.

Just as each individual has his own fortune, the family and the nation also have a family fortune and a national fortune, and beyond this there is the fortune of the world, and there is heaven's fortune for all of heaven and earth. Even though a person may have been born with a lot of fortune, when his family fortune declines he must endure hardship. For a person who has both good individual fortune and family fortune, when the national fortune declines, he cannot help but be ruined.

Going beyond this, the national fortune and the direction of the world is decided according to the direction and the progress of heaven's fortune which is above everything and includes everything. Establishing the way of heaven in the world means making the way the individual or nation is going correspond to the fortune of heaven.

Today, let us think about the evils of Korea and the problems of the world: economic depression, environmental pollution, political irregularity, racial and religious strife, the decay of ethics and morality, and the collapse of the sense of values. Is there anyone who can fundamentally solve these many evils and problems? It has not been possible through human wisdom or effort. We have not been able to find a solution to these problems by mobilizing economic power or governmental power; rather, the evils of humankind are gradually becoming worse.

Now humanity has to humbly listen to the voice of heaven and find the road of resolution directed by God. This country and its people must accept my teachings. This is not because I am trying to raise myself up, but because it is the will of God. God has revealed the principles of heaven through me, and He has given me the answers to the fundamental problems of humankind.

My life has been truly difficult. I have been beaten, persecuted and unfairly imprisoned by successive governments, and due to the prejudice and malicious opposition of some Christian leaders, all types of rumors have been spread about me. But, thanks to the protection of God, I have laid a miraculous and victorious worldwide foundation. Such a foundation has been without precedent since the dawn of history.

In America, which is a prepared nation representing world Christianity, I have a record-breaking foundation that no other non-white person has been able to achieve. Of course, I had to suffer from racial discrimination and religious prejudice; I even had to surmount unfair imprisonment. Nevertheless, I rebuilt the Christian foundation, which was shaking at the roots; I educated and trained the youth who were suffering from drugs and immorality, and I gave hope to America. Neither the government of America nor the people can ignore my foundation.

The same is true for Japan and Europe. Already there are Unification missions in 160 countries which are developing every day. Each of these missions has become the symbol of each kind of religious activity and the symbol of the movement to rebuild ethics and morality.

Unification by Giving True Love to Others

From the early 1980s I ordered world-level academic meetings to be held with the theme of the collapse of the Soviet empire. In 1985 an academic journal published an article, which has now become world famous, prophesying for the first time the collapse of the communist Soviet empire.

On the basis of such a foundation, I visited the Soviet Union and I met Mikhail Gorbachev. Now in three of the fifteen republics of the former Soviet Union, there is a movement to make Unificationism the national religion.

Already tens of thousands of university students have studied my teaching, and the Collegiate Association for the Research of the Principle (CARP), which is the Unification Church university student organization, has been organized in over 700 universities. This year, tens of thousands of high school teachers and students will attend Divine Principle training workshops.

Do you think this kind of activity is the result of human power alone? It is real proof that the living God is working together with us. Miracles are taking place as confirmed atheists change their views of life and the universe to one centered on God, after five days of Divine Principle lectures.

I have established a huge foundation in China. I prepared important projects such as the construction of the Panda industrial city many years ago, and many underground missionaries have been working hard until this day. Only God knows how much I have done to bring about the unification of North and South Korea. The unification of North and South Korea is not merely a visible and external unification; it is a providential unification centered on God. It cannot be established without going through my foundation.

The unification required by God's providence is not for unification in itself; it is so that on the foundation of unification, eternal freedom, peace and happiness can blossom. It cannot be unification by force or where one side is miserable. It must be a unification by true love in which each lives for the other and gives and gives again. Therefore, the unification of the fatherland cannot be exploited for the benefit of any individual, political party or government. When all of our hearts and actions, colored with love, reach out to the hearts of our fellow countrymen in the north, then true unification will come.

In Order for World Peace to Come

Women leaders! Centered on God's true love, I have expanded supra-denominational and supra-religious movements of reconciliation to the worldwide level. Without reconciliation and interchange between the divided religions, how can world peace be realized? Isn't it true that today there is still appalling religious strife in the Middle East, in Ireland, in the Balkans and in other areas?

Last year on August 27, I gathered together all the highest religious leaders of the world and established the Inter-Religious Federation for World Peace. We joined together in order to realize world peace through the unity and cooperation of religious people. It is truly a precious organization. There may be important differences among religions, but there are just as many common points and all have the purpose to seek for the Absolute Being.

It is an important fact that God established all religions with a providential purpose for the whole. Therefore, they must unite together. Just as President Han mentioned in her address, Christianity teaches that man ate of the fruit of the tree of knowledge of good and evil; this means that our human ancestors committed the sin of disbelief and fell. If our human ancestors had not fallen, as God's precious son and daughter—namely, God's prince and princess—they would have inherited God's blood lineage; they would have inherited their Father God's possessions—namely, the creation. They should have grown to perfection and become the ideal husband and wife of love. However, through the fall, they changed from God's blood lineage, they were robbed of God's possessions, and they lost God's heart.

God's providence of salvation as the providence of restoration for complete recovery must take responsibility for the mission to restore the blood lineage, to restore the realm of ownership and to change the realm of the human heart. As a result of the fall, Adam and Eve came to be one with Satan and they followed him to hell. The eldest son Cain followed Eve and the second son Abel followed behind him.

God's providence of restoration has been carried out in such a way that the condition to separate from Satan is established through the second son, who starts later and represents the side of goodness, subjugating the eldest son, who starts first and represents the side of evil.

The basis of the providence of restoration is to send the restored Adam—namely, the Messiah—who will change the blood lineage, ownership and heart. However, the heartistic position of the original son cannot be restored at once. The providence must be accomplished gradually, starting from the position of the servant of servants.

In this world which is held under the power of Satan, Abel who is on the side of good should complete the mission of the servant of servants by living for Cain with true love. Then Satan cannot accuse him, but instead cannot help but praise and recognize him. After that, the missions of the servant, the adopted son, the illegitimate son and the direct son are restored following the order of love and affection. Restoration can only take place on each level when the Abel side lives for Cain's side through true love, so that Satan cannot accuse him.

If Abel in the position of the true son and daughter makes Cain surrender and they become one, the mother Eve can stand on that foundation, and when Eve fulfills her responsibility, Adam can stand on that foundation. Then for the first time God can come to dwell on that foundation and the eight necessary stages of the vertical course of the providence of restoration can be completed.

If we look at the stages of the providence of restoration horizontally, there are also eight stages: the individual, family, tribe, race, nation, world, cosmos and God. Jesus came as the second Adam, the Messiah, but unfortunately the chosen people of Israel did not know who he was.

Will today's Christians be able to recognize the Lord when he returns? The Lord of the Second Advent will not literally return in the air on the clouds. There are people who believe and are proclaiming that on October 28 of this year, they will be taken up to heaven on the clouds, but it will not happen like this. Please believe me, this kind of event will never happen. The Lord who went through the cross will return through the cross.

When Jesus died on the cross, there were three types of people connected with Jesus' crucifixion. There was the first type, the thief on Jesus' right who repented of his sins and testified to Jesus; there was the second type, the thief on Jesus' left, who was a sinner who did not repent and who vilified Jesus. The third type was Barabbas, a criminal who surely should have been crucified, was saved when Jesus was crucified instead.

At the time of the Second Advent, these three types are realized on the world level. Western Christianity is the first type in the position of the thief on Jesus' right. Although they still have original sin, they believe in the Lord and they are in the position of good. The materialistic, atheistic communist bloc is the second type and is in the position of the thief on the left. Islam in the Middle East is the third type and is in the position of Barabbas. Because Jesus died instead of him and because Israel caused Jesus to die on the cross, Islam came to occupy the land of the Middle East which had been divided between the twelve tribes of Israel. The Lord of the Second Advent, who is in the position of the reborn Jesus, has to straighten out the worldwide achievements of these three types which came about through Jesus' death.

In order to straighten out the Western world of Christianity, he has to bring about a new movement of religious reformation, overcome the atheistic ideology of communism, and bring all the communist world back to God's side. The ideology that can overcome the left-wing and right-wing ideologies and bring about a unified harmony between them is my proposed Headwing ideology of Godism.

I Have Fulfilled my Mission as the Lord of the Second Advent, the Savior and the True Parent.

As I have mentioned before, the left-wing and right-wing worlds are already being straightened out through the Headwing ideology. Also, the religion of Islam has started to promote reconciliation and cooperation. A miracle took place last April when representatives from eight Middle East countries took part in a mass holy wedding of the Unification Church. I conducted the blessing ceremony through which fallen people can be cleansed of sin. I solved the historical conflict and settled the tension between the left and the right; furthermore, I established the miracle of bringing about reconciliation with the world of Islam.

These kinds of works cannot be performed through the ability or planning of an individual alone. God chose me to be the Messiah and during this time He has been performing His work of salvation.

I have fulfilled my mission as the Lord of the Second Advent, Savior and the True Parent. I am proclaiming this in this place because the time has come to do so. Those who accept this will be blessed. If this race listens to me, how good that would be for this country. How good it would be if the statesmen listen to me. Whether a person listens to me or not is his individual responsibility; however, the time is coming when all people of the world will want to listen to me.

People generally believe that the Messiah is thought only to be the Lord of Glory and have the authority of judgment, but they are wrong.

God does not want to look at this sinful world. He has thought about judging the world and wiping it out in an instant. However, the God of true love always worries about the eternal life of humankind. You have to know God's heart which has endured for so long, trying through true love to make humanity comply of its own free will.

From the point of view of fallen man, the Messiah is the Savior; but from God's point of view he is the True Parent, the True Son who will realize the ideal of creation of true love, which was lost at the beginning. The Messiah is the person who has pioneered the way of sacrifice, dedicating his life to liberate God from His grievous sorrow which was caused by the fall. He is not a person who stands only in a glorious position. He always weeps together with God's heart, and he is concerned about how to make Satan surrender.

He is deeply concerned and anxious about realizing God's purpose of creation. He knows better than anyone else the heart of God who is like a servant of servants, wandering and shedding endless tears in the satanic world in search of His lost children, and unless he completely liberates God from His sorrow, he cannot receive glory.

Complete the Ideal of the True Family

Leaders of the Women's Federation for World Peace! It must have been difficult for you to have a succession of rallies, and you probably complained when you heard this rally was going to be held within ten days. However, if together with me you devote your heart sincerely every day, then God's will of goodness shall be accomplished. I have no intention of exploiting you. You need me. You must become one with President Han and be like an extension of her, and in your family you must educate your children and your husband properly. I want all of you, under the ideal of true love, to receive God's blessing.

What I am most concerned about is for each of your families to complete the ideal of the true family by becoming one through true love. City, town, village, county, ward and block leaders of the Women's Federation for World Peace: through you, morals can be restored. If you expand this movement of true love, what movement could be more patriotic than this?

There is a mountain of work to do. We have to spread a movement for proper morals, a movement for the eradication of drugs, a no-smoking and no-drinking movement, a movement for the removal of the red light districts, a movement to expose immorality in the leaders of society and to inspire and encourage the youth. When the Korean society based on you women leaders becomes purified, and harmony is realized through true love, then the cherished hope of the Korean race, the unification of North and South Korea, will be achieved. Not only that, our nation will come to lead the world, and a peaceful world will be realized.

You Must Become One with True Parents' Family

Women leaders! Until this day I have never directed my followers to do anything that I have not first done myself. I sincerely ask you to practice true love and devote yourself, even if it is one hundredth of how much I have, and raise up a great movement of national salvation.

The most effective units of the Women's Federation Movement are the town, village, county and ward. When the movement of true love rises up in these basic units, then it will go through the level of neighborhood and come to settle in the family. We have to go through the original homeland before the fall and recover the family which has been separated from God before we can hope for eternal settlement. God has worked so hard. He has suffered so much to raise up the perfected Adam. That is why the True Father came about. The true man of heaven has been born.

Because the satanic world knows this man is the true groom, the master who comes as the king of the Kingdom of Heaven and earth, individuals in the world are trying to destroy him by uniting individuals, families, nations, the world and the universe against him. From the position of having to suffer all kinds of persecution, plotting and slandering by Satan, he has gained victory on the individual, family, national, world and cosmic levels and has become one with God. As the first victor of history, he came to the satanic world of the individual, family, nation, world and cosmos.

The True Mother, who has been in the position of following after the True Father, has for the first time in history come to stand in an equal position. Through her worldwide declaration of the liberation of women, the True Father and the True Mother will take their children, go before God, and inherit all the authority and power of heaven. They will establish the original family, and reclaim the tribe, race, nation, world and cosmos, and reorganize the perfect world of God's will.

All men are in the position of the archangel. Therefore, they stand in the position of having to give back all women. Women stand in the position of being the extension of the True Mother, the perfected Eve. From the position of the extension of Eve and on the condition of becoming one with the True Mother, they come to the condition of becoming one with the True Father. From this position they must educate their sons and daughters in the thought of the True Parents.

Through this education the sons and daughters come to have the status of being true sons and daughters and they should become one with their mother. Then they should reeducate the worldly father and receive True Parents' blessing. From the position of being grafted to the True Parents, they come to learn the family duty of the True Parents.

Because Adam and Eve fell on the family level, restoration also has to be accomplished on the family level. Restoration has to go beyond the levels of county, ward and block, and settle in the family, and then the families must meet the True Parents. The True Parents have gone over the individual peak, the national peak, the world peak and the cosmic peak, and have been victorious. However, in order to save each family they have to come back to the cosmos, the world, the nation, and return to the family. That is the meaning of this meeting.

The rally on April 10 was the True Parents' world rally, and its purpose was so that rallies could be held on the national level, the city level, the district level, down through the town, village, county, ward and block levels, until they arrive at the family level. By becoming one with True Parents' family, it is possible for you leaders of the Women's Federation for World Peace to attain family restoration and become absolute victors. You have to connect this to your tribe. The True Parents have already assigned tribal messiahs all over the world; if you receive education from them and become one with them, the restoration of the nation also will be accomplished naturally.

In this way the unification of North and South Korea, unification of the world, and the unification of heaven and earth will be realized; God, too, will be liberated. After this happens, we will come to see an age of peace centered on God.

Let the True Mother and the women of the world join together to meet the True Father who comes as the groom and, standing in the position of the bride, let us restore the ideal family of creation.

I pray that you become members of the Family Federation for World Peace and create families which will receive much blessing.

Thank you very much.

True Parents and the Completed Testament Age

Mrs. Hak Ja Han Moon, President, Women's Federation for World Peace
This address was given May through July, 1993 on a 44-city American tour.

Honored Guests,
Ladies and Gentlemen:

I want to express my heartfelt gratitude to you for coming here today. The promise of a peaceful and prosperous future depends directly upon the collective actions we take today.

As we all know, our world today is not a world of peace and happiness, but a world of conflict and despair. We are confronted with the breakdown of our families and the moral decline of our society. We have become a nation of talk shows. We debate the issues over and over again and yet find no solutions. Why is this? This is because a true solution must include God and deal with the root of the problem and not just the symptoms.

To find this root, we must first understand God's purpose of creation and realize that we, today, face the most important turning point in the history of God's providence.

At this crucial time in history, God has asked me to bring a new revelation to the American people. My wife, Mrs. Hak Ja Han Moon, the International President of the Women's Federation for World Peace, has been supporting me in this work.

In 1992 she conducted a tour that took her to 12 countries, where she spoke on the role of women and families in creating true world peace. Last year her speaking schedule took her to all 50 states of the U.S., where she spoke on the topic, "True Parents and the Completed Testament Age."

Last July, she addressed members of the United States Congress in Washington, and a few weeks later she delivered this speech to representatives of the world at the United Nations. Since then she has delivered this message in 27 cities of Japan and to the Japanese Diet, at 40 major universities of Korea, and the Korean Parliament. In December of last year, she completed a dramatic speaking tour of 40 countries. Now, our entire family is visiting 100 colleges and universities across America. Today, I would like to take this opportunity to convey to you this important message.

God's Original Ideal

God's ideal in creating the first human ancestors, Adam and Eve, was that they perfect themselves through true love so that they could then create a good family of true love, true life and true lineage. Such a good family would have been formed on the basis of unified

---

heart and mind among family members in front of God.

When God created Adam and Eve, His first son and daughter, God wanted them to be better than Himself. Traditional thinking would say that this is absurd. But please take a moment to think about this. When we as parents look into the faces of our children, we wish upon them an infinite amount of love and hope. We want them to grow and achieve things we ourselves only dreamed of.

Similarly, God wants to give limitlessly to His children. God is not content in giving just 100 percent. God's desire is to give a thousand times more than what He has given. The nature of God's love is to give completely and then forget what He has given. Unlike some who calculate how much they have given and decide that it is enough, for God enough is never enough. Moreover, God's purpose in creating the world was to have an object of love. His purpose in creating parents and children, husbands and wives, and all things in this world in complementary pairs was to substantiate true love throughout His creation.

Likewise, parents are to live for their children, and children for their parents. Husbands are to live for their wives, and wives for their husbands. All beings in creation are to live for and give to others. If God's ideal of true love had been realized through Adam's family, that family would have become the beginning of the heavenly kingdom. It would have expanded throughout all of history to the clan, to the nation and to the world. This would have been the world of true love—the Kingdom of Heaven on Earth. Furthermore, there would have been a parallel expansion of the heavenly kingdom in the spiritual world.

Human History's False Start

If God's original ideal had been realized, then there would have been no need of a Messiah or of God's providence to save humanity. Adam's family, though it was merely a single family, would have been the center of the clan, of the nation, and of the world. It would have been the blueprint for all future families. It would have been the model for the realization of God's ideal world. Because of the fall of the original human ancestors, God's work of salvation had to begin. Salvation history had to be repeatedly extended through the complicated and suffering courses of the Old and New Testament Ages, culminating in today's Completed Testament Age.

God's ideal of the true family and the heavenly kingdom, which He wanted to realize through Adam's family, was destroyed because Adam and Eve fell away from God. Due to the fall, this present world is far from the good world of God's ideal. In fact, today's world is a "false" world, in that it is flooded with self-centered love.

This came about because Adam and Eve became false parents based on false and self-centered love with Satan. They multiplied evil rather than goodness, creating a false family and passing on false life and a false lineage to their descendants. Thus, false clans, false nations and a false world came into being.

Therefore, the goal in God's dispensation of salvation is for a man and a woman, representing Adam and Eve, to be restored as True Parents centered on God's true love, so that the true family can be formed. From them would eventually flow the true clan, the true nation and the true world. In other words, the seed from which God's true love, true life and true lineage can grow must be created.

Formula for the Reconciliation

My dear friends, have you ever wondered how a world filled with such evil and corruption could come from a God of love and goodness? If you read the Bible carefully, you will see that the fall of man involves the loss of Adam's entire family. First, the position of parents was lost through the fall of Adam and Eve. Second, the position of children was lost as Cain murdered Abel. God's blueprint for an ideal family and world perfection was lost. Therefore, to restore the original family, God works in reverse to reclaim the positions of Cain and Abel, and then the positions of True Mother and True Father.

This pattern of reconciliation of Cain and Abel as the foundation for restoring the True Parents has been God's consistent formula throughout the history of restoration. The separation of fallen mankind into a Cain-Abel division occurs over and over again in Judeo-Christian history. God first of all separated fallen mankind into two "brotherly" sides of Cain, symbolizing Satan, and Abel, symbolizing God, to work out the hatreds resulting from the fall.

God used the method of having Abel be hit first and sacrificed. As a result, Abel could stand on that very foundation to embrace Cain and recover the blessing given to the elder son. For example, the religion that most advances the purpose of salvation always receives Satan's most severe persecution. It walks the path of constant opposition yet continues its sacrificial effort to save the sinful world. Likewise, good people always stand in the position of being struck first and sacrificed.

Looking almost anywhere in our fallen world, it is easy to notice struggles between good and evil, similar to the struggle between Abel and Cain. These struggles start in the conflict between each individual's mind and body. The mind, which represents the Abel side, struggles to overcome the body, which represents the Cain side. The struggle within individuals has expanded to the family, nation and world. As a result, humankind has always been divided into two opposing camps, one good, or Abel-like, and the other evil, or Cain-like, locked in struggle at every level. It has always been God's intention, however, that both sides be restored, not that one triumphs over and destroys the other.

Some examples of this division are the thief on the right side of Jesus' cross, who represented Abel, and the thief on the left, who represented Cain, and South Korea versus North Korea, which represents the last conflict between right wing and left wing on the world level. So the key to God's work of salvation has always been to unify such divided sides, based on His ideal, in order to build a foundation on which to reclaim the True Mother and True Father.

The Root of Social Problems

Ladies and gentlemen, if a family is not centered on God's ideal of love, there will be conflict among the members of that family. Without God's love as an absolute center, such a family will ultimately break down. Moreover, a nation of such families will also decline.

Because illicit, self-centered love invaded the first family, selfishness and greed have continued to dominate human history from the individual to the family, society, nation and world. For this reason, God's work of restoration begins at the individual level. Since Satan knows this, he focuses his efforts also on the individual level.

It is not by chance that self-centered individualism has become the dominant way of life in these last days. People feel increasingly alienated from those around them, and bear little sense of responsibility for the well-being of their country, society, or even their own families. Rising divorce statistics indicate that husbands and wives feel little responsibility toward their marriages; parents do not take proper responsibility for their children; and individuals, devoid of any sense of human dignity, fail even to take responsibility for themselves.

America has seen such phenomena at work beginning with the youth movement of the sixties. Idealistic youth rejected the materialism around them in order to seek love and peace, but in the process, they also abandoned morality and responsibility. Unable to attain the true love they sought, many disillusioned young people resorted to suicide, drug abuse and free sex.

Of all these, what pains God most is free sex. A world of free sex is absolutely contrary to the will of God and the ideal of the family. Love comes from the stimulation of unblemished emotion, but free sex is totally devoid of purity or true emotion. How many of us have been touched by the cruelty of infidelity and divorce? Where is God in all the one-night stands? What about the nightmare of the children who are sexually abused by a parent? Is free sex worth the price of a broken child?

Equally alarming is the policy of giving schoolchildren condoms, teaching the illusion of safe sex, and surrendering to the assumption that premarital sex is inevitable. Indeed, where there is homosexuality, free sex, drugs and alcoholism, the world of true love is far away.

In this world, Satan openly tells people, "Drink! Take drugs! Have sex!" Those who do God's will, on the other hand, live a lifestyle that is 180 degrees different from this. Throughout history, those who chose to walk a spiritual path of self-sacrifice have been bitterly opposed and persecuted by the rest of the world. For example, it is only God's love and blessing that have allowed the Unification Church to prosper, despite worldwide opposition. The fact that our church has risen from obscurity in war-torn Korea, to become a world-level religious movement in only 38 years, testifies to God's continued guidance and support.

There are those who continue to oppose the Unification Church, spreading wild rumors or trying to prevent our teachings from being heard. Again, Satan's way is always to attack that which is most precious to God. Yet those who go against the will of God can never prosper. The principle holds true that those on God's side, who can endure unjust persecution, will win the right to take back the blessing. God's strategy is always to be hit first, and then take back what is rightfully His.

Restoring True Love

Ladies and gentlemen, the Bible teaches that Eve was the first to disobey God and enter into a relationship with Satan. Due to the Fall, not only Eve, but also Adam and their sons Cain and Abel, inherited Satan's lineage, based upon selfishness and false love.

As the descendants of the original couple which was compromised by Satan, we have all inherited a satanic lineage. This is why Jesus said in John 8:44, "You are of your father, the devil."

The Old Testament described a process of restitution according to the formula "an eye for an eye and a tooth for a tooth." In the Divine Principle, we refer to making restitution for a wrong as "paying indemnity."

To make restitution for her wrong actions, fallen Eve needed to take the entire responsibility upon herself. She should have reversed the actions of the fall and made spiritual and physical restitution for each step of the fall. It was God's will that Eve assist her younger son, Abel, to unite with the will of God. We know from Genesis that Abel had his offering accepted by God.

However, this was not all that was expected of Abel. Through Abel's love, Cain was supposed to recognize Abel as God's chosen person and unite with him, and Eve was supposed to help them bring about that unity. If Cain and Abel had united, the second of the two problems of the fall would have been solved. The unity between Cain and Abel centering on Eve would have created a foundation to restore the whole of Adam's family.

Throughout providential history, we see the same role played by special women called by God to help unite the positions of Cain and Abel as restitution for fallen Eve's role.

A Model Course

In the Bible, one of these special women is Rebekah, the spouse of Isaac. As the mother of Jacob and Esau, Rebekah held the same position in Isaac's family that Eve held in Adam's family. Unlike Eve, however, Rebekah understood God's providence and helped her second son, Jacob, representing Abel's position, to gain the blessing destined for the first son, Esau. Just as Cain killed Abel, Esau wanted to kill Jacob when the blessing went to his younger brother. But with Rebekah's help, these brothers eventually reconciled in a warm embrace, rather than resorting to violence.

This reconciliation was a major victory for God. This victory, nevertheless, was not complete, since the reconciliation represented only a symbolic purification of God's lineage. The substantial purification of His lineage had to be accomplished in the womb. This is the reason for the paradoxical story of Tamar.

By understanding that Tamar, like Rebekah, was in the position of fallen Eve, it becomes possible to understand why Jesus was born of her lineage, the tribe of Judah. I am sure that many of you have read the story about the birth of her twins. She conceived with Judah, her father-in-law, the twins Perez and Zerah. The Bible tells us that the two sons struggled even in the womb for the position of first-born. During Tamar's labor, Zerah's hand was the first to emerge, and the midwife tied a red string around his wrist. Then, Zerah's hand disappeared back into the womb and Perez, the younger, was born as the elder!

Thus, the positions of Cain and Abel were restored even before birth took place. It was from this point that the Israelite people became the nation chosen to receive the Messiah. In terms of conventional morality, the stories of Rebekah and Tamar would be questionable at best. Why God blessed them has been a theological mystery until today. As we now see, God needed to reclaim His lineage from Satan so that Jesus could be born. Purified, true-love lineage was the point from which the Israelite nation started expanding. The word Israel means victory. Their victory was the purification of God's lineage.

Mary's Life-Risking Course

The lineage of Judah developed for generations, expanding to the levels of tribe, society and nation. From this same lineage, Mary was born in Israel 2,000 years later.

Mary had the responsibility to unite Cain and Abel figures on the family, clan and national levels through paying appropriate indemnity and restoring elder sonship. Mary responded to God's call and conceived Jesus even though, in the eyes of others, she had betrayed her parents and Joseph, to whom she was engaged. At that time, it was customary to stone to death any woman who became pregnant out of wedlock. However, Joseph, standing in the position of Adam, courageously protected his fiancee and resisted abandoning her.

Because of Mary's faith, and the work of Rebekah and Tamar, Satan could not claim sovereignty over Jesus in Mary's womb. Jesus was born in the position of a true son under God's complete, direct lineage. He is the first true son of God after the purification of the fallen lineage. That is why Jesus, the first-begotten son of God, is the saint of all saints and the ancestor of God's true lineage. His birth represented the conclusion of the Old Testament Age at the national level and the dawn of the New Testament Age at the worldwide level.

Mary, in the position to restore fallen Eve, had to build a unity between Jesus, who was in the position of Abel, and his elder cousin, John the Baptist, who was in the position of Cain. This unity was essential for the people of Israel to identify Jesus as the Messiah.

John was the elder. He had a great following and was widely respected. As Jesus explained to his disciples, the ministry of John was the fulfillment of the Old Testament prophecy that Elijah the prophet would return to "make straight the way of the Lord." But did John fulfill his role in God's providence?

The Gospel of Luke tells us that John came "in the spirit and power of Elijah." John, however, denied that he was Elijah, and doubted the messiahship of Jesus even after he had received a clear revelation at the Jordan River at the time of Jesus' baptism. John was a well-respected religious figure, while Jesus was seen as only the illegitimate son of a poor carpenter. Without the support of John, it was impossible for the Jewish people to believe in and follow Jesus. Alone, Jesus undertook the difficult path of proclaiming himself.

John the Baptist should have helped Jesus reach the religious leadership of Israel. If John had fulfilled his role, then Judaism, in the position of Abel, and the nation of Israel, in the position of Cain, could have united centered on Jesus.

This Cain-Abel unity would have laid the foundation for the marriage of the Lamb. Jesus would have stood as the True Father of humanity and his bride would have stood as the True Mother of humanity. In less than seven years, his teachings would have expanded rapidly to the worldwide level, winning Asia and Rome to his side before he was 40.

Eventually, Jesus and his bride would have achieved the individual heavenly kingdom, family heavenly kingdom, clan heavenly kingdom and national heavenly kingdom.

A Dream Unfulfilled

However, this glorious destiny could not be realized. It was the religious people themselves who rejected Jesus' words and called for his crucifixion. Confronted by the disbelief in Israel, Jesus determined to give his life to achieve spiritual salvation for humankind. However, he knew that Christ would have to come again in order to bring both physical or earthly salvation as well as spiritual salvation.

This is why the mind can draw close to God through Jesus, but the body continues to be tempted by evil. Even Saint Paul anguished over the contradiction of the desires of the flesh and the desires of the spirit. Many great Christian evangelists have also suffered because of this contradiction. At the dawn of the Completed Testament Age, the crucial challenge is to accomplish both physical salvation and spiritual salvation.

Because of Jesus' death on the cross, the conflict between left wing and right wing appeared, symbolized by the two thieves who died with him. This is like the separation into

Cain and Abel necessitated by Adam's fall. Likewise, Islam and Christianity appeared and began struggling. Because such separation was caused by the crucifixion of Jesus, Christ will work for unity of these Cain-Abel divisions at the time of the Second Coming.

The Unity Imperative

God's preparation for the Second Advent required a world-level foundation of successful Cain-Abel reconciliation. This dispensation was carried out through the events surrounding World War II. The Allied countries of Britain, America and France represented Christianity and were in the position of Abel. The Axis countries of Germany, Japan and Italy were under the influence of nationalistic militarism and stood in the position of Cain. This war represented the expansion of the conflict between Cain and Abel to the world level.

Immediately after the Allied victory, great strides were made toward creating a world of peace centered upon Christianity. With Britain in the world-level position of Eve, and America and France representing Abel and Cain respectively, these Allied nations stood in the position ready to receive the Lord of the Second Advent. Despite all of this preparation, God's dispensation was not fulfilled at that time. God's representative came to bring His word, but was met with tremendous persecution and almost universal misunderstanding.

This paralleled Jesus' situation 2,000 years ago. Just as the Israelites of Jesus' time awaited the Second Coming of Elijah on a chariot descending from heaven, Christians awaited the Second Coming by expecting Jesus himself to descend on a cloud from the sky. In the Book of Revelation, Jesus reveals to the Apostle John that he will come again with a new name. This foreshadowed that Jesus would come again through another man, just as Elijah had done.

At this crucial time after World War II, God instructed me to bring a new message of truth to Christians in Korea. Korean Christian leaders, however, rejected the possibility that I, a humble young man, had been chosen to bring this new message. They could not believe that the Second Coming would be born as a man on earth any more than the Jewish people could believe the same about Elijah at the time of Jesus.

If the Christian churches had become one with me, the heavenly kingdom would already have been established on earth as well as in the spiritual realm. During the seven-year period from 1945 to 1952, marking the end of World War II and the end of the New Testament Age, the entire world could have united in accordance with the providence of God.

A Thorny Path

Instead of uniting with me, however, these religious leaders became jealous of the growing number of my followers. They blindly opposed me without hearing me out. They even spread lies about me. Rumors of sexual misconduct and greed, the very antithesis of my teachings, were used to assassinate my character.

God had expanded Christianity and had raised up a mighty Christian nation like America for the purpose of preparing the way for the Second Coming. Whether they realized it or not, those ministers in Korea represented all of Christianity. Because America and worldwide Christianity failed to unite with me after World War II, they began to decline in their power and moral authority.

After World War II, the nation of the United States and the religion of Christianity stood on a victorious foundation of Cain-Abel unity. The time was ripe to receive the Second Coming.

However, this opportunity failed to materialize and the whole world opposed my work. I was expelled into the wilderness. I was forced to the bottom and have been climbing back up ever since.

Thus, the Cold War began. Starting with the Korean War, the world separated again into two worldwide spheres of Cain and Abel, just as it had during World War II. Denying God, just as the thief on the left denied Jesus, communism represented the Cain-type world. Christian democracies, which affirmed the existence of God, represented the thief on the right, and the Abel-type world.

In the world today, the two most significant Cain and Abel figures are Premier Kim Il Sung, a Cain-type father in North Korea, and the Reverend Moon, an Abel-type father in South Korea. Following God's will, these two fathers must establish the foundation for world peace by achieving the reunification of Korea.

Moreover, it will be the Messiah of the Second Coming who unites these two hostile blocs worldwide. That is why we mobilized our church to help settle conflicts between the right wing, represented by the free world, and the left wing, represented by communism. We have also worked on behalf of Christianity and Judaism as a peacemaker with our Islamic brothers and sisters. During the Cold War period, I fought to break down barriers on the individual, family, clan, national, worldwide and cosmic levels in order to rebuild the lost foundation to receive the Messiah.

I knew that I would have to indemnify all of history in just 40 years. During this period of four decades, I restored the 4,000-year history before Jesus, and the 6,000-year biblical history since the creation. After this indemnity was paid, the Cold War ended through the unity of Cain and Abel blocs. This was consummated by the Unification Church at the 1988 Seoul Olympics, where 160 nations of the world came to Korea.

For decades, I have been completely misunderstood. For three years, I was imprisoned in a North Korean communist concentration camp. Altogether, I have been wrongfully imprisoned six times for doing God's work. Moreover, the media have mocked me as a monster who brainwashes the young for self-benefit.

Can anyone disagree when I say that I am the most persecuted religious leader in the world? But I always am comforted and reassured to know that God has deep compassion for those persecuted for doing His work.

My wife and I have purposefully walked a path of indemnity, or restitution, in order to restore the failures of the past, including those of the Old and New Testament eras. Korea can be compared to the Old Testament Age, while America, a mostly Christian civilization, can be compared to the New Testament Age.

For the first 20 years, we walked the road of indemnity of the Old Testament Age, centering on the Korean nation and the Unification Church, representing the positions of the Israelite nation and Judaism, respectively. On the foundation of this work, we established in 1960 the Holy Wedding of True Parents on the national level. Then, in 1971, we came to America. During the next 20 years in the United States, we walked the path of indemnity to fulfill the New Testament Age and begin the Completed Testament Age. Thus, we established the True Parents' family, the origin of true love, true life and true blood lineage based on God.

The reason why America is still essential in the providential dispensation is because of her close ties with Judaism, Israel and the Christian Churches, representing the Old and New Testament Ages. Even though America dismissed and opposed my work, I continue to pray for America to realize her providential responsibility. It is my sincere desire that America avoid repeating her failure.

A failure to unite with God's will would create the need for further indemnity and would deprive America of the blessing that God wishes to bestow upon this great nation. Indeed, without the help of our Unification movement, America would have waned long ago.

Rome thought that the world existed only for the sake of Rome. She did not realize that God had raised her up for the purpose of uniting with the Messiah and serving the world. Now, ruins are all that remain of that civilization. America faces a similar situation today. People must realize that God blessed America not for herself but for the sake of the world. America's pilgrim fathers did not come here for wealth. They came here to attend God. If America fails to remember the purpose for which she is blessed, then her blessing will cease and she will perish.

We desperately want to prevent this. We must save America. For more than twenty years, we have struggled in this country, trying to bring God's message to the American people. American leaders, prominent Christians and other leading figures of the world have only a faint idea of the forces that shape the future. They can offer little insight, hope or guidance to their people. In these chaotic times, humankind is longing for a true direction and purpose, yet America and Christianity have shown no confident answer.

God, however, has granted me an understanding of the forces involved in His providential history. I know the direction that humankind must go, and with the help of God, I will lead the world there.

What the Unification Church Offers

The truth that God revealed to me is contained in the Divine Principle. Looking at the history of humankind and the stories of the Bible from the providential viewpoint, the Divine Principle unlocks the answers to questions unsolved for thousands of years. Those who have sincerely studied its contents have found it to be a true gift from God, providing the only solutions to the problems facing our society today.

Even in the formerly communist C.I.S., government leaders and thousands of young people have found their lives renewed through their studies of our teachings, known as "Godism" or "Head-wing Ideology." Finally free from the oppression of communist ideology, they are hungry for the spiritual truth to guide their nations.

There are countless other testimonies to the power of the Divine Principle to give hope and new life to young people. In 1992, in Korea, my wife and I held a wedding celebration for 30,000 couples, all dedicating their lives to one another, to God and to the world. In most families today, parents cannot effectively guide their children, especially on such intimate matters as love and marriage.

Yet, we brought together young people from 131 different nations and realized their most cherished dreams of love in an historic way. This was indeed a great miracle of the modern world. In the future, as people come to understand the value and quality of these precious families, millions will seek such marriages. Through them, God can restore the family that Satan has destroyed. Such restored, God-centered families are the very building blocks of an ideal nation and world.

My dear friends, when Jesus taught about the coming of the Messiah, he told the parable of the virgins who were awaiting the arrival of the bridegroom. According to the Book of Revelation, Christianity is portrayed as a bride. America, representing Christianity, can also be seen as a bride nation.

Women's Crucial Role

Therefore, America must take the responsibility of creating a foundation for worldwide unity upon which the bridegroom can finally be received. This signifies the restoration of the original positions of man and woman, restored Adam and Eve, to the realm of true equality.

When Christianity failed to meet her bridegroom the first time, God's dispensation had to be delayed 40 years until 1992. During this time, my wife and I worked and prayed to bring about the unity of Korea, Britain, America, France, Japan, Germany and Italy. At this turning point in the history of restoration, a woman in the position of True Mother must prepare the world to receive the True Father. This is why, in April, 1992, Reverend and Mrs. Moon founded the Women's Federation for World Peace.

In that year, with the heart of a True Mother, my wife visited these seven countries, as well as Russia and Oceania. She gathered together the women of these nations to form chapters of the Women's Federation for World Peace.

With these events, the nations that had been the worldwide Cain and Abel countries since World War II united together to receive the True Mother and prepare again the foundation to meet the True Father. Based upon this foundation, my wife and I can now stand on a worldwide level as the first True Parents. As the True Parents, we are ushering in the Completed Testament Age.

At this historical turning point, we have to practice on the worldwide level the principle that an individual's mind and body must be united centered on God. To facilitate this, we have founded two organizations working for world peace. The Inter-Religious Federation for World Peace represents the world mind, and carries out the internal mission of uniting all the world's religions on the basis of God's love.

The Federation for World Peace, on the other hand, represents the world body, and pursues the external mission of building up ideal societies with leaders in the fields of politics, economics, media, academia, science and the arts.

Completing the Family Foundation

Looking from the vertical perspective of love, Adam and Eve should have related directly with God by developing in themselves the four types of love: child love, brother-sister love, conjugal love and parental love. Therefore, Adam and Eve should have originally grown through the four spheres of the heart, centering on God's true love, as completed children, completed brother and sister, loving couple and perfected parents.

They would have thus achieved the completed family. Adam and Eve should have become the role models for everyone in their family. Their children would have looked to their parents as ideal role models. They would have become brothers and sisters who loved each other as their parents loved them. They would have become a married couple resembling the husband-wife relationship of their parents. Finally, with the birth of children, they would have established another completed family, identical to that of their parents.

Thus, all the families in the world, originating from the same God-centered ancestors, Adam and Eve, would have had equal, divine value. By establishing ideal, unbreakable families that fulfill the vertical and horizontal unity between parents and children, brothers and sisters, and husbands and wives, we will finally build the eternal basis for God's kingdom on earth as well as in heaven. In every completed family, grandparents will be in the position of kings and queens, representing God and good ancestors. Parents will be in the position of kings and queens, representing present humanity, and children will be in the position of princes and princesses representing all future descendants. When all three generations are united, past, present and future will live together in harmony.

Ladies and gentlemen, it is my great privilege to announce to you the establishment of the first True Family. My wife and I, together with our 13 children and 20 grandchildren, are absolutely dedicated to serving God and humanity. With three generations in one family, we have achieved, on the family level, the central root, the central trunk, and the central bud of the "Tree of Life" mentioned in the Bible.

It is our sincere hope that you will symbolically graft into this tree by joining us in our efforts to create an ideal nation and world. This marks the beginning of the Completed Testament Age.

Extension of the Messianic Ideal

Ladies and gentlemen, at the dawn of the Completed Testament Age, the time has come for each family to take up the messianic mission of completing the work of salvation all over the world. After restoring your family, the next step is to restore your community, tribe and nation. We call this process "Tribal Messiahship."

In the Completed Testament Age, the mother's role will be crucial. She must unite her children and her husband, and link her family with the True Parents. Already, we have sent thousands of tribal messiah missionaries around the world. Soon, the original ideal of the family will be achieved worldwide.

As the world enters the Completed Testament era, we will live with God again. Realizing this, we must accomplish the unity of our mind and body, parents and children, and husbands and wives. Then we can establish ideal families centered upon God's love.

With such families, the symptoms of our decaying society will vanish. As confident children of God, we will no longer be enslaved by the temptations of alcohol and drug abuse. Moreover, by understanding the holiness of love between a husband and a wife, we will possess the moral strength to stand strong against infidelity and promiscuity. Finally, we will work as a whole to eliminate war, racial prejudices and world hunger. Based upon this foundation, we can realize a world of true happiness, freedom and peace.

God is very much alive, and His original ideal for humankind is unchanging and absolute. It is our destiny to fulfill this ideal and liberate God's heart. In such a world, there would be heartfelt compassion for the needs of others, and the nations of the world would naturally cooperate to preserve peace and justice. Therefore, understanding that this is God's vision for humanity, let us join together to bring peace and reconciliation to every corner of the world.

It is my hope that all Christians, and people of all faiths, will understand this message with a deep heart and an open mind. I sincerely pray that by upholding the will of God, we can all reach the place of God's blessing.

May God bless you and your families.

Thank you very much.

The Proclamation of the Complete Testament Age

View of the Principle of the Providential History of Salvation

Reverend Sun Myung Moon, President, Federation for World Peace
This address was given April 16, 1996 at the inaugural banquet of the Washington Times Foundation.

Distinguished Guests, Ladies and Gentlemen,

Today, I sincerely thank God that you and I can meet as we face this era of great historical change. God is the absolute One, the only, unchanging and eternal One. His will is the same. If the human beings Adam and Eve had become one body under the love of God, everything would have been complete and perfect. God's origin, purpose and process of creation, as well as cause, effect and direction, are all absolute.

The human ancestors Adam and Eve entered into chaos after they fell through their ignorance. This ignorance and chaos expanded from the individual level to the levels of family, nation and world. It has been the task of religion and the Providence of Salvation to liberate us from this sphere of the Fall.

In the Last Days, the Messiah comes and teaches clearly the absolute, the only, unchanging and eternal cause, direction and effect, from God's viewpoint. He will cleanse the world of ignorance and chaos and return it to the original bosom of God. This is the completion of the will of God. If this does not happen, then in the Last Days all religions, "isms," systems of thought, and nations will pass away.

To bring about completion and perfection between God and humankind, centering on True Love, God required that man accomplish a condition of responsibility in order to reach unity with Him. Therefore, God needed to give the Commandment to the first ancestors. In other words, God knew that they were in the growth period, on the way to reaching perfection, so He established the Commandment as the condition for His children to inherit the most precious thing, True Love.

Originally, True Love was to be gained through life experience and understood through internal realization. True Love is not something that can be learned through words, a written text or schooling. It is experienced completely only in life. Created as newborn infants, Adam and Eve were to grow and perfect themselves gradually through experiences of the heart of True Children, True Brother and Sister, True Husband and Wife, and True Parents encompassing their whole lives. Only after experiencing the True Love of God in its entirety can one perfect the Purpose of Creation and become an ideal human being.

Every person desires that his object of love be ten million times more valuable than himself, or even infinitely more valuable. In the same way, God desires that humankind, His object of love, become infinitely valuable. If a human being perfects himself, then that person obtains God-like value by attaining God's divinity and perfection.

God's Ideal of True Love

God is absolute, but His ideal of True Love cannot be realized by himself. That is because love always requires an object—a beloved. At this point, we should understand the relationship between God's True Love and humankind's True Love, and how they begin and are perfected. What would have happened if God had not chosen human beings as His absolute objects of True Love, and instead had sought to begin and perfect True Love in some other way? In that case, God and man would have pursued the ideal of True Love with different motivations, directions and purposes. God would have had to achieve His ideal of love through an object higher than humankind; and by the same token, humankind's ideal of love would have had no direct relationship with God.

But God, as the subject of True Love, did establish humankind as the object of His True Love. Accordingly, God can fulfill His ideal of True Love only through humankind. The fulfillment of God's Purpose of Creation is the ideal world where God and mankind are united through absolute love. Human beings were created as the greatest object of God's love. They alone in all Creation embody the nature of God. They are born the visible bodies of the invisible God. If a person perfects himself, he becomes the temple of God, a visible, substantial body in which God can freely and peacefully dwell. God's overall ideal of absolute True Love is realized and perfected through humankind in a vertical parent-child relationship.

God created Adam first. He was to be the son of God and at the same time the substantial body of God Himself. Later, God created Eve as the object of Adam so that Adam and Eve could perfect the ideal of horizontal love, which is conjugal love. Eve was to be the daughter of God, and also, as a bride she was to perfect substantially the ideal of the horizontal love of God.

The place in which Adam and Eve are perfected, consummating their first love by marrying under the blessing of God, is precisely the place where God meets His substantial bride. This is because God's ideal of absolute love descends vertically and joins where the ideal of conjugal love between Adam and Eve is realized horizontally. The True Love of God and the True Love of humankind join and perfect themselves at the same point, although they came from different directions, one vertical and the other horizontal.

Why God Needs Humankind

God's act of creation was inevitable. And we cannot imagine Creation without a purpose. There was only one reason God needed the Creation: to realize the ideal of True Love. God developed life from the simplest and lowest levels up to the human level in pairs, subject and object and positive and negative, to form reciprocal relationships under the ideal of love. The Creation's ideal of love and God's ideal of ultimate love are not separate or different. This Principle of Creation is at work to perfect the absolute love of God through the perfection of the love of man and woman in the human world. This is the reason why in the beginning God created one man and one woman, Adam and Eve.

God's Purpose of Creation called for Adam and Eve to obey the Commandment of God, who is the subject of True Love, and perfect themselves as True Man and True Woman. Furthermore, they were to become a True Couple united in the True Love of God. Then, by having sons and daughters through that True Love, they would have become True Parents and lived in happiness. Had Adam and Eve perfected themselves in True Love, they would have fulfilled God's desire to have a substantial body. And when they perfected themselves as a True Couple, the ideal of God's absolute love would have been fulfilled.

By Adam and Eve having children of goodness and becoming True Parents, God would have established Himself substantially as the Eternal Parent and achieved His ideal: Citizenship in the Kingdom of Heaven would expand infinitely in the afterlife of the spirit world based on myriad generations of descendants in the physical world.

But Adam and Eve, the human ancestors, fell away from God. When they were expelled from Eden, they had not yet had children. Having driven them out, God had no basis to follow behind them to bless their marriage. The entire human race has thus descended from our failed ancestors. Humanity has multiplied without any direct relationship whatsoever to the love of God.

Could the Fall of Man have been the result of eating the fruit of a tree? The fall of Adam and Eve was an immoral sin against the ideal of the True Love of God. The fact that Adam and Eve needed to obey the Commandment shows that they fell in a stage of imperfection, that is to say, during their period of growth. The Archangel, who is symbolized by a serpent, tempted Eve to eat of the fruit of good and evil, and she fell spiritually. She later tempted Adam (who was also too immature to eat of the fruit), and they then fell physically.

The only possible sin that could have been fatal in the Garden of Eden, where Adam and Eve were in communication with God and living in joy, was the sin of illicit love. The first consummated love of the human ancestors, because it was supposed to have been the perfection of the love of God Himself, should have marked the beginning of a celebration that would continue throughout history, filled with the never-ending intoxication of joy and blessing for God, Adam and Eve, and the universe. It should have been a joyous occasion in which the love, life and lineage of God would have been established within humankind. To the contrary, however, Adam and Eve covered their lower parts and hid themselves among the trees, trembling in fear. By disobeying heavenly law, they established an immoral relationship as the basis for false love, false life and false lineage. As descendants of Adam and Eve, all human beings are born with Original Sin. The Fall gave rise to conflict of mind and body within every person and caused our societies to be filled with tainted love, and people to do things that contradict the desire of their original minds.

Taking Responsibility for Love

According to the ideal of love, all love relationships in the animal and plant kingdoms are for reproduction only. Human beings are the sole exception. Humankind enjoys freedom in the conjugal relationship of love. This is humanity's special privilege as the lord of all creation. God gave the blessing and infinite joy of love to His sons and daughters. However, the True Freedom that God allowed requires human responsibility. If an individual were to insist upon and practice freedom of love without responsibility, how much confusion and destruction would take place! Achieving the highest ideal of human love is possible only when one takes responsibility for love.

We can think of this responsibility in three ways. The first responsibility is for one to become the master of True Love—truly free and thanking God for the freedom of love and knowing how to cultivate and control oneself. This responsibility for a love relationship should not be taken merely because of law or social convention. Instead, a person should establish responsibility through his own self-control and self-determination within the life-committing vertical relationship with God.

Second is one's responsibility toward the object of love. By nature, people do not want their spouse's love to be shared with others. Horizontal conjugal love, which differs from the vertical love between parents and children, loses its potential for perfection the moment it is divided. This is because the Principle of Creation requires husband and wife to become one in absolute love. Each spouse has the responsibility given by love to live absolutely for the sake of the other.

The third responsibility of love is toward children. The love of parents is the basis for children's pride and happiness. They would wish to be born through the total and harmonious unity of their parents in True Love, and they would wish to be raised in that kind of love. The most precious responsibility of parents is not only to rear their children externally, but also to offer them life elements of True Love that can perfect their spirituality. This is why the family is so valuable. The daily experience of the heart of True Children, True Brothers and Sisters, True Spouses and True Parents cannot be acquired in any place other than the True Family.

If Adam and Eve had become a couple of True Love centered upon God, God could have dwelt in Adam as His substantial body and thus loved Eve. What is more, Adam and Eve could have become True Parents who substantially embodied God, and become the origin of the love of goodness, a life of goodness, and a lineage of goodness.

Due to the Fall, however, Adam and Eve became the substantial body of Satan and ended up becoming the original evil couple, evil parents and evil ancestors. Their union became the root of evil love, evil life and evil blood lineage. Because human beings originated from this root, they descended from the adulterous Satan, who is the enemy of God, and inherited this lineage of evil parents.

How great must have been the pain of God when, by the Fall, our human ancestors destroyed His ideal of True Love! Humankind should have been the sons and daughters of God, but they do not know God Himself as their Original Parent. Yet even though His sons and daughters serve Satan, God has worked for the Providence of Salvation. Because He is an absolute being, and His ideal of creation is also absolute, He has carried out the Providence of Salvation even amid great sadness. God's Providence of Salvation is the Providence of Restoration, which means to recover the lost Purpose of Creation, centered on True Love. The Providence of Salvation is also the Providence of Re-creation.

The Essence of God's Providence

Based on this point, the root of the Providence of Salvation is the re-creation of the seed of the original child, the human being who will fulfill the ideal of creation. That which God abhors—the life and blood lineage that began with the false love of the adulterer Satan—must be cleansed. The essence of the Providence is the task of setting up the birth of the True Parent, the Savior united with the True Love, Life and Lineage of God.

Since the ancestors of humankind failed to fulfill their responsibility, inherited the immoral lineage of Satan, and came under the dominion of Satan, God Himself could not directly intervene and return human beings to their original position. Furthermore, God can neither unconditionally accept humankind, who chose to go to the side of the evil Archangel, nor punish them. So God uses the strategy of placing a central figure on the side of the good Archangel; by being struck first, that figure establishes the indemnity condition to recover what was lost. Satan strikes first but as a result, he must take the losing position. The First, Second and Third (Cold War) World Wars are good examples of this. The side that struck first, lost.

From the overall perspective of the Providence of Restoration, the foundation of cooperation between mother and son is very important. This was so at the time of Jacob, Moses and Jesus. God was working His Providence to separate people from satanic life and lineage by establishing the foundation of cooperation between a mother—who had to fulfill the responsibility of Eve, the originator of the Fall—and the second son of the family.

God cannot directly relate to the first son because he is in the position of having a direct blood relationship with Satan, who through the Fall was the first to dominate humankind. God has been restoring the blood lineage of goodness by having the second son, who represents the side of goodness, establish a condition. Then God has had the first son, representing the side of evil, take a position subordinate to the second son.

In the family of Adam, God carried out the providence of establishing the second son, Abel, and having him subordinate the first son, Cain. Even though Eve had fallen, as a mother she could have made an effort to create unity between the two brothers. In the end, however, Cain murdered Abel (Genesis 4:8), and the Providence of Salvation, not being fulfilled, was prolonged.

There was also a required formula of cooperation between mother and son at the time of Noah. But that formula of meaningful cooperation was not realized until the time of Rebekah and Jacob.

The human Fall was committed by three beings: Adam, Eve and the Archangel. The Archangel seduced Eve, causing the spiritual fall, and later fallen Eve seduced Adam, causing the physical fall. As a result, they turned their backs on God, and the fallen Archangel became Satan. Since the Providence of Salvation is the Providence of Restoration, the Principle of Restoration can be carried out only by going in a direction 180 degrees opposite of the Fall.

God lost Adam, who had the seed of True Love and True Life. Thus, God had to find a son with the new seed free from satanic accusation. Just as God created Adam first at the time of the creation, God must prepare a son first who has no relationship to the Fall, according to the Providence of Restoration, which is the Providence of Re-creation. This is the basis for the idea of the coming of the Messiah. The Messiah rejects the sinful lives of those with a fallen lineage under the dominion of Satan. He comes as a True Person who engrafts fallen humanity into the seed of new life. The Messiah has his roots in God, and comes as the Second Adam, who wipes away all that was committed by the first Adam. This is the reason God cannot send a superman Messiah who will work only through miracles.

For a son to be born on earth with this seed of God's love and life, there first must exist a mother. And the mother cannot give birth to this child in a conventional way. Conception must happen through the formula of restoration. All the cooperation between mothers and sons in the Providence of Restoration is a preparation and a condition for the Son of God to be born with the seed of new life, free from satanic accusation. By making conditions to avoid Satan's attacks, and by subordinating the firstborn son who represents evil, mother and son restore the love, life and lineage that were taken over by Satan.

The Meaning of Jacob's Victory

The Bible, which records the providential work of God, contains many stories that are difficult to understand. For example, Rebekah deceived her husband Isaac and her first son Esau, and helped her second son Jacob receive the blessing. (Genesis 27) God took the side of that mother and son, and although they used methods that at first glance seem unjust, God still blessed them for their actions.

In Adam's family, Cain and Abel fought outside the womb. Their struggle resulted in the death of Abel, the second son. Then came Jacob. On the merits of many godly people who paid indemnity and sacrificed after the time of Abel, Jacob at last caught up to the level at which Satan first dominated humankind. Then Jacob dealt with his twin brother, Esau. At the ford of Jabbok, Jacob set up the condition of spiritual victory over the angel. (Genesis 32:28) And through winning over Esau (Genesis 33), who was in the position of the substantial body of the Archangel, Jacob consequently was blessed as the first victor in history and was given the name "Israel." But by then he was already in his fortieth year.

Satan sowed the seed of false love within the womb of Eve, which gave birth to evil life. Therefore, God needed to purify a mother's womb from which the heavenly Son could be born. That purification period of separation from Satan had to begin at the time of conception and continue to age forty, so even though Jacob was victorious he did not meet that criteria. The great mother who assumed the responsibility to meet this condition was Tamar.

Tamar's Providential Role

Tamar had married Er, the eldest son of Judah. (Genesis 38) But Er displeased God and he died. According to the custom of that time, Judah gave Tamar his second son, Onan, that they might bear a child for Er. But Onan, knowing that Tamar's child would not be his own, spilled his semen on the ground. This was a sin in the eyes of God, for which Onan died.

Then Tamar wanted Shelah, the third son of Judah, for a husband, but Judah did not give him to her. Judah thought that his two sons had died because of Tamar, so he was afraid that Shelah would die and end the family lineage.

But Tamar had the conviction that she was to carry on the lineage of the chosen people. To do that, she disguised herself as a prostitute and slept with her father-in-law, Judah, and became pregnant with twins. At the time of birth, one of the twin sons, Zerah, stretched out his hand from the womb to be born first. But he was pulled back into the womb, and the second son, Perez, was born first, taking the position of the elder brother. Thus, within the womb of Tamar, the first and second sons fought, and their reversal of position separated them from Satan. That became the condition for restoration in the womb. Upon this condition, the Messiah could be conceived within the blood lineage of the chosen people, on the base of the nation of Israel which could stand up to the Roman Empire two thousand years later. The victorious foundation on the national level could then be formed in the womb of a mother free of satanic accusation, prepared for the seed of the Son of God. On this foundation, the Holy Mother Mary emerged in the mainstream of God's Providence.

Mary Receives God's Will

Mary, when she was engaged to Joseph, received from the Archangel Gabriel the surprising message that the Messiah would be born through her. (Luke 1:31) In those days, if an unmarried woman became pregnant, she would be killed. But Mary accepted the will of God with absolute faith, saying, "Behold, I am the handmaid of the Lord; let it be to me according to your word." (Luke 1:38)

Mary consulted with the priest Zechariah, who was her relative and was highly respected. Zechariah's wife Elizabeth, with the help of God, was pregnant with John the Baptist. She said to Mary, "Blessed are you among women and blessed is the fruit of your womb. Why is this granted to me that the mother of my Lord should come to me?" (Luke 1:42-43) With these words she testified to the coming birth of Jesus. In this way, God let Mary, Zechariah,and Elizabeth know about the birth of the Messiah before anyone else. All of them had the absolutely crucial mission of following the will of God and serving Jesus. Zechariah's family let Mary stay in their house. Jesus was conceived in the house of Zechariah.

Elizabeth and Mary were cousins on their mothers' side. But according to God's Providence, they were considered sisters, with Elizabeth as the elder (Cain) and Mary as the younger (Abel). Mary received Elizabeth's help in the presence of Zechariah. Through this cooperation, Zechariah's family, on the national level, indemnified the lack of unity between mother and son with Leah and Rachel in Jacob's family. (Genesis 29-30) This allowed Jesus to be conceived. For the first time in history, there could be born on earth, free of satanic accusation and through a prepared womb, the seed of the Son of God—the seed of the True Father. In this way, the only begotten Son of God, the owner of the first love of God, was born for the first time in history. Mary had to achieve something that could not be understood by common sense, nor easily tolerated under the law of those times. Mary, Elizabeth and Zechariah had been spiritually moved. They followed the revelation that came from God and unconditionally believed that it was the will and desire of God.

Although the Son of God could be born on earth, he needed a wall of protection to grow up safely in the satanic world and fulfill the will of God. God had hoped that these three people in the family of Zechariah would establish that protective foundation. There are many points to consider with regard to how seriously the three had to dedicate themselves to protecting and serving the Son of God, and how long they should have been united with each other.

In the Bible it is recorded, "And Mary remained with her [Elizabeth] about three months, and returned to her home." (Luke 1:56) After that, there is no biblical record of any further communication between Mary and Elizabeth and Zechariah. From the time Mary left Zechariah's house, difficulties began for Mary and Jesus. The family of Zechariah should have been the wall of protection for Jesus until the very end.

A short time later, Joseph discovered that Mary was pregnant. How great must have been his shock at that moment! Mary, his beloved fiancée, without having had any relationship with him, had become pregnant after a three-month stay in another place. It was natural for Joseph to question Mary about who the baby in her womb belonged to. What would have happened if at that time Mary had explained everything candidly? If she had exposed everything, it could have been the end of a clan. So Mary simply responded that she was pregnant by the Holy Spirit.

Mary's pregnancy began to show, and the people of the surrounding area became aware of it. What would have happened if Joseph had declared that he didn't know anything about it? But Joseph was a righteous man. He believed in the revelation of God and defended Mary, saying the pregnancy was his responsibility. Mary may have been ridiculed for becoming pregnant during her engagement, but she had avoided death by stoning. Joseph, who loved Mary, protected her this way in the beginning. However, there was a great deal of anguish deep in his heart. Once Jesus was born, Joseph's suspicions about the father of Jesus only increased and his heart ached. As Jesus grew older, the two became more and more distant in heart. And because of this, family problems frequently arose. Jesus was viewed as an illegitimate son, and lacking the protection of Zechariah's family and the love of Joseph, he grew up with an indescribable loneliness in his heart.

No Bride for Jesus

Jesus was aware of his path as the Messiah, and he lamented by himself these lonely circumstances and the serious obstacle they presented to fulfilling the will of God. The Messiah is the True Parent, and to fulfill that mission he needed to receive his substantial bride. Jesus had to reverse, at the very root, the false love by which the Archangel had caused the fall of Eve, who was growing up as the sister of Adam. Consequently, Jesus, in the place of Adam as the Son of God, should have received as his bride the younger sister of someone in an archangelic position. That bride was to have been none other than Zechariah's daughter, the younger sister of John the Baptist. To fulfill this in a world where Satan plays the role of owner and lord, Jesus needed a foundation of protection formed by absolute faith. Tragically, the entire foundation ended up collapsing around him.

This would not have happened if Zechariah and Elizabeth, who had received the revelation and spiritual support from God, had maintained absolute faith. If they had fulfilled their responsibility, Mary would have been in contact with them continually, even after her three-month stay at their house. God chose Zechariah's family as the foremost representatives of the entire world, so that even after the birth of Jesus they would protect, serve and witness to him as the Messiah. They not only should have served Jesus as the Son of God and Messiah with utter devotion, but they should have learned the will of God through Jesus and followed him absolutely. Also, John the Baptist was born to serve Jesus and should have fulfilled his responsibility to guide everyone he led to repentance, to believe in Jesus and receive salvation. But unfortunately, although Zechariah, Elizabeth and John the Baptist testified at first to Jesus as the Son of God, there is no evidence that they served him as such. The respected priest Zechariah was simply a spectator. John the Baptist stood separate from Jesus. These circumstances blocked the people from following Jesus and made his path very difficult. And once this family lost faith in Jesus, looking at him through human eyes, there was no room for them to help him receive his bride.

We should also consider the influence that Joseph and Mary's relationship had on Jesus. Mary had to restore the position of Eve and Tamar through indemnity, so she should have remained as only the fiancée of Joseph. Providentially, they could not be husband and wife. It was God's desire that they not have sexual relations either before or after Jesus' birth. Joseph still loved Mary after Jesus was born, but Mary should have wanted to separate from Joseph to raise Jesus as the Son of God.

But the real circumstances did not make this easy to do. Even though Mary's original mind told her that she should not do so, she had sexual relations with Joseph. They had children, which was a repetition of Eve's mistake. With this condition, Satan invaded them. With the exception of Jesus, everyone who should have protected Jesus came under the dominion of Satan: his father, his mother, his Abel-type brothers (John the Baptist and his brothers) and his Cain-type brothers (the children of Joseph).

Jesus Seen through Human Eyes

When someone is invaded by Satan, he loses all spiritual support and inspiration. Trust in God, as well as a sense of gratitude to Him, is lost. One begins to see everything through human eyes. Mary did not help Jesus with the wedding he desired. She even opposed it. This was the direct reason that Jesus could not receive his bride and could not become the True Parent; and this forced him to go the way of the cross.

Jesus' words to Mary during the wedding at Cana, "Oh woman, what have you to do with me?" (John 2:4), reveal a reproachful heart to a mother who helped in the weddings of others but neglected to help Jesus receive his bride, the most important requirement of the Providence. With this perspective, now we can understand why Jesus asked, "Who is my mother, and who are my brothers?" (Matthew 12:48)

Faced with the opposition of Mary, Zechariah, Elizabeth, and finally John the Baptist, Jesus gave up hope for their protection as he sought to fulfill his mission. Therefore, Jesus left his home in search of a new spiritual foundation to restart the Providence of Salvation.

Now without a family and household, Jesus lamented, "Foxes have holes, and birds of the air have nests; but the Son of man has nowhere to lay his head." (Matthew 8:20) With his family-level foundation lost, Jesus sought to replace it. That was his three-year course.

In the end, as people disbelieved and the disciples lost faith, Jesus endured Satan's attack. And as his foundation crumbled, he went the way of the cross. Originally, Jesus came to the earth as the Messiah to give blessings to his disciples and all humankind. He was to build the sinless Kingdom of Heaven. But because of the lack of faith in him, he could not receive his bride, he could not become the True Parent, and he could not accomplish his mission. This is why he promised to return.

Completing the Ideal of True Parents

The Lord of the Second Advent comes to perfect the foundation of God's Providence of Restoration left uncompleted by Jesus. That is to say, he comes as the seed of the original True Child to complete the ideal of creation. He comes to complete the ideal of True Parents, who are the origin of the True Love, True Life and the True Lineage of God. He comes on the victorious foundation of the fundamental providence of God's side up to the time of Jesus. He also stands upon the victorious foundation of Jesus' life and finds the bride that Jesus could not find. Together they become the True Parents to save all humankind.

Through the blessing of new marriages that pass on God's original blood lineage, the True Parents will be able to give salvation to all humanity. People will become True Persons engrafting into the True Love, True Life and True Lineage of God. Furthermore, the Messiah will establish a True Family, creating the Kingdom of Heaven on earth. Thus, it is the International Holy Weddings that establish this new blood lineage when the Lord of the Second Advent comes in the flesh.

On the level of the great worldwide family, the Lord indemnifies that which was lost in the family of Adam and restores the True Elder Sonship, True Parentship and True Kingship that should have been perfected in Adam's family. He will transform this world into the Kingdom of Heaven on earth under the dominion of God, opening the Kingdom of Heaven in the spirit world for registration. Humanity will enter into the era of kingship both spiritually and physically, centered on God; establish a world of victory, freedom, happiness and unity; and create the Heavenly Kingdom on earth and in the spirit world, which is God's ideal of creation. This is the View of the Principle of the Providential History of Salvation. I hope that in the future all of you can also receive this joyous new marriage blessing.

Distinguished writers and honored guests, I want to again express my appreciation that you have taken time from your busy lives to come together from so many nations to attend this important conference.

I have the highest hopes that your achievements from this gathering can be the beginning of the guidelines from which we can build an eternal future for our descendants.

May God bless you and your families.

Thank you.

In Search of the Origin of the Universe

Reverend Sun Myung Moon, President, Family Federation for World Peace
This address was given on August 1, 1996, at the Farewell Banquet of the Family
Federation for World Peace Convocation, Washington D.C.

Distinguished Guests, Ladies and Gentlemen:

With the end of the Cold War, new hope for peace and justice has spread rapidly across the globe. Leaders unable or unwilling to acknowledge the new international realities are being swept away by the tidal wave of change.

As we stand at the threshold of the new millennium, I believe it is time to review our traditional patterns of thinking and boldly seize these new opportunities. Thus it is my great honor to share with you my life-long advocacy for world peace and true family values.

In this world there are two kinds of human beings: men and women. Can they decide to exchange positions? Was your birth as male or female based upon your personal desire? Or were you born that way irrespective of your personal preference? The sex that we are given is an absolute and is not a matter of choice. We did not think it nor did we want it, but without knowing the cause, result or process of our birth, we were born a certain way.

Thus it is undeniable that no matter how great a person may be, he or she is not a causal being, but is a resultant being. Therefore, there must exist the first causal being. Who is that causal being? Is it male? Is it female? You can call that first causal being God or any other name, but this causal being must exist.

Here today are gathered some of the most distinguished writers of the world. You might say, "Where is God? Show me and then I will believe." But I warn you not to deny the existence of that causal being.

The topic of today's speech is "In Search of the Origin of the Universe." If we go deeper and deeper in our search for the origin of the universe, we arrive at God. We come to know that God possesses dual characteristics of male and female. How did the universe begin? Let us put aside our discussion of God for the moment and consider humankind. It is clear that humankind is comprised of man and woman, or subject and object. In the mineral kingdom, molecules are composed of anion and cation. Plants reproduce through stamen and pistil. Animals live as male and female, and human beings as man and woman. If we examine creation, whether the mineral kingdom, plant kingdom or animal kingdom, we observe that plus and minus on a higher level exist and develop by absorbing plus and minus from the lower level. Why does this phenomenon take place? It is because the existing world is responsible to perfect human beings, who are Lords of all creation.

In the mineral kingdom, plus and minus, that is, subject and object, unite centering on the ideal of love and thus exist. In the same way, in the plant kingdom, stamen and pistil, that is, subject and object, unite centering on love and thus also exist. Medical science today points out that even bacteria exist as plus and minus.

How do subject and object, or plus and minus, unite? By kissing? Love is a substantial reality, not merely a concept. What is the reality upon which love can settle? President Ford and President Bush, who attended the Inaugural World Convention of the Family Federation for World Peace, and all of you distinguished writers are famous, but there is something that you do not know. You do not know what makes man man, and woman woman. The answer is: the sexual organs. Is there anyone here who dislikes the sexual organs? If you like them, how much do you like them? Until now you may not have thought it virtuous to value the sexual organs, but from now you must value them.

What will the world be like in the future? If it is a world that values the sexual organs absolutely, will that world be good or bad? Will it prosper or perish? This is not a joke. When God was creating human beings, into which part did He invest the greatest creative effort? The eyes? The nose? The heart? The brain? All of these organs eventually die, do they not?

True Owners

What is the purpose of the Family Federation for World Peace? If humanity were to go beyond the traditional categories of virtue, religion and any other human norms, but was absolutely in harmony with the sexual organs, earning the welcoming applause of God, what kind of world would it be? When we are born as a man or woman, who is the owner of our sexual organ? Actually the owner of man's sexual organ is woman, and the owner of woman's sexual organ is man. We did not know that the sexual organ is owned by the opposite sex. This is a simple truth. We cannot deny this truth. Even after history progresses for thousands of years, this truth will not change.

Every man thinks his sexual organ belongs to himself, and each woman thinks her sexual organ is her own. That is why the world is perishing. Everyone is mistaken concerning ownership of the sexual organs. We all think that love is absolute, eternal and dreamlike, but when we come to clearly understand that the ownership of eternal love lies with the opposite sex, the world will not remain in its present condition. There are numerous scholars and Ph.D.s, but none of them have thought about this.

Can any of you deny this? If you ask your parents, your grandparents, your great-grandparents, the original ancestors, and even God, who is the origin of the universe, they all will agree with this. This is a universal law. This truth will remain even after the universe continues to exist for billions of years. The natural conclusion is that when you stand before God, He will judge you as righteous or unrighteous according to this immutable law.

Even the fall of Adam and Eve originated in the violation of this law. Adam and Eve both erred by thinking their sexual organ was their own possession. Think about it. Would God chase Adam and Eve away because they ate a literal fruit? God is not such a senseless being. God chased them out because they did not meet the most basic criterion by which the universe functions. Because of their mistake with the original point of love, they could not be acknowledged anywhere in the universe. In the mineral kingdom, plant kingdom and animal kingdom, the positivity and negativity, that is, the sexual organ, is reserved for the sake of the complementary partner of love. Adam and Eve did not know this.

Then why do the sexual organs exist? For love. Male and female exist in order to find love. What are characteristics of God? God is absolute, unique, eternal and unchanging. Then who is the owner of love? The owner of love is not man or woman. The owner of love is God. Centering on love and through love, God and humankind become one. This is because both God and human beings absolutely need love.

God is the Standard

Then, what kind of love does God need? God needs absolute love. What about you? It is the same for you and for me. Just as God needs absolute, unique, unchanging and eternal love, we also need absolute, unique, unchanging and eternal love. It seems that we all resemble God.

God himself has characteristics of masculinity and femininity, or positivity and negativity. Human beings, who were created as the substantial object of God, were created as man and woman. When man and woman marry, they become substantial plus and minus representing God. It is God's will that when we marry, we completely unite horizontally centering on God's vertical love.

The human body is horizontal, representing the earth. On the other hand, the conscience always loves the vertical and seeks the higher perspective. Thus human beings irresistibly seek the point at which they become one with the vertical standard of God. That point must be the center, and man and woman must meet each other at that point.

Thus when every person, who is born from that center, grows up through experiencing the love of a child, the love among brothers and sisters, and conjugal love, the mature body represents the earth, and the mature mind centers on God. At this ultimate point, body and mind become one vertically and horizontally, thus establishing a base for happiness. Only at that place will God, who is the Absolute Being, rejoice centering on absolute love. In that place, husband and wife, who are love partners, also will rejoice.

When the relationships of parent and child, husband and wife, and brother and sister, which represent respectively north and south, east and west, and front and back, unite perfectly centering on that one point, an ideal, global shape is created.

Thus in the East, there is a saying that parents and children form one body. Further, they see husband and wife, and brother and sister, forming one body. What is the basis for that traditional wisdom? It all is made possible when the three relationships form a sphere, extending in all directions centering on true love. Those relationships must form a sphere with one center. There should be only one center. Unification is possible because those relationships in reality have the same center. The relationship between God and human beings is a parent-child relationship. Thus, God and man must become one, centering on true love.

Which is More Important?

Distinguished ladies and gentlemen, how lofty is human desire? Your mind wants to reach higher than God. No matter how lowly a person is, he or she can desire a world even greater than that of God's desire. As a beloved son or daughter of God, if you say to God, "Father, please come!" won't He come? No matter how ugly a man's wife is, if he really loves her, he naturally will follow her when she calls. With unity centering on true love, the husband will respond to his wife's beckoning, the elder will follow the younger's call, and the younger will follow the elder's call. None of them will ever want to separate from the other.

If God is alone, does He feel lonely or not? How can we know that He feels lonely? Distinguished Ladies and Gentlemen, do you have love? Do you have life? Do you have sperm and eggs? Do you have a conscience? You affirm all these things, but have you seen love? Have you seen life? Have you seen lineage? Have you seen the conscience? Have you ever touched these things? You know their existence, but you cannot touch or see them. You know them only through your mind's intuition. By the same token, even though you have not seen or touched God, you cannot say that He does not exist.

Absolute Balance

What is more important, that which is visible or that which is invisible? I am sure you realize that the invisible is more important than the visible. You can see and touch money, position and honor, but you cannot see or touch love, life, lineage and conscience. We all have them, so why can we not see them? It is because they are one with us. When mind and body maintain absolute balance, you do not feel them.

Do you feel your eyes blinking? Try counting your blinks for three hours. Do you count the number of breaths you take every day? Touch the left side of your chest with your right hand. Do you feel something beating? You can feel the beating of your heart. How many times a day do you hear the sound of your heart beating? Through a stethoscope your heartbeat sounds like the explosion of a bomb. But when we are busy, we go for weeks and months without feeling that. Think about it! We immediately feel a small fly sitting on our head, but cannot feel our heart beating even when the sound of it is a hundred times greater than the lighting of a fly. It is because we are one with our own body.

You may think it rude if I share this with you, but I would like to give you an example. You use the bathroom each morning. When you defecate, do you wear a gas mask? This is not a laughing matter but a serious one. If you are near someone else defecating, you will quickly move a good distance away. But when you smell your own feces, you do not even notice it. This is because that fecal matter is one with your body. Therefore, you do not feel that it is dirty.

When you were young, did you ever taste the dried mucus from your nose? Does it taste sweet or salty? It's salty, right? Since you can answer, you must have tasted it! Why did you not feel that it was dirty? It is because it was part of your body. Reverend Moon has figured out something that no one in the world knew.

When you cough up phlegm, you sometimes swallow it, right? What about you who are here today? How you ever had that experience? Be honest. Why do you not feel it is dirty? Because the phlegm was one with your body. We all eat three meals a day, breakfast, lunch,and dinner. If you go about twelve inches down from your mouth, there is a fertilizer factory. By eating three meals a day, we are providing raw materials for fertilizer factories. After knowing that, can you still take food into your mouth with a fork and spoon? We know that there is a fertilizer factory in our stomach, but we live on without feeling its presence. Why do we not feel it? It is because we are one with it. In the same way, we have love, life, lineage and conscience, but because they are one with us in balance, we do not feel them.

Just like us, God has love, life, lineage and conscience, but He cannot feel them by

Himself. Because they are completely in balance, God cannot feel them. That is why God also needs an object partner. We understand the necessity of an object partner from this perspective. When one is alone, one cannot feel oneself. But when a man appears to a woman and a woman appears to a man, the stimulation of love and lineage will erupt like lightning and thunder. You must be fully awakened about this. We have lived without knowing this truth. Man has not understood that God absolutely needs His love partner.

Then who is God's love partner? Is it a monkey? If human beings are resultant, can monkeys be the being that caused us? Can monkeys be our progenitors? Don't even talk such nonsense. In order for life to have begun from an amoeba and reach the human form, it must pass through the gates of love on thousands of levels. Does life progress automatically? Absolutely not. It is the same with all animals. The division of species is very strict. Nobody can trespass the separation of species.

If materialists who believe that monkeys are our ancestors crossbreed a human being and a monkey, do you think a new life form will emerge? It will fail no matter how many thousands of years they attempt it. Why will it not work? You must think about this.

Then what would God need? What part of your body would God need most? Your eyes? Hands? Your five senses? Within Him, God has both masculinity and femininity, but to exist as Father, His being is that of a male, subject. With this in mind, would we say that God needs a love partner?

Then who or what within His creation could be His love partner? Is it man by himself? Or can woman by herself become God's love partner? What kind of partner does God want? Does God need a partner with great wealth? Does He need a partner of knowledge, or one of great authority? No, none of these things matters. God wants a love partner. Thus, centering on the place where husband and wife become one through their sexual organs, God wants to appear and meet us.

Love is Absolute

Why is that the place where man and woman become one centering on God? It is because love is absolute, and that place is where man and woman have the absolute desire to become one. Looking horizontally, man, who is plus, approaches that center, and woman, who is minus, also approaches that center. In God also, the masculine characteristic and the feminine characteristic become one as plus and minus. That union in God, as a bigger plus, becomes one with a bigger minus, namely, the union of man and woman. The question turns to the conditions by which that union can come about.

What is marriage? Why is marriage important? Marriage is important because it is the road to finding love. It is the road to creating life. It is the road where the life of a man and a woman unite into one. It is the place where a man's lineage combines with a woman's lineage. History emerges through marriage, and from marriage nations appear and an ideal world begins. Without marriage there is no meaning to the existence of individuals, nations,and an ideal world. This is the formula. Man and woman must become absolutely one. Parents and children must become absolutely one with God, love God, and live and die with God. And when they die and go to the spirit world, that is the place called Heaven. But there has been no individual, family or nation that has fulfilled that ideal; the world and humankind have not established that ideal, and for that reason the Kingdom of Heaven that God desires is empty. All people who died until now fell into Hell. No one entered the Kingdom of Heaven.

From this perspective, we can see that Jesus came as Savior of humankind but could not enter the Kingdom of Heaven. He instead went to Paradise. In order to enter the Kingdom of Heaven, Jesus would have had to form a family. That is why Jesus wants to come again. Jesus was to marry, form a family, serve and live with God in that family, and then enter the Kingdom of Heaven with that family. He could not enter the Kingdom of Heaven by himself alone. Thus it is said in the Bible, "What is bound on earth is bound in Heaven, and what is loosed on earth is loosed in Heaven." We must solve the problems on earth. Since the disease was contracted on earth, it must be cured on earth.

Traversing the Road of Death

Humankind descended from the fall. Therefore, we dwell in the realm of the fall and cannot enter the Kingdom of Heaven without making a foundation to rise above that realm. Man in the realm of the fall must destroy that realm no matter how difficult it is. Thus Jesus said, "Whoever seeks his life will lose it, and whoever loses his life for my sake will find it." In order to traverse this road of death, we must penetrate it and rise above by risking our entire lives.

Your families are in the realm of the fall. Your tribes and nations are the same. You must struggle and win. The fall occurred in Adam's family. Did Adam and Eve have children before or after they were chased out of the Garden? They had children after they were chased out; they created their family without any relationship to God. How can you go to the Kingdom of Heaven without knowing this? It is not conceivable; you cannot achieve the perfect ideal through ignorance. This is my warning to you.

Pray to find out whether Reverend Moon's words are true. No one knows how much hardship I endured in order to find this path. Even though I committed no crime, I suffered through six different prisons to find this path. Through this truth, I am able to straighten out and educate precious young people in the matter of an hour. Some people say that I am brainwashing youth, but in fact I am enlightening them with logical truth. Atheists have been silenced since they failed to prove scientifically and logically that God does not exist. On the other side, Christians entrap us, crying heresy because our doctrines differ, and they try to destroy us. But in this case, this so-called heretical cult is on the side of truth.

Satan hates whatever is on God's side, and God hates whatever is on Satan's side. Has anyone in the world liked Reverend Moon? You came here only on the basis of learning what Reverend Moon is doing. You did not come without knowing that.

Youth in the former Soviet Union, living in an ideological vacuum, are equipping themselves intellectually with a unification perspective through comprehensive ethics texts in middle schools, high schools, universities, and even in prisons. Thousands of schools in the former Soviet Union are using such texts. They believe that my teachings provide the only way to overcome the corrupting influence of the decadent Western culture of homosexuality and free sex. They are proclaiming, "We must surpass America, which opposes Reverend Moon!" They want to move ahead of America in attending Reverend Moon.

Ladies and gentlemen, do you like God? Would God enjoy watching Reverend Moon doing these works? Can the teaching of the Vatican harmonize with the teaching of Reverend Robert Schuller, who also attended the Inaugural Convention of the Family Federation for World Peace? Their teachings are different. Then ask God whose teaching is true. What is the benefit of my telling you that your understanding of Jesus and Mother Mary is wrong? But you must understand one fact very clearly: Without being loosed on Earth, it will not be loosed in Heaven. Reverend Moon, who knew this at an early age, has devoted his life to walking this path.

Should Jesus have married? Jesus should have married. Is Jesus a woman or a man? If there is a woman saint, would Jesus not desire to marry her? During the creation of Adam and Eve, God granted them their own sexual organs. Why would He have done that? Would God have married them when they reached maturity, or not?

The problem lies in their fall. Due to the fall, their blood lineage switched from God to Satan. Therefore, God chased them out of the Garden of Eden. Originally, Adam and Eve were to have become God's body, in the position of God's bride. The fall, in a sense, introduced a disease into God's body and ideal, as Adam and Eve acted like God's enemies. Can you imagine how much God's heart suffered as He watched this taking place? The human fall is the grave in which you bury yourself. It was an act of expropriation. It was the root of free sex as well as the origin of individualism.

What kind of nation is America today? It has become a nation of extreme individualism, a nation whose people are pursuing private interests, over-indulging themselves, gluttonous, practicing free sex. Does God favor these things? What is the goal of such extreme individualists? They abandon Heaven and Earth, the world, the nation, society, their extended family, and even their grandparents. Beyond that, they lose their parents and brothers and sisters. Therefore, they live as gypsies and wander around as hippies, having no place to go when it rains and snows. So they are driven to end their lives by suicide. That is the result of individualism.

Reaping What is Sown

The original mind does not want to protect this extreme individualism and ridiculous exaltation of privacy. The original mind wants to live receiving love from the universe, the nation, our village and our parents. But because people walk the opposite path, their consciences become dysfunctional and they feel a contradiction with their own original mind. Thus more and more people would rather die than live, and commit virtual suicide by taking drugs. We are witnessing the truth, "You will reap what you have sown," being proven.

What seed did Adam and Eve plant in the Garden of Eden? It was the seed of free sex. Can that be denied? That is the reason they covered their lower parts. Is it not true that even children know they must cover up, for example, after having eaten the cookies hidden by their parents. This is a function of human nature. If the fruit of the Tree of the Knowledge of Good and Evil were a literal fruit, then Adam and Eve should have covered their mouths or their hands. So, why did they hide their lower parts?

Reverend Moon is an intelligent man. I am not doing what I am doing because I am inferior to you. It cannot be denied that the fall was caused by fornication. To restore the fall of Adam and Eve, it is very logical to say that we must take a path 180 degrees different from that of the fall. We inherited a lineage on the path to Hell, due to the fall. That is why the Messiah must come.

The Messiah comes as the owner who should form the family, in the Garden of Eden as originally intended by God. We must understand this clearly. It must be logical. The

Messiah first should create a family that serves God. Through this family, he should establish a nation. Therefore, the family is the key. Centering on the Messiah's family, there should be an engrafting process. The problem is, "who can save me from this world of death?" That is why the opposite path is taken.

Look at the Old Testament era. The indemnification took place centering on the principle of "an eye for an eye, a tooth for a tooth." Look at Rebekah, the wife of Isaac. Isn't she the one who stole the blessing for Jacob by cheating her elder son, Esau, and her own husband, Isaac? Why would God love such a woman? How can we have faith in such a God? No one until now has answered these questions. Reverend Moon is the first person to provide the answers, because Reverend Moon is the only one who knows all the secrets of God.

The Serious Problem Facing Us Today

Now, let us discover the dividing line between Heaven and Hell. Is it up in the air? Where is it? It is your sexual organ. This is a serious matter. This has turned Heaven and Earth upside down. Who can deny this? This is explained in the chapter on the human fall in the Divine Principle, the teaching of Reverend Moon. If you doubt this, ask God. You cannot reject Reverend Moon's Divine Principle, which contains content beyond your wildest dreams presented through logical explanations and in a well-ordered structure.

If you wonder whether Reverend Moon will go to Heaven or Hell, please die and go to spirit world. There you will find out. If you feel upset by my talk tonight, you could go ahead and commit suicide, and you will really find out. You have to realize that Reverend Moon overcame death hundreds of times in order to find this path. Reverend Moon is the person who brought God to tears hundreds of times. No one in history has loved God more than the Reverend Moon has. That is why even if the world tries to destroy me, the Reverend Moon will never perish. It is because God protects me. If you step into the realm of the truth Reverend Moon teaches, you also will gain God's protection.

When a sexual organ is used in the same way a blind person wanders aimlessly and without direction, it will, undoubtedly, lead you as its owner to Hell. By the same token, one will be led high up into Heaven when he or she uses the sexual organ according to the standard of God's absolute love. This is a clear conclusion.

Today, we face a serious youth problem, because in the Garden of Eden Adam and Eve planted the seed of free sex in the shade through their fall during their youth. In the Last Days, harvest time, there must be the worldwide phenomenon of rampant free sex among the youth.

Satan knew that the Lord of the Second Advent would come in the Last Days with the strategy to save humankind, who are in the realm of the fall, by lifting them up to the realm of absolute love, centered on God's true love. Satan cannot find any other standard of love other than free sex, as the archangel introduced in the Garden of Eden. Therefore, we see that the entire world is stripped naked and being pushed in the direction of death by free sex. All humanity is being forced to walk this path in the Last Days as the archangel's descendants. Because today's humankind descended from Adam and Eve, who fell under Satan's dominion in the Garden of Eden, Satan can boldly claim in front of God that he has a right to do whatever he will with all men and women in this world.

God knows what Satan wants. Through free sex, Satan wants to stop every last person from returning to God. In other words, Satan wants to destroy all humanity and create

Hell on Earth. Is not the world in which we live today Hell on Earth? Therefore, we will find the road to Heaven by going 180 degrees opposite the direction of this Hell on Earth. When the Lord of the Second Advent comes, he will show us the 180 degrees opposite path, as a means to save the world and lead us to Heaven.

Opening the Path to Heaven

Then what is the road that is 180 degrees opposite the way of free sex? The path of free sex was laid because of the false parents. Therefore, True Parents have to come to straighten the wrong path. God cannot intervene. No authority nor any military, economic or political power can do it. It was caused by false parents. Therefore, it takes True Parents to cut it open with a scalpel. True Parents should operate with their scalpel; that is the only way humanity can be saved.

The one who sinned has to indemnify the sin. It was in the family that a false marriage took place, which corrupted the lineage 180 degrees. Therefore, True Parents must come and bestow marriage that is in a direction 180 degrees opposite, in order to open the path to Heaven.

Then, what did God expect from Adam and Eve? God expected absolute sex from them. You eminent writers gathered here tonight, please learn this truth and take it back to your countries. If you start a campaign to secure absolute sex in your country, your families and your nation will go straight to Heaven. When there is absolute sex, an absolute couple will emerge automatically. Words such as free sex, homosexual and lesbian will naturally disappear.

Reverend Moon has lived an entire life overcoming a suffering path in order to initiate this kind of movement worldwide. Now the time has come for Reverend Moon to trumpet the fanfare of victory and move the entire world. Therefore, I am grateful to God.

The family sets the cornerstone on the road to world peace. The family also can destroy that road. It was Adam's family in which the destruction of the foundation of human hope and happiness took place. Therefore, when we establish the Family Federation for World Peace, the road going 180 degrees opposite the direction of the satanic world will be open, and for this we cannot help but give thanks to God. Without following this road, there is no freedom, happiness or ideal!

I wish that you would center on the absolute sexual organ, unique sexual organ, unchanging sexual organ, and eternal sexual organ, and use this as your foundation to pursue God. You should realize that this foundation should become the foundation of love, life, lineage and conscience. We also have to realize that the Kingdom of God on Earth and in Heaven will begin on this foundation.

If all men and women admit that their sexual organ belongs to their spouse, we all would bow our heads and become humble when we receive our spouse's love. Love comes to you only from your partner. There is no love other than love for the sake of others. We must remember that we can find absolute love where we absolutely live for the sake of others. When you return home, you should expect to wage a war against the satanic world.

Wherever you may go, please try to spread Reverend Moon's message through television or other media. You will never perish. What force can turn around this world of Hell? It is impossible to achieve this unless our sexual organ is used in accordance with an absolute, unique, unchanging and eternal standard centering on God's true love, which is absolute, unique, unchanging and eternal love. God is the original owner of the sexual organs.

Let us go forward all together for this common cause. Let us become the vanguard that will carry out God's true love. This is the very mission of the Family Federation for World Peace. Now, please go back to your homes and affirm with your spouses that your sexual organs are absolute, unique, unchanging and eternal. Proclaim that yours is truly your spouse's and what your spouse has protected so well until now is truly yours. And please pledge that you will live your life with gratitude and in eternal service to your spouse. In such families, God will dwell eternally and, centering upon them, the world-level family will begin to multiply. I sincerely hope that each of you will participate in the next marriage blessing of three million six hundred thousand couples. By doing so you will form a true family that can register in the Kingdom of God on Earth.

Thank you very much.

True Family and True Universe Centering on True Love

Reverend Sun Myung Moon, President, Family Federation for World Peace
This address was given on July 18, 1997, at the Washington Times 15th
Anniversary Banquet, Washington D.C.

Respected guests from Washington D.C. and abroad, dear staff of *The Washington Times*, eminent world literary leaders, ladies and gentlemen.

I deeply appreciate your taking time from your busy schedules to attend this meeting.

Today, as we celebrate *The Washington Times'* 15th anniversary, I cannot help but feel deep emotion. Fifteen years ago, when the world was adrift on the stormy waves of the Cold War, I established *The Washington Times* to fulfill God's desperate desire to save this world. Since that time, I have devoted myself to raising up *The Washington Times*, hoping that this blessed land of America would fulfill its world-wide mission to build a Heavenly nation. Meanwhile, I waged a lonely struggle, facing enormous obstacles and scorn as I dedicated my whole heart and energy to enable *The Washington Times* to grow as a righteous and responsible journalistic institution.

Today The Washington Times Corporation can be proud of its development into a world-class global media enterprise. Since the end of the Cold War, the world began to realize that the direction taken by *The Washington Times* was correct. History will not forget our contribution. The efforts of *The Times* to revitalize the moral and spiritual values of the United States and the world are being recognized as absolutely urgent and necessary at this time.

I want to convey my warmest appreciation to all *The Washington Times* staff who have worked so hard together with me to develop *The Times*. I would also like to express my deepest gratitude to the American and world leaders who have offered their unwavering support.

The most precious thing that I can offer from the bottom of my heart as a token of my appreciation on this special day is to introduce you to what I consider to be the two most significant lectures that I gave during my most recent world tour.

I refer to "View of the Principle of the Providential History of Salvation" and "In Search of the Origin of the Universe." Today, we need a complete solution for the problems of sexual immorality, family breakdown and alienation among our young people. These two speeches provide fundamental solutions for these problems. When each one of you goes back to your home, I hope you will take some time for self-reflection. Whenever you want to bring more love into your family, read these speeches together with your family and think deeply. I believe this can help you and your family to achieve harmony and real happiness.

I suggest that you read these two speeches as many times as the number of your age.

If your age is over 80, then read them more than 80 times. The more you read these speeches, the more heavenly blessing and fortune will be with you. The more you read them, the more peace will flow in your family naturally and automatically. I invite you to read more!

The title of the first speech is "View of the Principle of the Providential History of Salvation." To summarize: Because of the failure and Fall in the family of the First Adam, Jesus came as the Second Adam to restore the failure of the first family at the national level. The First Adam had become fallen Adam. Thus, the Messiah, Jesus, came as the Second Adam. However, since Jesus was not able to realize a family based on being True Parents, the Messiah needs to come back as the Third Adam and restore the mission of True Parents on the world level. This is the mission of the Second Advent, who is coming as the Third Adam. This speech also introduces the fact that the fundamental issue of salvation is the restoration of the original lineage.

The title of the second speech is "In Search of the Origin of the Universe." Since the human Fall originated in the misuse of love, humankind lost True Love. Thus the problem arises: How can we recover True Love? The loss of True Love means falling through adultery. In other words, True Love became degraded by misusing the sexual organs, and in order to restore it, we need to use these organs in the right way. Just as the seed of fallen love was planted in the Garden of Eden during the first ancestors' youth, so in these final days, mankind will harvest the fruit of the Fall among our young people. That is the reason why today we find so much chaos and confusion, centering on the issue of sex. This problem can only be solved with what I call "Absolute Sex." Only the concept and practice of Absolute Sex can prevent the destruction of the family and reverse the corruption of our youth.

Becoming True Parents

This evening, because time is limited, I would like to share a speech with a new title: "True Family and True Universe Centering on True Love."

Everyone here has parents and teachers, and you also have the leader of your nation. Correct? These are things everyone undeniably needs. However, when compared to the true standard, there are many different levels of parents. What do you think? To what extent have you, yourself, become True Parents? In the same way, if a person is a professor at an Ivy League university such as Harvard, Yale or Columbia in the United States, or Oxford or Cambridge in England, does this mean that he or she can be called a True Teacher? Similarly, there are different types of leadership in a nation compared to the true standard of leadership. Even if someone is the president of a superpower such as the United States, does this mean he or she is a True President?

In fact, today in the family, children do not trust parents. Between spouses, there is no complete trust. Brothers and sisters also don't trust each other fully. Furthermore, students do not trust the teachers in the schools, and the people do not trust the leaders of their nation.

So the problem is, how can we attain the true standard of even one of these three most important positions of parents, teacher and leader?

When I say you should become True Parents, True Teacher or True Leader, what do you think is the highest standard or central model for those three positions? That is God. God is the True Parent among parents, True Teacher among teachers, and True King among kings. God is the Eternal True Parent, Eternal True Teacher, Eternal True Leader and King.

If we are children of God, we need to become True Parents first, just like God. We should also follow the way of the True Teacher, just like God. And we need to follow the way of the True Leader, just like God. This is the idea of the three primary positions. The ultimate model is God.

The Messianic Concept

Who is the Messiah sent to the people of Israel, as promised in the Old Testament? The Messiah is the one who comes as True Parents, True Teacher and True King. However, because Jesus was prevented from establishing the True Family and uniting his people, he needs to come again. In other words, because he did not accomplish the national-level foundation, the Messiah of the Second Coming will come as the Third Adam and teach the way of the True Parents, True Teacher and True King at the world level. This is the messianic concept. Wherever the family, nation, world and Heaven exist, the idea of the three primary positions of parents, teacher and leader should always be established.

To exist in the spatial dimension, human beings need to stand in relation to what is above and below, right and left, front and back. In this way, one's position is determined. One's shape and situation depend upon where one stands relative to above and below, right and left, and front and back.

This same formula that applies in the relation of above and below, right and left, and front and back also applies to the family, the nation and the world. Just as there are above and below, right and left, and front and back centering on the individual, in the family there are parents and children, husband and wife, and brothers and sisters. Similarly, in the nation, centering on the leader, families should embrace all the civilizations of East and West and all the civilizations of North and South. Then they can embrace all people of the world as brothers and sisters. Ultimately every level will form a family pattern. All these models have the same pattern and the individual self is the central model. In the same manner, one's existence expands to the level of the family, nation, world, Heaven and Earth, and eventually reaches God. Each person has the desire to live as the center of the cosmos and the potential to make this a reality.

Thus, the core concept of the universe is the concept of the family. Heaven represents parents. Earth represents children. In the concept of East and West, East symbolizes man, West symbolizes woman. When a woman gets married, she usually follows wherever the husband goes, but they have equal value. When the West side reflects the sunlight, it has the same value as the East side. The relationship of brothers is the same. When the older brother works, the younger brothers naturally help him.

Therefore, people should exist in the relation of parents and children, husband and wife, and elder and younger siblings. And these three relations meet at one central point. There can be only one center. Above and below, right and left, and front and back should not have different centers. If the central point is different, then the balance of the relationships between above and below, right and left, and front and back will be broken. Eventually above, below, right, left, front, back and the central point all together comprise seven positions. Thus, the number seven represents all elements uniting to become one centering on God, with perfect True Love. Together, these seven elements form a complete sphere and eventually a family structure of harmony and unification. So, as you can see, seven is truly a lucky number.

When this sphere completes itself and revolves, it becomes a new entity based on the number eight. As long as True Love remains unchanging, the central point can revolve without change. But because of the human Fall, God was expelled from the central position. Since God's True Love was expelled, the True Family ideal collapsed.

There are many differences in lifestyle between East and West. In many ways, they are totally opposite. For example, when Koreans call someone to come to them, we motion with the palm down, like this. But if we do this in the West, people go the other way. We often misunderstand and wonder if people don't like us, because they go away from us when we are actually asking them to come closer. Also Western writing has a horizontal structure, proceeding from left to right. Oriental writing originally is vertically structured, starting from top to bottom and proceeding from right to left. So Western books open from left to right. But in the Orient we open a book from right to left. Thus Western civilization is more horizontally-based, while Oriental civilization is more vertical. As another example, shaking hands is a horizontal greeting, while bowing is vertical. In the Orient, there is a tradition that the ancestors are the core of the family system. But in the West there is no strong concept that considers the ancestors as the core. There is mostly a concept centered on the self.

All Are One In the Family

Because everything is connected through the core, without the movement of the core, the whole entity does not move. Therefore, all the positions of one, two, three, four, five, six and seven, the central core, have equal value. Once they are divided, they comprise twelve segments. These twelve will fit wherever they are placed. Whatever the grandfather wants, the grandchild is not against. The children of the grandfather also want whatever their parents want. Ultimately all three generations become united in one desire. All of the elements— grandfather and grandmother, father and mother, husband and wife, son and daughter—resonate with the center. Let us look at the family, centering on love. Since the relationship between parents and children is one of unity, they are said to be one body. The relation between husband and wife is also said to be one body, as is the relation between brother and sister. In the family, all are one body. Centered on what are these relations called one body? They are one body centered on God's True Love, which is the center of all love. Centered on True Love, parents and children become one, husband and wife become one, and brothers and sisters become one. Through this process, the value of each element becomes equal.

Then what did God want for His children? To become billionaires? To have more power than anyone else? What God wanted for His children, Adam and Eve, was for them to grow to become children of filial piety, loyal citizens, saints, and a Holy Son and Daughter. Did you ever consider that, in accordance with God's desire, we should become children of filial piety in the family, loyal citizens of the nation, saints in the world, and Holy Sons and Daughters before Heaven and Earth? In history the saints and sages have taught that we should become children of filial piety, loyal citizens, saints, and Holy Sons and Daughters.

This evening do you think you have mastered the way of filial piety, loyalty, sainthood, and Holy Sonship which is needed to become an ideal human being and to complete the human personality? Without knowing this, you cannot perform the function of True Parents in the family. True Parents need to teach their children progressively to complete the way of the filial child, loyal citizen, saint, Holy Son or Daughter, and eventually even to reach God.

If there is someone who truly teaches and exemplifies these things, then God will see that person as the ultimate True Parent, True Teacher and True Leader.

Following the True Way

When you are qualified as True Parents and True Teacher, you also will be qualified as a True Leader; and furthermore you will be qualified to become a True King or Queen. Fallen man lacks this concept of filial piety, loyal citizenship, sainthood, and of becoming Holy Sons and Daughters. That is why this world is perishing. Who wants Holy Sons? God does. Who wants saints? The world does. Who wants loyal citizens? The nation does. Who wants children of filial piety? The family does. This is the way of truth.

The truth centering on love continues eternally in one direction. We did not know this, and that is why we could not be True Parents, True Citizens, True Saints, and Holy Sons and Daughters. When Jesus came to this world, there was no True Parents in the family, no True Leader in the nation and the world, and ultimately there was no True King in all of Heaven and Earth. People did not know how to follow the True Way. However, now you should know.

True Parents do not tell their children, "Once you become children of true filial piety, do not become loyal citizens." True Parents should teach children of filial piety to sacrifice their family by following the way of a loyal citizen in service to the nation, and to sacrifice the nation to fulfill the way of saints in service to the world. And then parents should teach their children to sacrifice the world in service to Heaven and Earth, and to sacrifice Heaven and Earth to come to God.

To achieve this, individuals should sacrifice for the sake of the family. By sacrificing for the family, a person becomes a child of filial piety. To become a patriot, a person will sacrifice even their entire family to save the nation. That is the way to become patriots. To be a saint, you will sacrifice even the nation in service to the world. The Holy Son should establish the Heavenly Kingdom on Earth and in Heaven, even sacrificing the world. Therefore, among all parents, those who live more for the sake of their children are True Parents. Teachers who do more for the sake of their students are True Teachers, and the president who sacrifices more for the nation will be the True President. We did not know this concept of investing and sacrifice. But without it, we will never have one eternally peaceful and unified world.

Nothing is Alone in Nature

What is the basis of individualism? One cannot claim anything as "mine alone." When the child, through the love of its parents, grows from an egg in the mother's womb and is born, 99.999 percent of its existence is from the mother's bone, blood and flesh, which was combined with the 0.001 percentage from the father's sperm. There is no concept of "myself alone" in nature. Nobody had a concept of "myself" when they were born.

Anyone who considers that they are the best cannot say they became so by themselves, including Reverend Moon. Bone, blood and flesh are all received in the mother's womb. We should recognize that the important parts of our body are the extension of our mother's body. All the essential elements of our body were included in the egg and sperm. There is no exception. Therefore, there is no basis for self-centered individualism.

When we say the word "above," that word automatically recognizes "below." Can individualism stand only with the concept of "above" by itself? There is no way that a being can be only individual. Talking about the "right" side presupposes the existence of "left." In the relation between front and back, "front" presupposes "back." The word "man" also cannot exist by itself. It presupposes "woman." This is not just the claim of any one person, but a cosmic fact.

Why was man created? Usually, men say that they can live by themselves alone, so they don't care why they were created. But man was born for the sake of woman. Without woman, there is absolutely no need for man. Actually, nothing was created for man by himself or for woman by herself alone.

Look at our five senses. Were my eyes created to look at my eyes? Nose, ears, mouth, hands—all of them were created for the sake of the object. The force that mobilizes and focuses all five senses is True Love. Eyes, nose, ears, mouth and hands were created for True Love as a tool for the use of True Love.

Nothing is created only for myself. On the contrary, a person who says that what belongs to others is "mine" is called a thief. When someone takes the things of others and uses them as his own, isn't he a thief? Therefore, any man who uses his five senses and his body as he wants for himself alone is a thief, since these exist for the sake of woman.

What is the difference between man and woman? Their bodies, including the sexual organs. Then to whom is man's sexual organ absolutely necessary? Man's sexual organ exists for the sake of woman. The human sexual organs are shaped as concave and convex. Why are they shaped that way? Both of them could be pointed or both could be flat. Why are they shaped differently? Each is for the sake of the other. Woman absolutely wants what is man's. And man absolutely wants what is woman's. Until now, we did not know the fact that, absolutely, woman's sexual organ is man's and man's sexual organ is woman's. By owning each other's sexual organs, man and woman come to know True Love.

Only through the experience of two becoming one can we know the highest level of love. No one can absolutely deny these facts. Everyone should recognize this. At the place where husband and wife become completely one, the ideal couple will be created. In that very place, absolute love exists. That place of love, which is absolutely unchanging, is the dwelling place of God.

Absolute Sex and True Love

Absolute Sex is centered on God, and free sex is centered on Satan. Historically, world literature and the media have often stimulated free sex. But from now on, you literary figures and journalists should lead the way to prevent free sex. Free sex should completely disappear.

Now that you have heard Reverend Moon's speech, you can change your current position 180 degrees and become a new person, new nation and new world. Definitely you are being changed. It is an absolute necessity to change this evil world. This world must be transformed.

People in the evil world, including Satan, don't like people on God's side. Therefore, everyone in the world has opposed Reverend Moon; even at the level of the nation and the world they opposed me. But because Reverend Moon belongs to God, God has protected me. Satan doesn't like Reverend Moon; but God likes me. No matter how many times the world pushed Reverend Moon down or ignored me, I did not care. Reverend Moon never went down. Rather, he came up to the highest position. Therefore, now nobody can oppose me.

How could I establish this worldwide foundation even under all kinds of persecution? With what kind of power could Reverend Moon create these foundations to teach eminent world scholars and leaders? That was possible because God gave Reverend Moon a special kind of power. God has protected me and directed me, and even now God continuously protects and teaches me, so I am moving toward the way of success all the time.

Throughout history, there have been numerous religious leaders who could communicate with the spiritual world. You should know there is only one, Reverend Moon, who fully understood and unified the spiritual world and commenced work in this world. Since unifying the spiritual world, I received the Heavenly seal of recognition from God. Otherwise unification on the Earth cannot be done. You should know that in the same way that God has trained me and raised me in the spiritual world, He continuously leads me on the Earth.

For more than 20 years, since I came to the United States, I received enormous persecution. But I knew that God's plan for Christianity has endured through bloody sacrifice for 2,000 years, ultimately settling in the United States. Therefore, I could not give up on this country. Please consider, if America had accepted Reverend Moon even 40 years ago, how would this country be today?

Sacrificing and Giving Again

Then from where does True Love begin? This is True Love: After you sacrifice your own life and are resurrected, you try to invest again, more than three times. Since we have inherited fallen lineage, even at the cost of our own lives we have to persevere and overcome. Therefore, "whoever seeks to gain his life will lose it, but whoever loses his life will preserve it." (Luke 17:33) Jesus followed this way when he came to this world. That is why he could lead the world, not by selfish individualism, but by altruism. Therefore, although I have created great wealth during my life, none of it, not even one penny, is mine. I invested everything for the world and then I forgot what I had done for others, and then I sacrificed and invested again. I repeated this process again and again.

Which do you prefer, "One Nation under God" or "One World under God?" Among Americans, some people do not like the concept of One World under God. Some white people do not like black people. White Anglo-Saxon Protestants occupy dominant positions in the United States. America, led by this group, should have the idea that this country exists for the sake of the world. If America lives only for its own sake, America will ultimately perish.

Now the times are changing. The coming time is the age of One World under God. God is working for this kind of world and will always help those people who also are working for that kind of providence. But there is a problem with many people wanting to lead the world but not wanting to participate in that providence.

In order to make one peaceful world, I have poured myself into various efforts. Let me give a few examples. We need to establish an ideal, world-wide academic institution like a U.N. University, transcending the barriers of race, religion and language, in order to complete the foundation for the future world. Also, to exchange knowledge globally, we need a university system for distance learning. We also need to develop a unified medical science. We need not only to cure the diseases of the body caused by the Fall, but also to end the conflict between Orient and Occident through harmonizing Eastern and Western culture. By unifying Eastern and Western medicine we can cure formerly incurable diseases, such as AIDS. In Korea, among the people of the countryside who never had formal medical education, there are many gifted healers who can cure serious diseases that are incurable through modern medicine. These healers have received teaching from the spiritual world about special treatments. Without recognizing certain realities of the spiritual world, problems will continue to grow.

Already these projects are being implemented at the University of Bridgeport and Sun Moon University. I have also created *The Washington Times* and other newspapers to cover the entire hemisphere, and I am expanding this media foundation into 185 countries to help all the people of the world learn from each other and cooperate as one. Since I came to America, I never had any debt to the American people. Rather, America should feel indebted to me. I shared the blessing I received from Heaven with America. I didn't receive any blessing from America, but my entire blessing was given to her.

Regardless of the degree of opposition, the person who loves the most will become the owner. Those who love more, invest more, who give more and forget what they have given, will become central figures. This is cosmic law.

In the future, please follow the way that in the family you offer filial piety to your parents, become a loyal citizen before the nation, become a saint before the world, and become a Holy Son or Daughter before God. Whoever can stand without shame before the family, nation, world, and Heaven and Earth, will be protected in the center of the cosmos and can then realize a family that receives God's highest love.

Such a person shall transform this world into the Kingdom of Heaven on Earth, being registered in the Kingdom of Heaven in the spiritual world and entering into an era of kingship both spiritually and physically centered on God. Such a person shall receive the International Ceremony of Holy Blessing, which is to establish a world of victory, freedom, happiness and unity. I invite each of you to participate in this year's 3.6 million couple Blessing Ceremony, and so become a person welcomed by Heaven and Earth and find the way of eternal life.

Today literary leaders from all over the world are gathered together here. I hope the staff of *The Washington Times* and all the world literary leaders will become major figures to create a True Family and True World (cosmic) culture centered on God's True Love, ushering in a world of peace and unification in the forthcoming 21st Century.

May God bless you, your family and all your endeavors.

Thank you.

True Family and I

Reverend Sun Myung Moon, President, Family Federation for World Peace
This address was given November through December 1995 on a world speaking tour.

Ladies and Gentlemen:

I am truly grateful that you have granted me the opportunity to speak to you today. I am Reverend Moon. No doubt you have already heard about me through many rumors and stories. I have stirred up a good deal of controversy around the world. At the same time, I have initiated a number of events and accomplishments with worldwide impact. I must add that these things have resulted from the historical reality of my having served God to this day.

Today in this brief encounter I would like to speak to you for a time on the subject "The True Family and I," because the world's problems stem from the family. Let us ask what we mean by a "true family."

Why Are Mind and Body in Conflict?

Today, if we ask whether the world in which we live is good or evil, we must answer that it is evil. Why, then, is it evil? It is because whether we consider world history, American history, or the history of any country, there has been constant conflict. Conflict and struggle means that the parties involved will not develop, but will necessarily decline. To say that the world is evil implies that America is evil, that Americans are evil, and that we, ourselves, are evil. If we study ourselves, we cannot deny that within ourselves there is a struggle between mind and body. The origin and cause of this struggle remains a mystery which must be solved.

If an individual does not possess a foundation for peace within himself, then he will not be happy, no matter how peaceful his family, his nation or the world might be. This is because the individual is the true battlefield. As you know, World War I, World War II and the Cold War have already ended. In the midst of any other future conflicts, it will be possible to have a truce. However, the struggle between mind and body has existed from the beginning, without a moment's truce. It has continued throughout history and, of course, it continues today. We do not know how much longer it will continue in the future.

When we think of this and at the same time consider that God exists, the fact that God would permit the historical struggle between mind and body to continue is a major problem. But if we agree that human beings committed sin, we can understand that it is the human responsibility to indemnify it. God cannot take that responsibility upon Himself nor can He interfere with it.

Where does the struggle between mind and body originate? We inherit life from our parents and from the parents of their parents. If we continue going back in this manner, we eventually arrive at the first generation, that is, the first human ancestors. It is a fact that the struggle between mind and body originated through a problem in the conjugal love of Adam and Eve. Our life originates in our parents' love. Since this struggle began before any of us were born, we have to conclude that the problem relates to the circumstances in which our first parents entered into a love relationship with each other.

The love of Adam and Eve was not a love of true happiness. Instead, it was conflict-ridden love. Because the roots of our life are in this love, we must conclude that the conflicts in our inner self originate there. The Bible teaches that because Adam and Eve sinned, they were expelled from the Garden of Eden. After they were driven out of the Garden, they began to multiply children. God could not follow them and bless them in marriage, because it was He who had driven them from the Garden. Thus we must ask, under whose guidance did they marry? We must concur that, because of having fallen into sin, they married in the hands of Satan.

God Is Working to Recreate Love

The fall consisted of Eve being tempted by Satan and her later temptation of Adam. Therefore, when our ancestors, Adam and Eve, established a relationship of conjugal love, that relationship was not a happy one. Instead, it was conflict-ridden. Humanity, because of its roots in that relationship, cannot separate itself from that struggle between mind and body. This reality is very clear and my explanation is logical. The fall began with immoral love. Due to a love relationship which God did not desire, Adam and Eve united with Satan. They did not become the ancestors of goodness, but rather the ancestors of evil, planting the roots of evil love, evil life and evil blood lineage.

If this is true, then what began with one fallen family grew into tribes, nations and a world of five billion people who are descendants of Satan, incapable of denying that we inherited the lineage of evil parents. Satan betrayed God and stole Eve away from God. No one knew that the blood of this adulterer, Satan, is present within our bodies, or that this is so displeasing to God.

How are we going to eliminate those roots within us? Satan dug his roots into our physical body, our flesh. God cannot avoid working to separate good from evil and thus to reverse this situation. God is public-minded and continues on the path of living for the whole, going toward the goal of love and peace. On the other hand, Satan is selfish and individualistic. Satan is always trying to destroy the good side through hatred, evil and war. He intends to prevent the earth from ever returning to God's side.

God, who represents goodness, cannot severely punish humanity for having gone with Satan. God's strategy to regain humanity on His side is to allow evil to attack Him. He can then, later, claim indemnity for damage and abuse. Satan's strategy is to strike first, but in the end he loses everything. Satan has marched through history, wishing to ruin God's plan through hatred, evil and war. On the other side, God has been working to recreate humankind through love and peace.

When the Last Days come, Satan has to give over to God's side his spiritual power as a ruler over humanity and the respect which he once enjoyed. Satan retaliated by coming up with atheism, the ideology of no God, which supported the appearance of humanism, materialism and communism. After World War II, the struggle between God's side, the right wing, and Satan's side, the left wing, moved to the world level. Further, after World War II, because of the victory of God's side, the world entered a transitional period in which to welcome victory and peace based upon the realm of Christian culture.

The present era is the era of the realm of individualism: the era of free sex, the era of children denying parents, the era of parents denying children, the era of denying the couple. Through homosexuality, an attempt is being made to destroy completely the family ideal. It is this ideal that the Messiah, at his second coming, intends to establish in order to change this hell into the Kingdom of Heaven on earth. The Messiah, as the True Father, desires the unity of mind and body, the unity of husband and wife, and the unity of children.

The Relationship of Spirit and Matter

Problems must still be solved on a worldwide level. They include: (1) Which came first, matter or spirit? (2) Is the materialist theory or the idealist theory correct? (3) Which comes first, reality or concept? (4) Is evolution or creationism correct?

Let us attempt to answer these by way of an example. When we observe the animal kingdom, we discover that the first thing formed in a newborn animal is the eyes. The eyes are made of matter. Would those eyes know prior to birth that the sun existed? Being purely material, the eyes do not know, but something or someone prior to the material knew that the eyes were created to see sunlight. Someone knew.

Being purely matter, the eyes did not know that the atmosphere existed, but the eyes were formed with eyelids to assure that dust in the air does not damage the eye. The eyes, being purely material, did not know that steam and other heat radiations could dry the eyes and damage them, but someone knew and, for that reason, we blink so that our eyes can stay moist.

The conclusion is that through the simple example of the eye, we can solve the great debate over whether thought precedes existence, whether spirit precedes matter, and whether concept precedes reality. We can answer the debate of spirit versus matter, of creationism versus evolution. Given this, we cannot deny that everything was created by God. Therefore, we must return to the original world of creation, and realize the kind of self, the kind of family, and the kind of world God desires.

The Purpose of Religion

Thus, I would like to explain the complicated relationships that came to surround each one of us after the fall. It is logical that if Adam and Eve had not fallen, it would have been normal for their minds and bodies to have been one, just as God is one. Due to the fall, the body emerged as another positive, which was opposed to the positive of the conscience which relates to God. The repulsion between these two positives led to a history of struggle. We must be aware of this.

The body became the base of operation for hell, and the conscience became the base of operation for heaven. Man did not know that he contained, within himself, the division of two worlds.

From this perspective, we all should ask ourselves if our body leads our mind or our mind leads our body. In reality, throughout history, the body has had complete license to lead the mind. If the conscience were strengthened, we would automatically return to God and bring the world to be with God. The fact that the physical body leads the conscience, instead of the conscience leading the body, originated at the time that our ancestors established a relationship with Satan. This resulted in the power of false love.

The problem is that this power of false love, which tied the first ancestors to Satan, was stronger than the force of the conscience. God, who knows the situation of human beings very well, cannot abandon fallen humanity. Instead, He must establish a strategy to weaken the body-centered force that dominates our conscience. The historical system for salvation which was created and driven by God is religion. Religion was necessary in the past and it is still necessary today. God has established many religions. According to their different circumstances and antecedents, the world's cultural spheres formed. Until now, religious people did not know that the purpose of religion is to prevent the body from continuing to lead the mind. If there had been no fall, religion would not have been necessary.

Something bad happened, and religion became necessary to correct it. What does God intend to do through religion? He intends to discipline the body. You probably think that by believing in religion you will be saved, that by believing in Christianity you will go to heaven, or that by believing in Buddhism you will go to paradise. But it is those who are united with God's love who will enter heaven. To enter heaven, Adam's family should have been a family whose center was the love of God, a family that had a blood relationship with God. Until now, no one knew that the place where such families dwell is the Kingdom of Heaven. Therefore, to strengthen the power of the conscience, we must dominate the body. We must liberate our conscience, so that it can lead our body by our will. We can then return to the bosom of God's love as original beings, free from sin.

If we ask what religion should do, the answer is that it should motivate our body to do everything it hates to do. What does the body hate most? To fast! To serve! To sacrifice! Furthermore, religion asks us to be an offering. The offering is destined to shed blood; it must be capable of sacrificing its life. Therefore, the Bible tells us that he who is willing to lose his life shall gain it, and he who wishes to save his life shall lose it. This paradox teaches us that if we live according to the flesh, we are going to hell. If we win over the flesh and liberate our conscience, we will go to heaven. If we completely subjugate the body, and our conscience stands in a totally subjective position, our conscience will open us to unlimited desire and infinite hope.

The Nature of the Conscience

In the course of history, there have been many religions and religious leaders. Yet those who believed in those religions and in those leaders could not totally control their bodies and deny themselves. They could not liberate the conscience and position it to relate with God on the original basis. We sinful people did not become true olive trees. Instead, we became wild olive trees, with our roots in false love. Man should have had his roots in God's true love, yet we established roots in Satan's love. How are we going to solve the problem of being wild olive trees, instead of true ones? This remains an inescapable, extremely crucial task, which we must fulfill.

If you study yourself, you will notice that your conscience knows everything about you. Your conscience is closer to you than are your own parents. It desires to possess eternal love and to be embraced eternally in God's bosom. When we marry, we separate from our earthly parents, but not from our conscience. The conscience exists with us prior to our birth on earth. It loves us, and its mission is to transform us into eternal sons and daughters of God. In this sense, the conscience does not need a teacher.

Have you ever heard of a Secretary of Education announcing a plan to educate the conscience? If the conscience had gone the original way, we would have known clearly the course we should follow in life. It would have taught us and guided us to return to God's bosom. On the basis of our conscience, which knows everything about our life, there is a computer in the spirit world that registers everything we do on earth. When you go to the spirit world, you will discover this.

Until today, we did not know that the mission of the conscience is to convert us into unblemished, true sons and daughters of God. Is there anyone here who is convinced that he or she will never die? We all will go to the spirit world someday. When you enter the spirit world, they will immediately know you by your name. They will know about your entire life. They will also know about your ancestors, because the spirit world transcends time and space. We should not bring anything into that world that would stain our conscience. For that reason, know that the conscience is above all other teachers.

There are many distinguished personalities gathered here today. Some of you are professors. I can honestly say that there has never been a professor who possessed a teaching superior to that of the conscience. The role of the conscience for a man is the same as that of a compass for a ship.

God Is the Root of the Conscience

I would like to ask those of you who are married, "When you married, did you want your spouse to be inferior to yourself?" The answer is "No." If I asked you whether you wanted a spouse ten times or one hundred times better than you, no doubt you would reply that, if it were possible, you would prefer that he or she be one thousand, ten thousand or one million times better than you.

The conscience's ambition demands the maximum amount of love. It wishes to possess the Absolute Being. The same was true for our ancestors. The same will be true for our descendants. If we were to ask God, He would respond that it is true for Him. Is it not impossible for all of our desires to be fulfilled? A mayor will want to be governor. Later, he will want to become president. Ultimately, he will want to ascend to the highest position in the world. That is how far the ambition of the conscience extends. From the beginning of history, people have generally thought that the conscience's ambition cannot be satisfied completely. But Reverend Moon, the person who is standing here, has arrived at the conclusion that it is possible to satisfy even the highest ambition of the conscience.

How big is the conscience? How can we measure the conscience? Do you think that the day will come when the conscience possesses God? Do you think that if something bigger than God exists, the conscience will desire to possess it? What is it that the conscience's ambition is seeking? The conscience desires to possess whatever has the maximum value in the cosmos.

Then how big would God's conscience be? Which is bigger, the human conscience or God's conscience? If God's conscience is bigger than a man's, what would He do with it? The conclusion is that we, in our immense ambition, desire the same thing that God desires: true love.

The Conscience Desires True Love

What do you think? We know that God is absolute, but does He not feel lonely? Do you think that He feels happy? Ladies and gentlemen, even if a person becomes the president of the nation, if he lives alone, without a spouse, that person will feel neglected. If we do not have an object of love, we are unhappy. Doesn't God need someone? How would you feel in that situation? Even if God is God, He feels very lonely.

Human beings feel empty when they lack money, knowledge or authority, but God does not need money, knowledge or power. We must ask ourselves what God needs most. We call God "the King of Love"! God is the Creator of Love! If it is the case that God is the King of Love, then He is like a bridegroom. This means that He needs His object of love, whose position is that of a Queen of Love. This is an absolute principle. Who, then, can be the absolute object of God's love? My answer is: a true human being!

Ladies and gentlemen, you need money. You need knowledge. You need power. But if you do not have a spouse, all of that will be useless. A husband needs his wife and children. A wife needs her husband and children. The family is the place where we find these partners of love.

The individual serves God, the subject of love, in the position of an object of love who completely satisfies the ambition of God's conscience. The family in which a man and woman unite as objects of God's love, and where children live happily, should be the initial foundation of the Kingdom of Heaven on earth, centered on the true love of God.

Just as a man wants his object of love to be infinitely more valuable than he, God also wants man, His object of love, to have infinite value. A person of that value is a true person. We did not know that Adam and Eve were meant to be that kind of man and woman. No one has known that we were created with such value. If we were given such a high aspiration in our conscience, it is because God is the subject partner and He wants man to be in the position of His object partner. He did not want man and woman simply to be a part of Him, but rather to be completely different personalities. God allowed us to have such an elevated power of conscience because He hoped that we would be one thousand or ten thousand times more valuable than Himself. You must understand this very well.

True Love of God and Man

If, at the beginning of creation, God and man had united in a relationship of true love within a family, we would not have to worry about hell or heaven today, because we automatically would have entered the Kingdom of God. The problem here is that God's true love and man's love did not begin at a common point, united as a subjective and objective love. From the first family, God's love and man's love moved in two different directions with two different goals. Therefore, it has been impossible to realize the ideal world for which God and man are longing.

God's ideal of a common point of beginning was completely frustrated. False parents arose centered on Satan's love. As their descendants, we inherited that false love, false life and false lineage, and are thus destined for hell. We have nothing to do with the Kingdom of Heaven. A person may have money, knowledge and power, but if she loses the love of her life, none of those things have any meaning. We did not know that, by being people whose spirit dominates our body through willpower, we were supposed to conquer God's love through our conscience.

What does the conscience do to win the true love of God? If you unburden and liberate your mind completely, your conscience will automatically connect with the true love of God. If we compare the size of the conscience to that of love, we will see that the size of love is greater. We can know this from the fact that the conscience begins from love.

The Kingdom of Heaven is the place where we go to live in unity with God, in true love and with a free conscience. It is the place we go after having lived centered on love and after preparing ourselves to be in the lineage of God's love. Without winning this love, we cannot enter the Kingdom of God for thousands of years. Due to the fall, there will be no connection with the Kingdom of Heaven until humankind is illuminated by God's true thought and sustained by God's true love.

The person who lives in unity, with a true conscience and true love, will enter the Kingdom of Heaven automatically. No matter how much a person believes in Jesus, he cannot enter the Kingdom of Heaven if he is not linked to the love of God. The struggle of our mind and body prevents us from entering the kingdom. The person who remains in Satan's lineage cannot enter the kingdom. The religions which have the mission of opening the way are struggling among themselves. They will meet a sad end in the Last Days.

God cannot be found where there is conflict. Catholicism and Protestantism must become one. Religion is not a key to open the doors to salvation; rather, it is a movement to subjugate the body and liberate the conscience. We have to know that we cannot receive the key that opens that door if we fail to inherit the love, the life and the true lineage of God. We will not receive salvation just by believing in religion. In reality, religion only exists to discipline the body.

When our conscience is liberated, its ambition for love can be raised to encompass God. How does this seem to you? Reflect first about what you are doing with your life. Will you try to find out more about this? Who is the first to know what someone is doing? Who knows first, the conscience or God? The conscience knows first. Man is distinct from God because he occupies the object position. In the same sense, husband and wife are distinct. The characteristics of each are clearly different. If we were to conclude that God knows everything prior to its happening, we could say that we are a part of God, as if we and God were a single entity. But if such were the case, we could not be the object partners of God's love.

A person who stands alone cannot realize the ideal. After Adam and Eve sinned, they hid themselves among the trees. God asked, "Adam, where are you?" and Adam answered, "I am here." God understood, and said, "You hid yourself because you have sinned." Since man began from God, he should return to the position of object partner to God. We must return to God.

Friends of God

Ladies and gentlemen, your sons and daughters grow up. When you reach the age of one hundred and your children reach the age of eighty, the relationship of father and son also becomes a relationship of friends. Friends! We cannot compare the physical strength of a woman with that of a man. Women can never defeat men physically; but, through love, wife and husband are attracted to one another and they come to resemble each other. If Adam and

Eve had become the objects of God's love, would that have been pleasing to Him? Absolutely, yes! God created the universe before Adam and Eve perfected themselves as the objects of His love. God had the ambitious hope that in the future they would be His ideal objects. If, after having perfected themselves as the objects of God's love, they had asked God to create something greater than what He had already created, do you think He could have done so?

Given the infinite ambition of our consciences, we should know that God can create everything we desire. God created us with the value of true love object partners. Because this absolute value was lost, it must be restored. This restoration is the purpose of human life and history. God established religions and promised that someday each of the founders of those religions would return.

Christianity has taught that Jesus will return. In Buddhism, they speak of the return of Buddha. Confucianism alludes to a new Confucius. Likewise, in Islam, believers await the return of Mohammed. What could be the reason God established the different religions? We need to understand that the Will of God is accomplished centered on His beloved children, children who are like God's flesh and blood. With that type of son and daughter, God wants to form families, tribes, races and nations.

We need to understand, then, what the Messiah is. The Lord in his second coming is the person who completes the ideal for which all religions have longed, descending to the earth with the root of true love from the eternal God. He will become a True Father. Through the restoration of that lost true love, he will work to establish a true family on earth, on the foundation of true life and true lineage.

That is the purpose of the providence of salvation. Due to the fall, God lost the true mother as well as the children of Adam's family. This means that God could not have true children. There was no family connected to the blood lineage which was to come from God's love. Through fallen parents, blood ties originated from false love and false life, and the struggle between mind and body began. Adam and Eve became enemies to each other. There was a fight to the death between Adam's sons.

The providence of salvation is the providence of restoration, which God has been leading in order to restore his lost sons and daughters, restore the absolute unity of mind and body, restore the absolute unity of husband and wife, and restore the absolute unity of parents and children in the true love of God. This true family, which is qualified to live eternally with God, should be connected to Christianity, which is in the position of the bride to the Lord. By establishing such a blood relationship with God, we can realize united families, united tribes, united races and united nations, which thus will bring about the united world, the culmination of the providence of salvation.

The Necessity of True Parents

Distinguished people of America, is it not true that America would like to receive God's Blessing? To do so, you must become a people whose minds and bodies are united in God's true love. You must also unite as absolute husbands and wives. When the number of families that unite as absolute children of God grows, then God will come to live in this nation. If this happens, then automatically this nation will be the central nation of the world.

Man has this nature. If his beloved lives in poverty in the countryside, he wants to live there with her. In the same way, wherever God's beloved sons and daughters dwell is the

Kingdom of Heaven, even if it is a place of poverty. If it is prosperous, it will be the Kingdom of Heaven as well.

Today, the founder of the Unification Church is here speaking to you. If you ask me, "What is the mission of the Unification Church?," I will say that it is a place where God's true love is present. It is the place where we want our mind and body to unite in true love. It is the place where we want to form ideal marriages with absolute unity between husband and wife. We are carrying out the mission that God has given us, by means of an ideology that can make all people into inseparable brothers and sisters.

Centering on the love of the True God, my wife and I are cleansing all the polluted elements that originated in the false family formed through false marriage. This false marriage was caused by false love, false life and false lineage, which stemmed from the false, fallen parents. My wife and I established Headwing Ideology, an external ideology through which we can overcome and defeat both left-wing ideology and right-wing ideology. We also introduced the internal ideology of Godism. In other words, through True Love, we have purified the world of conscience and the spirit world. By doing so, we have achieved True Parents' position. Thus we are able to sow the seed of True Love, the seed of True Life, and the seed of True Lineage, which signifies the unity between God and human beings, to the couples participating in the International Holy Wedding, the ceremony of resurrection bequeathing this great Blessing.

This is the ceremony, then, that opens the path by which mankind will reach the new and true family. By having families from around the world participate in these marriage ceremonies, we want to connect the world to God's great Blessing. It is my fervent desire that all the world's people receive this great Blessing and become families and peoples that can establish the Kingdom of Heaven on earth.

The purpose of the Unification Church is to establish relationships of brotherhood that transcend nations through this means. Through this means, we want to realize the ideal of one great universal family, centered on God, and thus proclaim the ideal of True Parents, true spouses, and true brothers and sisters. In this way, we will begin the world culture of heart. From earth to heaven, we will be liberated to fulfill the Kingdom of Heaven on earth.

Since the end of World War II, for the past fifty years, the entire world has persecuted and criticized Reverend Moon. The time has come for you to know that such persecution was not the result of my committing a crime. Instead, it was to save you. And now, unlike in the past, people realize that I am a man of goodness.

I was instrumental in bringing about the collapse of communism. It was Reverend Moon who reached out to Mikhail Gorbachev and Kim Il Sung. To save the United States, which is going toward collapse, I built a foundation for the sake of creating hope. There are difficult political circumstances between North and South Korea which Reverend Moon is resolving. The same is true for the Middle East.

What I have proclaimed has come to pass. The entire world did everything it could to put an end to me, yet I did not die, and today I am firmly standing on top of the world. If I can boldly proclaim the truth to you today, it is because of God's love. You need to know that if I survived, it was because God absolutely protected me. For this reason, I believe that you should study the Unification Church with this same seriousness.

We have met together today and this is a day of deep significance. I have shared a very important message with you and I have placed my trust in you. I kindly ask that you not forget this. I also ask that, based on this new awakening, you determine to follow the path to bring God's Blessing to your families and your nation. In that way, ideal families will begin to appear on this earth.

As you probably know, Reverend Moon and his spouse are known throughout the world as the True Parents. If it is true that as the True Parents, we are connected to God in true love, true life and true lineage, I would like you to remember one thing. Beginning from a true family and you, a realm of liberation, liberty, unification and happiness will begin. This will allow the hope of peace to sprout upon the earth.

Thank you very much.

True Parents
and True Family

Mrs. Hak Ja Han Moon, President, Women's Federation for World Peace
This address was given at the inauguration of the Family Federation for World
Peace in 185 nations, Sao Paolo, Brazil, and on her Autumn, 1996 world
speaking tour.

Respected guests, members of the Family Federation for World Peace, ladies and gentlemen:

It is my great pleasure today to be able to share with you distinguished leaders a message about the True Family. As you know, the family is the cradle of human life and the cornerstone for a peaceful world.

It is my hope that at this gathering we will begin to find the way to build true families that are healthy and vibrant in the love of God.

God is the absolute One, the only, unchanging, and eternal One. His will is the same. If the human beings Adam and Eve had become one body under the love of God, everything would have been complete and perfect. God's origin, purpose and process of creation, as well as cause, effect and direction, are all absolute.

The human ancestors Adam and Eve entered into chaos after they fell through their ignorance. This ignorance and chaos expanded from the individual level to the levels of family, nation and world. It has been the task of religion and the Providence of Salvation to liberate us from this sphere of the Fall.

In the Last Days, the Messiah comes and teaches clearly the absolute, the only, unchanging, and eternal cause, direction and effect, from God's viewpoint. He will cleanse the world of ignorance and chaos and return it to the original bosom of God. This is the completion of the will of God.

If this does not happen, then in the Last Days all religions, "isms," systems of thought, and nations will pass away. Now humankind is facing the twenty-first century, entering the new historical era of the Third Millennium in just a few years. At this important moment, I would like to deliver this speech on the "View of the Principle of the Providential History of Salvation," so that we can resolve to prepare ourselves for the new era.

To bring about completion and perfection between God and humankind, centering on True Love, God required that man accomplish a condition of responsibility in order to reach unity with Him. Therefore, God needed to give the Commandment to the first ancestors. In other words, God knew that they were in the growth period, on the way to reaching perfection, so He established the Commandment as the condition for His children to inherit the most precious thing, True Love.

Originally, True Love was to be gained through life experience and understood through internal realization. True Love is not something that can be learned through words, a written text or schooling. It is experienced completely only in life. Created as newborn infants, Adam and Eve were to grow and perfect themselves gradually through experiences of the heart of True Children, True Brother and Sister, True Husband and Wife, and True Parents encompassing their whole lives. Only after experiencing the True Love of God in its entirety can one perfect the Purpose of Creation and become an ideal human being.

Every person desires that his object of love be ten million times more valuable than himself, or even infinitely more valuable. In the same way, God desires that humankind, His object of love, become infinitely valuable. If a human being perfects himself, then that person obtains God-like value by attaining God's divinity and perfection.

God's Ideal of True Love

God is absolute, but His ideal of True Love cannot be realized by Himself. That is because love always requires an object, a beloved. At this point, we should understand the relationship between God's True Love and humankind's True Love, and how they begin and are perfected. What would have happened if God had not chosen human beings as His absolute objects of True Love, and instead had sought to begin and perfect True Love in some other way? In that case, God and man would have pursued the ideal of True Love with different motivations, directions and purposes. God would have had to achieve His ideal of love through an object higher than humankind; and by the same token, humankind's ideal of love would have had no direct relationship with God.

But God, as the subject of True Love, did establish humankind as the object of His True Love. Accordingly, God can fulfill His ideal of True Love only through humankind. The fulfillment of God's Purpose of Creation is the ideal world where God and mankind are united through absolute love. Human beings were created as the greatest object of God's love. They alone, in all Creation, embody the nature of God. They are born the visible bodies of the invisible God. If a person perfects himself, he becomes the temple of God, a visible, substantial body in which God can freely and peacefully dwell.

God's overall ideal of absolute True Love is realized and perfected through humankind in a vertical parent-child relationship.

God created Adam first. He was to be the son of God and at the same time the substantial body of God Himself. Later, God created Eve as the object of Adam so that Adam and Eve could perfect the ideal of horizontal love, which is conjugal love. Eve was to be the daughter of God, and also, as a bride she was to perfect substantially the ideal of the horizontal love of God.

The place in which Adam and Eve are perfected, consummating their first love by marrying under the blessing of God, is precisely the place where God meets His substantial bride. This is because God's ideal of absolute love descends vertically and joins where the ideal of conjugal love between Adam and Eve is realized horizontally. The True Love of God and the True Love of humankind join and perfect themselves at the same point, although they come from different directions, one vertical and the other horizontal.

Why God Needs Humankind

God's act of creation was inevitable. And we cannot imagine Creation without a purpose. There was only one reason God needed the Creation: to realize the ideal of True Love. God developed life from the simplest and lowest levels up to the human level in pairs, subject and object and positive and negative, to form reciprocal relationships under the ideal of love. The Creation's ideal of love and God's ideal of ultimate love are not separate or different. This Principle of Creation is at work to perfect the absolute love of God through the perfection of the love of man and woman in the human world. This is the reason why, in the beginning, God created one man and one woman, Adam and Eve.

God's Purpose of Creation called for Adam and Eve to obey the Commandment of God, who is the subject of True Love, and perfect themselves as True Man and True Woman. Furthermore, they were to become a True Couple united in the True Love of God. Then, by having sons and daughters through that True Love, they would have become True Parents and lived in happiness. Had Adam and Eve perfected themselves in True Love, they would have fulfilled God's desire to wear a substantial body. And when they perfected themselves as a True Couple, the ideal of God's absolute love would have been fulfilled.

By Adam and Eve having children of goodness and becoming True Parents, God would have established Himself substantially as the Eternal Parent and achieved His ideal: Citizenship in the Kingdom of Heaven would expand infinitely in the afterlife of the spirit world based on myriad generations of descendants in the physical world.

But Adam and Eve, the human ancestors, fell away from God. When they were expelled from Eden, they had not yet had children. Having driven them out, God had no basis to follow behind them to bless their marriage. The entire human race has thus descended from our failed ancestors. Humanity has multiplied without any direct relationship whatsoever to the love of God.

Distinguished Leaders: Could the Fall of Man have been the result of eating the fruit of a tree? The fall of Adam and Eve was immoral conduct against the ideal of the True Love of God. The fact that Adam and Eve needed to obey the Commandment shows that they fell in a stage of imperfection, that is to say, during their period of growth. The Archangel, who is symbolized by a serpent, tempted Eve to eat of the fruit of good and evil, and she fell spiritually. She later tempted Adam (who was also too immature to eat of the fruit), and they then fell physically.

The only possible sin that could have been fatal in the Garden of Eden, where Adam and Eve were in communication with God and living in joy, was the sin of illicit love. The first consummated love of the human ancestors, because it was supposed to have been the perfection of the love of God Himself, should have marked the beginning of a celebration that would continue throughout history, filled with the never-ending intoxication of joy and blessing for God, Adam and Eve, and the universe. It should have been a joyous occasion in which the love, life and lineage of God would have been established within humankind. To the contrary, however, Adam and Eve covered their lower parts and hid themselves among the trees, trembling in fear. By disobeying heavenly law, they established an immoral relationship as the basis for false love, false life and false lineage.

As descendants of Adam and Eve, all human beings are born with Original Sin. The Fall gave rise to conflict of mind and body within every person and caused our societies to be filled with tainted love, and people do things that contradict the desire of their original minds.

Taking Responsibility for Love

According to the ideal of love, all love relationships in the animal and plant kingdoms are for reproduction only. Human beings are the sole exception. Humankind enjoys freedom in the conjugal relationship of love. This is humanity's special privilege as the lord of all creation. God gave the blessing and infinite joy of love to His sons and daughters. However, the True Freedom that God allowed requires human responsibility. If an individual were to insist upon and practice freedom of love without responsibility, how much confusion and destruction would take place! Achieving the highest ideal of human love is possible only when one takes responsibility for love.

We can think of this responsibility in three ways. The first responsibility is for one to become the master of True Love, truly free and thanking God for the freedom of love and knowing how to cultivate and control oneself. This responsibility for a love relationship should not be taken merely because of law or social convention. Instead, a person should establish responsibility through his own self-control and self-determination within the life-committing vertical relationship with God.

Second is one's responsibility toward the object of love. By nature, people do not want their spouse's love to be shared with others. Horizontal conjugal love, which differs from the vertical love between parents and children, loses its potential for perfection the moment it is divided. This is because the Principle of Creation requires husband and wife to become one in absolute love. Each spouse has the responsibility given by love to live absolutely for the sake of the other.

The third responsibility of love is toward children. The love of parents is the basis for children's pride and happiness. They would wish to be born through the total and harmonious unity of their parents in True Love, and they would wish to be raised in that kind of love. The most precious responsibility of parents is not only to rear their children externally, but also to offer them life elements of True Love that can perfect their spirituality. This is why the family is so valuable. The daily experience of the heart of True Children, True Brothers and Sisters, True Spouses, and True Parents cannot be acquired in any place other than the True Family.

If Adam and Eve had become a couple of True Love centered upon God, God could have dwelt in Adam as His substantial body and thus loved Eve. What is more, Adam and Eve could have become True Parents who substantially embodied God, and become the origin of the love of goodness, a life of goodness, and a lineage of goodness.

Due to the Fall, however, Adam and Eve became the substantial body of Satan and ended up becoming the original evil couple, evil parents and evil ancestors. Their union became the root of evil love, evil life and evil blood lineage. Because human beings originated from this root, they descended from the adulterous Satan, who is the enemy of God, and inherited this lineage of evil parents.

Ladies and gentlemen: How great must have been the pain of God when, by the Fall, our human ancestors destroyed His ideal of True Love! Humankind should have been the sons and daughters of God, but they do not know God Himself as their Original Parent. Yet even though His sons and daughters serve Satan, God has worked for the Providence of Salvation. Because He is an absolute being, and His ideal of creation is also absolute, He has carried out the Providence of Salvation even amid great sadness. God's Providence of Salvation is the Providence of Restoration, which means to recover the lost Purpose of Creation, centered on True Love. The Providence of Salvation is also the Providence of Re-creation.

The Essence of God's Providence

Based on this point, the root of the Providence of Salvation is the re-creation of the seed of the original child, the human being who will fulfill the ideal of creation. That which God abhors, the life and blood lineage that began with the false love of the adulterer Satan, must be cleansed. The essence of the Providence is the task of setting up the birth of the True Parent, the Savior united with the True Love, Life and Lineage of God.

Since the ancestors of humankind failed to fulfill their responsibility, inherited the immoral lineage of Satan, and came under the dominion of Satan, God Himself could not directly intervene and return human beings to their original position. Furthermore, God can neither unconditionally accept humankind, who chose to go to the side of the evil Archangel, nor punish them. So God uses the strategy of placing a central figure on the side of the good Archangel; by being struck first, that figure establishes the indemnity condition to recover what was lost. Satan strikes first but as a result must take the losing position. The First, Second, and Third (Cold War) World Wars are good examples of this. The side that struck first, lost.

From the overall perspective of the Providence of Restoration, the foundation of cooperation between mother and son is very important. This was so at the time of Jacob, Moses, and Jesus. God was working His Providence to separate people from satanic life and lineage by establishing the foundation of cooperation between a mother who had to fulfill the responsibility of Eve, the originator of the Fall and the second son of the family.

God cannot directly relate to the first son because he is in the position of having a direct blood relationship with Satan, who through the Fall was the first to dominate humankind. God has been restoring the blood lineage of goodness by having the second son, who represents the side of goodness, establish a condition. Then God has had the first son, representing the side of evil, take a position subordinate to the second son.

In the family of Adam, God carried out the providence of establishing the second son, Abel, and having him subordinate the first son, Cain. Even though Eve had fallen, as a mother she could have made an effort to create unity between the two brothers. In the end, however, Cain murdered Abel (Genesis 4:8) and the Providence of Salvation, not being fulfilled, was prolonged.

There was also a required formula of cooperation between mother and son at the time of Noah. But that formula of meaningful cooperation was not realized until the time of Rebekah and Jacob.

The human Fall was committed by three beings: Adam, Eve and the Archangel. The Archangel seduced Eve, causing the spiritual fall, and later fallen Eve seduced Adam, causing the physical fall. As a result, they turned their backs on God, and the fallen Archangel became Satan. Since the Providence of Salvation is the Providence of Restoration, the Principle of Restoration can be carried out only by going in a direction 180 degrees opposite of the Fall.

God lost Adam, who had the seed of True Love and True Life. Thus, God had to find a son with the new seed free from satanic accusation. Just as God created Adam first at the time of the creation, God must prepare a son first who has no relationship to the Fall, according to the Providence of Restoration, which is the Providence of Re-creation. This is the basis for the idea of the coming of the Messiah. The Messiah rejects the sinful lives of those with a fallen lineage under the dominion of Satan. He comes as a True Person who engrafts fallen humanity into the seed of new life. The Messiah has his roots in God, and comes as the Second Adam, who wipes away all that was committed by the first Adam. This is the reason God cannot send a superman Messiah who will work only through miracles.

For a son to be born on earth with this seed of God's love and life, there first must exist a mother. And the mother cannot give birth to this child in a conventional way. Conception must happen through the formula of restoration. All the cooperation between mothers and sons in the Providence of Restoration is a preparation and a condition for the Son of God to be born with the seed of new life, free from satanic accusation. By making conditions to avoid Satan's attacks, and by subordinating the firstborn son who represents evil, mother and son restore the love, life and lineage that were taken over by Satan.

The Meaning of Jacob's Victory

The Bible, which records the providential work of God, contains many stories that are difficult to understand. For example, Rebekah deceived her husband Isaac and her first son Esau, and helped her second son Jacob receive the blessing (Genesis 27). God took the side of that mother and son, and although they used methods that at first glance seem unjust, God still blessed them for their actions.

In Adam's family, Cain and Abel fought outside the womb. Their struggle resulted in the death of Abel, the second son.

Then came Jacob. On the merits of many godly people who paid indemnity and sacrificed after the time of Abel, Jacob at last caught up to the level at which Satan first dominated humankind. Then Jacob dealt with his twin brother, Esau. At the Ford of Jabbok, Jacob set up the condition of spiritual victory over the angel (Genesis 32:28). And through winning over Esau (Genesis 33), who was in the position of the substantial body of the Archangel, Jacob consequently was blessed as the first victor in history, and was given the name "Israel." But by then he was already in his fortieth year.

Satan sowed the seed of false love within the womb of Eve, which gave birth to evil life. Therefore, God needed to purify a mother's womb from which the heavenly Son could be born. That purification period of separation from Satan had to begin at the time of conception and continue to age forty, so even though Jacob was victorious he did not meet that criteria. The great mother who assumed the responsibility to meet this condition was Tamar.

Tamar's Providential Role

Tamar had married Er, the eldest son of Judah (Genesis 38). But Er displeased God and he died. According to the custom of that time, Judah gave Tamar his second son, Onan, that they might bear a child for Er. But Onan, knowing that Tamar's child would not be his own, spilled his semen on the ground. This was a sin in the eyes of God, for which Onan died.

Then Tamar wanted Shelah, the third son of Judah, for a husband, but Judah did not give him to her. Judah thought that his two sons had died because of Tamar, so he was afraid that Shelah would die and end the family lineage.

But Tamar had the conviction that she was to carry on the lineage of the chosen people. To do that, she disguised herself as a prostitute and slept with her father-in-law, Judah, and became pregnant with twins. At the time of birth, one of the twin sons, Zerah, stretched out his hand from the womb to be born first. But he was pulled back into the womb, and the second son, Perez, was born first, taking the position of the elder brother. Thus, within the womb of Tamar, the first and second sons fought, and their reversal of position separated them from Satan. That became the condition for restoration in the womb. Upon this condition, the Messiah could be conceived within the blood lineage of the chosen people, on the base of the nation of Israel that could stand up to the Roman Empire two thousand years later. The victorious foundation on the national level could then be formed in the womb of a mother free of satanic accusation, prepared for the seed of the Son of God. On this foundation, the Holy Mother Mary emerged in the mainstream of God's Providence.

Mary Receives God's Will

Mary, when she was engaged to Joseph, received from the Archangel Gabriel the surprising message that the Messiah would be born through her (Luke 1:31). In those days, if an unmarried woman became pregnant, she would be killed. But Mary accepted the will of God with absolute faith, saying, "Behold, I am the handmaid of the Lord; let it be to me according to your word." (Luke 1:38)

Mary consulted with the priest Zechariah, who was her relative and was highly respected. Zechariah's wife Elizabeth, with the help of God, was pregnant with John the Baptist. She said to Mary, "Blessed are you among women and blessed is the fruit of your womb. Why is this granted to me that the mother of my Lord should come to me?" (Luke 1:42-43) With these words she testified to the coming birth of Jesus.

In this way, God let Mary, Zechariah and Elizabeth know about the birth of the Messiah before anyone else. All of them had the absolutely crucial mission of following the will of God and serving Jesus. Zechariah's family let Mary stay in their house. Jesus was conceived in the house of Zechariah.

Elizabeth and Mary were cousins on their mothers' side. But according to God's Providence, they were considered sisters, with Elizabeth as the elder (Cain) and Mary as the younger (Abel). Mary received Elizabeth's help in the presence of Zechariah. Through this cooperation, Zechariah's family, on the national level, indemnified the lack of unity between mother and son with Leah and Rachel in Jacob's family. (Genesis 29-30) This allowed Jesus to be conceived. For the first time in history, there could be born on earth, free of satanic accusation and through a prepared womb, the seed of the Son of God—the seed of the True Father. In this way, the only begotten Son of God, the owner of the first love of God, was born for the first time in history.

Mary had to achieve something that could not be understood by common sense, nor easily tolerated under the law of those times. Mary, Elizabeth and Zechariah had been spiritually moved. They followed the revelation that came from God, and unconditionally believed that it was the will and desire of God.

Although the Son of God could be born on earth, he needed a wall of protection to grow up safely in the satanic world and fulfill the will of God. God had hoped that these three people in the family of Zechariah would establish that protective foundation. There are many points to consider with regard to how seriously the three had to dedicate themselves to protecting and serving the Son of God, and how long they should have been united with each other.

In the Bible it is recorded, "And Mary remained with her [Elizabeth] about three months, and returned to her home." (Luke 1:56) After that, there is no biblical record of any further communication between Mary, Elizabeth and Zechariah. From the time Mary left Zechariah's house, difficulties began for Mary and Jesus. The family of Zechariah should have been the wall of protection for Jesus until the very end.

A short time later, Joseph discovered that Mary was pregnant. How great must have been his shock at that moment! Mary, his beloved fiancé, without having had any relationship with him, had become pregnant after a three-month stay in another place. It was natural for Joseph to question Mary about who the baby in her womb belonged to. What would have happened if at that time Mary had explained everything candidly? If she had exposed everything, it could have been the end of a clan. So Mary simply responded that she was pregnant by the Holy Spirit.

Mary's pregnancy began to show, and the people of the surrounding area became aware of it. What would have happened if Joseph had declared that he didn't know anything about it? But Joseph was a righteous man. He believed in the revelation of God and defended Mary, saying the pregnancy was his responsibility. Mary may have been ridiculed for becoming pregnant during her engagement, but she had avoided death by stoning.

Joseph, who loved Mary, protected her this way in the beginning. However, there was a great deal of anguish deep in his heart. Once Jesus was born, Joseph's suspicions about the father of Jesus only increased and his heart ached. As Jesus grew older, the two became more and more distant in heart. And because of this, family problems frequently arose. Jesus was viewed as an illegitimate son, and lacking the protection of Zechariah's family and the love of Joseph, he grew up with an indescribable loneliness in his heart.

No Bride for Jesus

Jesus was aware of his path as the Messiah, and he lamented by himself these lonely circumstances and the serious obstacle they presented to fulfilling the will of God. The Messiah is the True Parent, and to fulfill that mission he needed to receive his substantial bride. Jesus had to reverse, at the very root, the false love by which the Archangel had caused the fall of Eve, who was growing up as the sister of Adam. Consequently, Jesus, in the place of Adam as the Son of God, should have received as his bride the younger sister of someone in an archangelic position. That bride was to have been none other than Zechariah's daughter, the younger sister of John the Baptist. To fulfill this in a world where Satan plays the role of owner and lord, Jesus needed a foundation of protection formed by absolute faith. Tragically, the entire foundation ended up collapsing around him.

This would not have happened if Zechariah and Elizabeth, who had received the revelation and spiritual support from God, had maintained absolute faith. If they had fulfilled their responsibility, Mary would have been in contact with them continually, even after her three-month stay at their house. God chose Zechariah's family as the foremost representatives of the entire world, so that even after the birth of Jesus they would protect, serve and witness to him as the Messiah. They not only should have served Jesus as the Son of God and Messiah with utter devotion, but they should have learned the will of God through Jesus and followed him absolutely. Also, John the Baptist was born to serve Jesus and should have fulfilled his responsibility to guide everyone he led to repentance, to believe in Jesus and receive salvation.

But unfortunately, although Zechariah, Elizabeth and John the Baptist testified at first to Jesus as the Son of God, there is no evidence that they served him as such. The respected priest Zechariah was simply a spectator. John the Baptist stood separate from Jesus. These circumstances blocked the people from following Jesus and made his path very difficult. And once this family lost faith in Jesus, looking at him through human eyes, there was no room for them to help him receive his bride.

We should also consider the influence that Joseph and Mary's relationship had on Jesus. Mary had to restore the position of Eve and Tamar through indemnity, so she should have remained as only the fiancé of Joseph. Providentially, they could not be husband and wife. It was God's desire that they not have sexual relations either before or after Jesus' birth. Joseph still loved Mary after Jesus was born, but Mary should have wanted to separate from Joseph to raise Jesus as the Son of God.

But the real circumstances did not make this easy to do. Even though Mary's original mind told her that she should not do so, she had sexual relations with Joseph. They had children, which was a repetition of Eve's mistake. With this condition, Satan invaded them. With the exception of Jesus, everyone who should have protected Jesus came under the dominion of Satan: his father, his mother, his Abel-type brothers (John the Baptist and his brothers) and his Cain-type brothers (the children of Joseph).

Jesus Seen through Human Eyes

When someone is invaded by Satan, he loses all spiritual support and inspiration. Trust in God, as well as a sense of gratitude to Him, is lost. One begins to see everything through human eyes. Mary did not help Jesus with the wedding he desired. She even opposed it. This was the direct reason that Jesus could not receive his bride, and could not become the True Parent; and this forced him to go the way of the cross.

Jesus' words to Mary during the wedding at Cana, "Oh woman, what have you to do with me?" (John 2:4), reveal a reproachful heart to a mother who helped in the weddings of others but neglected to help Jesus receive his bride, the most important requirement of the Providence. With this perspective, now we can understand why Jesus asked, "Who is my mother, and who are my brothers?" (Matthew 12:48)

Faced with the opposition of Mary, Zechariah, Elizabeth, and finally John the Baptist, Jesus gave up hope for their protection as he sought to fulfill his mission. Therefore, Jesus left his home in search of a new spiritual foundation to restart the Providence of Salvation.

Now without a family and household, Jesus lamented, "foxes have holes, and birds of the air have nests; but the Son of man has nowhere to lay his head." (Matthew 8:20) With his family-level foundation lost, Jesus sought to replace it. That was his three-year course.

In the end, as people disbelieved and the disciples lost faith, Jesus took Satan's attack.

And as his foundation crumbled, he went the way of the cross. Originally, Jesus came to the earth as the Messiah to give blessings to his disciples and all humankind. He was to build the sinless Kingdom of Heaven. But because of the lack of faith in him, he could not receive his bride, he could not become the True Parent, and he could not accomplish his mission. This is why he promised to return.

According to the Bible, "Whatever you bind on earth shall be bound in heaven, and whatever you loose on earth shall be loosed in heaven." Today, therefore, I clearly reveal this truth about Jesus and Mary in order to liberate them despite opposition from established churches such as the Catholic Church and Protestant churches.

Completing the Ideal of True Parents

The Lord of the Second Advent comes to perfect the foundation of God's Providence of Restoration left uncompleted by Jesus. That is to say, he comes as the seed of the original True Child to complete the ideal of creation. He comes to complete the ideal of True Parents, who are the origin of the True Love, True Life and the True Lineage of God. He comes on the victorious foundation of the fundamental providence of God's side up to the time of Jesus. He also stands upon the victorious foundation of Jesus' life and finds the bride that Jesus could not find. Together they become the True Parents to save all humankind.

Through the blessing of new marriages that pass on God's original blood lineage, the True Parents will be able to give salvation to all humanity. People will become True Persons engrafting into the True Love, True Life and True Lineage of God. Furthermore, the Messiah will establish a True Family, creating the Kingdom of Heaven on Earth. Thus, it is the International Holy Weddings that establish this new blood lineage when the Lord of the Second Advent comes in the flesh.

On the level of the great worldwide family, the Lord indemnifies that which was lost in the family of Adam and restores the True Elder Sonship, True Parentship and True Kingship that should have been perfected in Adam's family. He will transform this world into the Kingdom of Heaven on Earth under the dominion of God, opening the Kingdom of Heaven in the spirit world for registration. Humanity will enter into the era of kingship both spiritually and physically centered on God; establish a world of victory, freedom, happiness and unity; and create the Heavenly Kingdom on Earth and in the spirit world, which is God's ideal of creation. This is the View of the Principle of the Providential History of Salvation. I hope that in the future all of you can also receive this joyous new marriage blessing.

My dear Leaders and Distinguished Guests, I want to again express my appreciation that you have taken time from your busy lives to attend this important meeting. I hope you are able to have a clear understanding of the direction of providential history so that you can become true leaders in establishing a peaceful world. May God bless you and your families. Thank you.

Section 3

True Family

The Path of Life
For All Humankind

Mrs. Hak Ja Han Moon, President, Women's Federation for World Peace
This address was given January through February, 1999, on her American speaking tour.

Distinguished guests, ladies and gentlemen,

I am deeply grateful that you have taken the time from your busy schedules to help me make today's gathering such a success. Our theme for today is "The Path of Life for All Humankind."

Today the world is lost in great confusion and cries out in agony. We face endless conflict as individuals, in our families, in our nations and in the world. As individuals, we are confronted with inner turmoil between our mind and body. Our families are plagued with the moral decadence of our young people and the breakdown of family-centered traditions. Historical rivalries lead to distrust and even war among our nations, fanning the embers of uncertainty and hopelessness in the world. The solution to all these problems lies in experiencing an ideal love relationship with God.

Throughout history, humankind has sought to answer the basic question: Why are we born? Some have concluded that they were born for the sake of their country. Others have decided that they were born for the sake of their parents. Still others believe they were born for their own sake. People of faith believe they are born for the sake of God.

Yet, it is not enough to say that God created the universe for the sole benefit of human beings, or even for Himself. The creation of humankind involved the cooperation of many beings and elements. Although each had its own inherent purpose, they had to be aligned to initiate the creative process. God's purpose in creating, the angel's purpose in assisting, nature's purpose in providing the materials, and even the human purpose for being created must all be consistent. Each one must be pleased. There must be some common content that will be pleasing to God, to the angels, to the rest of creation, and to human beings themselves.

This common content must be something that gives greater happiness and joy the longer it is possessed. It should be something that, once we possess it, we would never let it go. It cannot be external in nature. It must be something internal and invisible. Things like knowledge, money and power are merely collateral conditions that are needed in people's lives. We are not born into the world for the purpose of possessing them. Such external things may exist in a reciprocal relationship with humankind, but only temporarily, not eternally.

God has no need for money. If Almighty God ever needed money, He could create as much as He desired. Also, we know that God is the root of all knowledge, since He created the universe through certain principles and laws. Furthermore, the Creator God is the subject of power, so He has no need to seek power.

What, then, is this common content? It is something we cannot achieve through human effort alone. This is because human effort cannot control the fundamental origin of life. This content must be something capable of directing the motivation, course, and even final destination of each person's life.

From this perspective, this common content can only be true love. Human beings are born in love and are destined to go the path of love. People even die for love. This shows that love is more valuable than life itself. Moreover, we see that love precedes life. That is why people willingly offer even their lives for the sake of love.

Love is eternal. When human beings reach the state of consciousness in which they are able to love the universe, all the doors of the universe open to them. For example, I am just a tiny being occupying this space right here. But centered on love, I can reciprocate in relationship with a being of any size or magnitude. Let us say that God is an extremely large being. Then by the power of love, I can rise to a position reciprocal to that of the Absolute God. This is possible because love is an attribute of God.

Thus, a person who recognizes and keeps God's covenant of love can enjoy freedom anywhere in the universe. Such an individual, called by God to represent all humankind centering on this cosmic love, would be the Messiah. Jesus is that representative. We can never find this cosmic love without going through the Messiah. It is reasonable to say that all people on Earth will have to follow the Messiah. Jesus said: "I am the way, and the truth, and the life; no one comes to the Father, but by me" (John 14:6). The meaning of this would be clearer if the word love were added: "I am the way, and the truth, and the life, and the love; no one comes to the Father, but by me."

Parents and Children

The Divine Principle of the Unification Church teaches that energy is produced when a subject and object become one. In a family, parents hold the position of the subject partner and children hold the position of object partner. Once they reciprocate in a relationship of love, they become one entity—a true family. This entity then becomes a new object, which can enter into unity with a larger subject. If God is that subject, then the parent-child unity becomes one with God. We can also say that when a perfect subject-object relationship is formed with God, centering on His ideal of love, God and humankind can exist in total oneness. When the realm of love between God and humanity becomes a reality, the light of love will shine throughout the universe as bright and constant as the sun.

Not only is each person a life-connecting entity in whom the lives of both parents are brought together as one, but we are also partners in our parents' love. We are one with their love. Furthermore, we are one with their ideals, including happiness and peace.

Each person is connected to the lifeline, love-line and ideal-line of their parents, and no one can sever these lines. Even God cannot sever them, nor can the universe. In fact, all the forces of the universe work together to safeguard these lines. This is because the parents are the cause and the children are the result. The parents and children are one, centering on love. Cause and effect become one to form a substantial realm of love. This is a principle of the universe.

Three Stages of Life

Each person comes into the world through three sets of parents. The first parent is the material world. Elements from the world of matter combine to form each person as the center of the material world and as a complex material being. Thus, it can be said that these physical elements themselves are the ancestors who gave us birth. On the other hand, the material world is an extension of us. The universe is created so that matter can settle only in the ideal of love. It is only in the ideal of love that all cells can live in tranquility. But this is all ruined whenever a person becomes angry.

Our second set of parents is our physical parents. By giving birth to us, our parents gave us a particular form, and to this extent they are the masters of our lives. However, no matter how hard they may try, these parents cannot be the masters of our love.

The master of love is God. In this context, God exists so that love can be expanded into the entire universe and made eternal. Because God is the subject of love, He becomes the parent centering on love. That is why God is our third parent. So we have three sets of parents.

Human life can be divided into three periods: life in the womb of about ten months, a physical life of about a hundred years, and life in the spirit world that lasts tens of thousands of years into eternity.

If we look at our own faces, we also see three stages: the mouth, the nose and the eyes. These reflect the three periods of our lives. The mouth symbolizes the period in the womb, which is a world of material. The nose symbolizes the period on Earth, which is the world of humanity. The eyes symbolize the period in Heaven, which is the spirit world.

To the fetus, the aquatic world of its mother's womb is a world of total freedom. Interestingly, although it is constrained within the confines of the womb, the fetus feels completely free. In the womb, it can't stretch its legs as much as it would like, and the fetus relies on an umbilical cord to breathe and receive nutrients for survival since its nose and mouth are both useless in this world. Nevertheless, to the fetus, the world in the womb is one of complete freedom.

As soon as the baby is born, it begins to cry. At the same time, it starts to breathe through its nose and becomes linked to the second world, the world of air.

As the baby leaves the womb to enter the world of air, the umbilical cord is destroyed along with the water sac and everything it needed in the world of the womb. With the death of these things, the baby is born into the bosom of its new mother, the planet Earth. Once born, the baby begins to eat with its mouth and breathe with its nose. The food we eat on Earth nourishes our physical bodies, but it does not contain the essential element of life. This life element is nothing other than love. Thus, while we are in this world, we also need to breathe the air of love. We need to inhale this air of love from our mother and father.

Growing in Love

A newborn baby automatically searches for its mother's breast, following the vibrations of her love. Whether she is beautiful or ugly does not matter to the baby. The only thing that matters is that she is its mother. It is a sacred scene manifested in limitless variety. We are born in love and we grow by receiving love.

Once we are born, our parents take responsibility to see that we become good human beings during our life on Earth. Our parents act on behalf of the world, the nation and the family to teach and provide for us. We receive material things and education from our parents so that we may become complete as individuals. Based on this, we then become linked to a horizontal foundation of love, which is marriage.

Parents take responsibility for us until we marry. After marriage, we inherit the love shared by our mother and father. When we marry and start rearing our own children, we begin to understand how much our parents loved us and thus come to inherit parental love. In this way, the individual becomes capable of receiving and giving love completely. This is how each of us matures as a complete man or woman.

We are born and mature in the vertical love of our parents, and later we engage in horizontal love. This is the only way we can find the integrated realm of love. Heaven and Earth together form a spherical world, covering all the dimensions of top and bottom, left and right, as well as front and back. When the vertical and horizontal love relationships are linked, they interact, revolve, become integrated, and finally emerge as a single center of harmony. Once the vertical love of Heaven and Earth is firmly established as the axis internally and externally, then the need for horizontal love arises. This takes place during adolescence.

During adolescence, even the sight of an autumn leaf blowing along the ground can seem inspiring. Girls who used to be so reserved when they were younger suddenly start doing things to their hair, putting on make-up and trying on all sorts of clothes and accessories. Their interests expand as well. These are horizontal phenomena of love.

The Path of Life

When a husband and wife love each other, it symbolizes the planting of God. Parents represent God's original position. Here, the husband and wife each embody different sides of God. Also, each child is like a small God. Since God is the original entity of true love, when the various members of the family link themselves to true love, they become one body with God. Here, parents are the living embodiment of God representing Him. Husband and wife each represent God, and the children represent Him as well. Thus, three generations, centering on true love, stand in the position of God.

This is why all members of the family—parents, husbands and wives, and children—need true love. A family formed in this way, centering on true love, is the foundation for the Kingdom of Heaven. Unless we first establish such a foundation, the Kingdom of Heaven can never be established. This is the formula. The family is the center of the entire physical universe. People today do not realize that their family represents their country, world and universe. They do not know that their family is the center. Breaking apart a family is an act of rebellion against the country, world and universe.

Because a perfect family is the foundation for a perfect universe, a person who loves the universe as she loves her family can travel freely everywhere. In such a case, God, as the Parent of the entire universe, sits in the central position to these manifold relationships of love.

When a man and woman become one centering on true love, they form an ideal couple, and build an ideal family. By doing so, they stand in a position representing God and thus are connected to everything in the universe. If this happens, then all of God's possessions become theirs. Think how wonderful that would be! This is the reason we naturally desire to have dominion over all creation.

Men and women come together as pairs to build families, societies, nations and the world. Thus, the family centering on one man and one woman must be the model for the tribe. This tribe, in turn, must be the model for the nation. Families must strive to achieve the ideal family, tribe and nation. Therefore, until ideal families appear, ideal nations will never emerge.

God and My Family

Respected guests! The greatness of true love is that it enables us to become God's object partners and also enables God to become us. The Bible speaks of God being in us and Jesus being in us. This is similar to the idea that the parent is in the child, the grandchild is in the grandparent, and the grandparent is in the grandchild.

A grandmother and grandfather should bind their hearts together centering on their grandchildren. This is necessary so that the vertical line of love can have a beginning. Also, grandchildren must become one with their grandparents. Grandparents are in the same position as God, so we should attend them as we would attend God. Grandchildren will not be able to find the vertical axis of love without doing this.

After the formation of this axis, the horizontal expansion can develop. The horizontal can be connected to all directions, but the vertical has only one direction. The horizontal can turn north, south, east or west; it has a range of 360 degrees. The vertical can move centering on one point only and cannot be split.

Our first task is to create mind and body unity, centering on love. Then, we need to know how to love the spirit world, which is the vertical world centered on God. Furthermore, if in the future a central country emerges, we should love humanity centering on that country. When we love the spirit world and the whole of humankind by means of sacrifice, service and dedication, we can automatically become the central figures who can have dominion over the two worlds, and make them into one. Then God will surely dwell there.

The entire spirit world, combined with the entire physical universe, is called the cosmos. The spirit world and the universe yearn for the unification of the cosmos centering on true love. True love can unify the cosmos. True love can transform all families into ideal families and make them one. Thus, we can conclude that true love is the only thing that humanity needs absolutely, whether we are alive on the Earth or are in the spirit world.

We can conclude, therefore, that nothing in this world is more precious than a true person who possesses true love. As the highest being in creation, human beings are in a reciprocal position equal to God's. Thus human beings should be able to act even more quickly than electricity or light, which travels at three hundred thousand kilometers per second. It is our spiritual selves that make such a thing possible. The fastest action in the world is not electromagnetic waves.

In the world of God's original ideal, a person who has experienced true love has the ability and authority to possess instantly anything God wants.

People need to experience such a state while on Earth. One can rise to this position only if the physical and spiritual selves become one while establishing a love relationship with God, centered on the true family. We can feel God's love by loving our countrymen, the people of the world, and creation. Each of us, regardless of nationality, must develop the heart to love people of all races. We should love not just people but even the smallest microorganism. This love has to spring naturally from within. When a flower blooms, its beauty and fragrance come naturally. The blossom of love has to bloom in the same way. The fragrance of love should fill the air naturally.

To do this, we need to receive the nutrients that make it possible for the blossom of love to bloom. In the same way that plants receive nutrients from the soil and sun, we receive nutrients through our physical body and spirit self. We receive vitality elements through our physical bodies, and then we receive living spirit elements through our spirit selves.

This is how we become beings who are totally equipped to love and how we develop the ability to fly anywhere. When this happens, the solar system and the entire universe become the stage of our activity.

The Next World

When we finish our physical life, we go through a second birth. This is called death. The place into which we are born this second time is the spirit world. We go into the spirit world and, on behalf of the entire universe, receive love from God, our third parent. That is to say, we receive ideal love. Thus in the spirit world, unification is inevitable.

In the spirit world, people breathe and live centered on love. We are born in love, live in love, and give birth to sons and daughters through love as God's representatives. Eventually, we reach the resting place of love, and return to God so that we may live eternally in His presence. In other words, our lives begin in love, ripen in love, and are finally harvested as the fruit of love. When a person dies, he harvests the fruit of his love.

During our life, we receive the love of our parents, share love with our husband or wife, and give love to our children, bringing to fruition all the seeds of God's love sown in the internal world of love. Eventually, we harvest this fruit and go into the next world. Thus when we become completely one in love, we come to resemble God. If a husband and wife work together to complete the three stages of love and then go to the spirit world, they will exist as creators and lords in a reciprocal relationship with God, who is the eternal subject. That is what happens when a husband and wife die centering on love. We begin and end in God.

To die means to move from a world of land, where we crawl and walk, to a world where we fly freely. We pass through death in order to become qualified travelers who, with love, can enjoy the entire universe. That is why death is, in reality, a new birth.

The Suffering of God

Ladies and gentlemen, our life course is not a smooth path. This is because human beings fell. The Fall of the original human ancestors did not result in misery only for human beings. God, also, suffered misery. For this reason, we do not dedicate our lives only to the accomplishment of the ideal world. An even more important goal for our life is to clear away the sorrow and agony in the heart of God, who is the origin of all life. Thus, when human beings finally attain happiness, then God, too, will be happy. God and humankind have gone through the course of history in the same situation, pursuing the same goal.

As a result of losing Adam and Eve, God has walked the most difficult path, a path that no one would choose to walk. Human beings, too, have walked this inevitable path of destiny brought about by the Fall, always hoping for the coming day of salvation.

Humankind's most fervent hope in relation to God is to become His sons and daughters. This is because no relationship is more intimate than that of parent and child. We were born when the love and life of our parents converged, and thus we represent their ideals. But words like love and ideals never refer to just one person. Life cannot be created by one person alone, but must come from a love relationship between husband and wife. Thus when God created humankind, He created us to be the object partners of His love, His life and His ideals. This is amazing and incredible.

If I did not exist, my parents' love could not become visible. The love, life and ideals of my parents exist in relation to me. I am the fruit of my parents' love, life and ideals. That is why the child's position is the most precious of all.

Had Adam and Eve not fallen, they would have been the children of God's direct lineage, and His royal descendants. That is, Adam and Eve were the prince and princess who stood to inherit the Kingdom of Heaven in the spirit world and on Earth. At the same time, because they were created as the objects of the invisible God, who is the subject, Adam and Eve were substantial beings who could receive His love. They were substantial manifestations of the invisible God.

It is the special privilege of a child of God to say, "God is mine. All that is His is also mine. Even His love, His life and His ideals are mine." It is up to human beings to recover this amazing and incredible value that was originally ours.

The Messiah's Mission

If God is the subject of love, who exists eternally, then the reciprocal partners of His love must also exist eternally. When I become one with God's love, God becomes me.

Had Adam and Eve not fallen, their bodies would have been the homes where God could dwell. They would have placed God at the center of their hearts and become entities of love, life and lineage who were unified eternally through true love. If they had done this, our mind and body would not be in conflict today.

The Fall meant that we inherited the life and lineage of evil, centering on evil love. We were born from false parents. We, therefore, have to rebuild the lineage. We have to take the false olive tree and change it into a true olive tree. To do this, we should be engrafted onto the true olive tree, go through at least three generations, and produce the fruit that becomes the true olive tree representing the original standard. Only then will fallen human beings be restored to the original state. That is when the Providence of Salvation will be completed.

In this way, God is trying to make human beings become children of the parents of goodness, centering on love that is one with Him. This is why He sends the Messiah to the Earth as True Parents. The Messiah is the one who comes to return the lineage of all humankind to God and establish the original ideal of creation.

Before seeking to excel on the world stage, humankind should have first excelled in the original family of Adam and Eve. Had Adam and Eve taken their places as lineal prince and princess before God, they would have been the most exalted among all men and women. They, however, fell and lost their entitled positions of the elder son and daughter, the crown prince and princess. This tragedy has remained throughout human history. That is why humankind has traveled a path of life in search of the positions of first son and first daughter so that we might recover God's true love.

If we are to receive His true love, we cannot live selfishly, centering on our own self. Instead, we should live for the sake of God and humankind as our brothers and sisters. The more a person sheds blood and tears for her brothers and sisters in place of her parents, the deeper, wider and higher will be the love she receives. This is the son and daughter we must become if we are to inherit everything from our parents. Every man and woman must go this path. Even if we have to face death ten times or a hundred times, we must continue our search for God's true love. This is the supreme path of life.

The Original Homeland

The Divine Principle of the Unification Church teaches that the Fall occurred when human beings left the realm of God's true love. Restoration means to return to that realm. When a person enters the realm of such love, he can merely look at his body and praise it tens of thousand of times. In that world, you know that your own body is one that receives God's true love. Words cannot express such joy. This wonderful world is called the Kingdom of Heaven.

Until now, people knew relatively little about the spirit world. It is a world where people are recognized depending on how closely they followed God's principle of existence— the principle of living for the sake of others. A world built on this content is the ideal Kingdom of Heaven.

This is the original homeland for which all humankind must search. Today, we live as fallen people who have been expelled from our homeland, so it is our destiny to return there. However, we cannot do this on our own.

God has worked through history to resolve this problem by establishing numerous religions in accordance with the different cultural backgrounds, customs and traditions of various nations. He has done this so that human beings would have a path to lead them back. Religion is the training ground where we can cultivate the qualifications that enable us to return to our homeland. In accordance with the cultural background of each region, God is guiding us toward one unified world of religion that can advance us to a higher ground.

Let us make the new millennium an age of true peace and true ideals in which people will practice the way of true love. I hope we will recover the value of true original human beings centered on God, establish true families, and live for others eternally, centering on God and the True Parents.

May your families and country be filled with an ever greater abundance of God's love and blessings.

Thank you very much.

Blessed Marriage and Eternal Life

Mrs. Hak Ja Han Moon, President, Women's Federation for World Peace
This address was given on April 1-16, 1996, on a 16-city North American speaking tour.

Distinguished guests, ladies and gentlemen, colleagues and friends:

Thank you for coming tonight. My husband, the Reverend Sun Myung Moon, and I are speaking throughout the world. We are sharing our desire to work with each one of you, beyond race, nation and religion, to create a world of peace. Therefore, I know that you will consider my message seriously.

Humanity is now facing the challenge of the Last Days. In this era, families the world over are breaking down. Husbands and wives, parents and children are becoming enemies to one another. What is the cause of this tragedy?

The cause is a lack of true love. Equally significant is the fact that we are ignorant of our most important responsibility. That responsibility is to prepare for eternal life. If we are clear about the concept of eternal life, and if we accept its reality in our hearts, then we can lead our children and our families properly. But in truth, most people are unsure if the spirit world even exists.

If we truly understand the reality of the spirit world, we cannot sin, even when temptation presents itself. We cannot live selfishly, even if told to do so. On the other hand, if we do not understand the spirit world, we cannot enter the Kingdom of God, no matter what our religion.

On the larger scale, without knowing the meaning of eternal life, we cannot create a true social revolution. If it is not connected to eternal life, social revolution may make things worse. No one desires that.

To this day, religions have neither embraced nor encompassed the secular world. As a result, secularism now controls culture. Secularism overpowers the influence of religion. This happened because religions were unable to establish a clear concept of eternal life.

Christianity also faces this challenge. Although people have practiced Christianity faithfully for many centuries, many churches today are confused. In the Last Days, they are objective to the changes taking place in the world. Even Christianity does not have a clear and logical understanding of eternal life.

In short, no one has complete confidence concerning eternal life. In fact, people do not even know with certainty whether or not God exists. When faced with the obstacles and temptations of this world, most people waver. They fall away from their faith, and follow the secular way.

The Reason We Should Understand Eternal Life

As we reach our forties and fifties, we come closer to the end of our life. We naturally become serious about the concept of eternal life. The older we become, the more serious we are. Ordinarily, the intensity of love declines as people age. But if our perception of eternal life has strong roots, then our love will grow and deepen as we get older.

How often have you been confused by the changes taking place in our world today? If our focus on eternal life is clear and unchanging, we will overcome the insecurities of our changing environment. We will be able to digest all the circumstances of our lives, the joys and sorrows that come our way.

God created Adam and Eve as His partners of true love. Accordingly, we should live as God's true love partners. This should not be a theory. We should allow this dynamic to work in our lives and put it into practice each day.

Once we realize the power of true love, we will strive against adversity to walk the road of true love. In daily life, we will always feel the security that comes from belief in eternal life. When this conviction overflows within us, our lives will be secure.

This has important implications for education of our children. If it is clearly explained to them, young people readily embrace the concept of eternal life. They are uniquely blessed to feel eternal life resonate in their mind and body.

Until reaching age sixteen, boys and girls possess an unfallen purity of character. They reflect the original character of Adam and Eve, who did not fall until they were sixteen. Because of this, it is vital that young people know God deeply.

Through knowledge of God, we can understand our inseparable relationship with Him. But in order to know this, young people must first understand the concept of eternal life.

Earthly Life and Eternal Life

How long do you think you will live? All of us think we will live until we are seventy or eighty years old. It is hard to imagine that we will die before then. In this regard, we can all be considered greedy.

But in truth, even those who seem confident that they will live a long time have no idea when they are going to die. It could be as soon as today or tomorrow. We may even die during a meal or while we are sleeping. Does God guarantee anyone a long lifespan?

Imagine that you knew you would die within a year. You would have to prepare for your passing in a very short period of time. With this newfound urgency, you might actually be happier. After all, you would be able to prepare for death in less time. The less time you use to prepare for death, the less time you will waste in your life. And if you prepare well, you can build a home for your eternal life.

How long do you wish to live? What if God told you that you had to die tonight? What legacy would you leave behind? Would you leave behind something of which God would be proud? While we are living in this world, we should always give our best. We should invest 24 hours a day to bring even one more person to God's love.

The highest standard of dedication to God is to not even want to stop to eat or sleep. We should not be consumed by worry over worldly needs. If you live with such sincerity, you will have eternal life in the next world.

The shorter we expect our physical life to be, the more value we will find in it. In this context, we should ask ourselves, "How much do I love others?" "How much do I love my family?" "How much do I love my clan?" "What does it mean to love others, to love my family, to love my clan?" This serves as the foundation to love all humanity. It is a wise approach to life. You will not lose if you live this way.

The Reason to Live an Eternal Life

The purpose of a life of faith is to seek the world of eternal life and God's eternal love. The way of a life of faith is to discover and rejoice in God's joy as our own. By living this way, we become one with God's eternal love and eternal life.

Accordingly, it is most important for people of faith to invest unceasing energy for God's life and love. The world's religions have expanded through history, against the backdrop of every culture. This is because our human destiny is to live an eternal life.

We are to live not just in our own era, but also in harmony with the entire universe. Once we reach the limit of life on Earth, we continue life in an eternal, unlimited world. Such a world exists in reality. Even those who do not believe it exists, or who do not fully comprehend it, have postulated eternal life. They did this in order to help and comfort humanity through their suffering and pain.

But God's existence is a reality beyond time and space. When we internalize the depth of this eternal truth, it becomes our starting point. Then we can find the answers to our questions concerning eternal life and God.

For what purpose and in what position did God create humankind? God created man and woman as His partners of true love. We were to have God's absolute and unique value. This is a startling revelation! In this light, the value of each person's life is infinite. Even the entire universe cannot replace the value of one person in the eyes of God.

All people are meant to be born in true love, to live and grow in true love, and even to die in true love. God is eternal, unchanging and unique. We stand as the eternal object of God's true love. Therefore, we are created to live eternally. Our eternal life has its roots in our relationship with God, as His partner of true love.

The Eternal Love Partner of the Creator

God's love is absolute. Since God's love was lost through the human fall, God has experienced indescribable misery and almost hopeless sorrow throughout history. No one has ever understood this; no one has been able to fully comfort God.

God, in the depth of His heart, wants to recreate His long-awaited love partner. God wants to embrace His children. He will travel any distance to meet them. Only by meeting His sons and daughters can He express His joy to the fullest. In actuality, God created the entire universe for His children.

Consider the earth's atmosphere. When a low pressure system forms, a high pressure system appears automatically. Through this phenomenon, air circulation is self-sustaining.

God has taught us to forget the good that we do for others. This creates a spontaneous and natural circular motion of give and take in our daily lives. It is similar to the natural phenomenon we observe in the atmosphere. This constant cycle of give and take leads to eternal life.

Eternal life can begin with nothing other than eternal commitment. To be specific, as long as one lives for the sake of others, one will never perish. A life of giving will surely grow and progress steadily. The person who lives thus will eventually take a central position as the nucleus of society.

If God were to seek an absolute love partner, who would merit such a position? It is natural to conclude that God's love partner would have to be humankind. That is why human beings are held to be the most precious beings among all of God's creation.

When we are able to accept that we are the eternal true love partner of the Creator, we can easily understand that we live for eternity. The concept of eternity naturally follows from this. It takes place right here! The religious world must bear in mind that the foundation of eternal life is the relationship of true love. In its simplest terms, eternal life stems neither from man nor from woman but from God's true love.

Only True Love Provides Salvation

Today, Christians proclaim that any individual can possess eternal life just by believing in Jesus. If I ask them how one can secure eternal life, they answer, "Just believe." Of course it is essential that we have absolute faith, but I would like you to consider a further perspective based on the meaning of eternal life.

Consider the aspect of continuity. The functioning of the physical body has continuity. For instance, our blood circulation, nervous system and brain should function continuously and smoothly.

From this perspective, what would you answer if someone asked you how you plan to secure eternal life? The life of the spirit also should have continuity. Then are you truly able to claim, "My eternal life is guaranteed through belief alone"? Does salvation come from belief and nothing else? Absolutely not. True salvation requires a continuity of the practice of true love from this physical world to the spirit world.

According to the principles by which God created this world, only a true person can become God's true love partner. Only with true love can one become such a person and obtain eternal life.

The key is to rid ourselves of the ignorance and burdens of the Fall. The fundamental question is how to free ourselves from evil love, an evil life and an evil lineage. Only in this context does liberation have any meaning. Only complete liberation from evil brings true freedom. True freedom is self-sustaining.

The Idea Necessary for Eternal Life

We are created to live an eternal life. We are similarly created to practice true love. Furthermore, we are to practice true love here on the Earth. We engage ourselves with many things in this world. These things become the material that insures our eternal life. In other words, everything we do in this world is training for eternal life.

We are fully capable of living forever! We desire an eternal life! In our search for eternal life, what does not change? Only true love does not change! Everything in this universe changes, but true love does not change.

This is because true love is the center. The center will remain intact even if everything that surrounds it disappears. True love is the center of the universe. It is one with God's love. Consequently, as long as God is unchanging, true love is unchanging.

What does true love mean? A husband desires that his wife be better than he is. A wife also wants her husband to surpass her. Are there any parents who do not want their children to surpass them? Why do we share this feeling? It is because we all are created in the very image of God. In other words, even God wants His love partner to be better than Himself, in the same sense that parents want their children to surpass them.

God is absolute, but at the same time He is our Parent. Can God impose an absolute standard upon us, and not upon Himself as well? No, He cannot. In light of this, our value is the highest in the universe.

In fact, in the realm of true love, we can have a value even higher than that of God Himself. This is why our minds have the highest of aspirations. Thus, we truly should feel that nothing is impossible.

God originally intended that His children rule this universe from the position of highest value. We were not to have been sidetracked or manipulated in any way. We were never to have been under the dominance of any force or being.

To confirm this, simply look into your mind. The mind desires complete freedom. No one wants their mind to be controlled. Once we secure the position of true love, we are totally free. We can travel anywhere. We can travel to God's throne and become God's friend.

God is eternal and absolute. Therefore, since God created us as His partners of true love, it is natural to conclude that we can enjoy eternal life. Clearly then, in order for a man to live an eternal life, he must dwell in the realm of true love. Only through true love is abundant eternal life possible.

The origin, motive and process of God's creation center on true love. No result can come without a process taking place, and the process of perfection is based upon the practice of true love. The perfection of mind and body is possible only when they both belong to the realm of true love.

Only true love can bring about the ideal. This is because God Himself exists for eternity upon the foundation of true love. Upon what, do you think, does God center His own eternal existence? Without question, God's eternal life is centered on true love.

Therefore, we also live with true love as our center. In this way we create the realm of eternal life. In order to find this realm, we practice true love in daily life.

I would like you to know that Reverend Moon has poured his life, his heart, and the resources of his church into America. Through this practice, true love was actualized. Without actualizing true love, there is no eternal life.

To Know God, Eternal Life and True Love

Even though we are not sure where in the spirit world God dwells, we should at least clearly understand that God is the center of true love. The power of true love is the fastest and the most direct. True love travels in a straight line. Why do you think I emphasize true love so fervently? It is because of my direct experience of this truth. Once you experience God and the eternal world, you too will never be able to have an indifferent attitude toward life.

First, we must know God. Second, we must know our eternal life. Third, we must know true love. True love means giving more than 100 percent of oneself. In this way, we can find eternal life. Without true love, there is no eternal life. Without eternal life, we can never meet God.

How should you prepare for the world of the future? First, be altruistic. Second, practice true love. Third, seek eternal life. With the sincere practice of these virtues, we can manage the world in the coming age. The opposite way is the self-centered way of life. That is the ideology of Satan. In contrast to satanic love, what is true love? True love is to invest yourself beyond the point of life and death. It is only through this intensity of life that we can find true love.

The fundamental root of evil life is the satanic lineage. Our lineage belongs to Satan. Our love belongs to Satan. But God's love transcends satanic love. And so the Bible teaches, "You shall love the Lord your God with all your heart, and with all your soul, and with all your mind. This is the great and first commandment." (Mt. 22:37-38)

What does this really mean? Loving God with all your soul and with all your mind means to give your life completely to God. This is the first great commandment.

The second commandment is, "Love your neighbor as yourself." What does this mean? It tells us to love others even at the cost of our lives. We have to invest ourselves in this way of life.

Then why should we commit ourselves with total intensity? Unless we commit ourselves to this degree, first, we cannot make Satan surrender. Second, we cannot free ourselves from the satanic environment in which we live. Third, we cannot eradicate our satanic lineage.

Even if we were able to separate from the satanic environment, we cannot eradicate the satanic lineage by ourselves. We need the power of true love, which is greater than our life.

The World after Death Is Related to Love

There is no concept of time for God. This means that the beginning and the end are the same in eternity. Likewise, the past, the present and the future are the same. Then what within God harmonizes everything and enables God to dwell in peace? This is a serious question. It is not God's almighty power. It is not His omniscience. It is nothing other than the power of love. Even God Himself responds unconditionally to true love. This is because God does not need anything other than true love.

Most people agree that we will enter the spirit world upon our death. But the spirit world is not just the dwelling place of the departed. The spirit world is connected to true love. The starting point of God's creation is true love. Therefore, once we secure true love in the physical world, this too will become the spirit world. This alone tells us how powerful true love is.

Through the perfect relationship of vertical and horizontal, harmonious movement in all directions—up and down, right and left, forward and back—can take place. But when vertical and horizontal are disconnected, there is no harmony. In that case, there can be no unification.

True love alone can connect vertical and horizontal. This brings about unification and harmony. The central thought of the Unification Church, based on the perspective of the Divine Principle, is that the ideal world is centered on true love.

Ladies and Gentlemen, God wants to guide humankind. God breathes through true love. Since the rhythm of the universe is in harmony with God, the universe exists for eternity. In God's true love, we can find eternal life. That is why when husband and wife connect with true love, they find complete joy. When the rhythm of true love is in balance, we can love one another. In this atmosphere there is only one direction in our life. That direction is centered on God.

The Kingdom of God and the Gate of the Blessing

Both the spirit world and the physical world move in conjunction with true love. The universe maintains a natural balance, centering on the vertical axis of true love. What is the common denominator of the universe? What is the universal norm, by which people of the past and the present can live together for eternity? What is the origin of human desire? The answer to all these questions is the same. The answer is true love. The norm is not selfish love; it is true love. Only the practice of true love can embrace people of all races, all nations and all religions.

There are over five billion people living in this world at present. Yet there are not many among the world's population who understand the meaning of the Blessing. My husband and I have been the first to adopt the word "blessing" in the context of marriage. Many such marriage Blessings have now been conducted.

Where will humanity head in the future? Humanity can enter the Kingdom of God by passing through the gate of this Blessing. There are millions of Christians in our world today, and Christianity itself can enter the Kingdom of God through the gate of the Blessing.

Some Christians complain that Reverend Moon's teaching is self-righteous. Of course, nothing can be done about this point of view since it is their own. Nonetheless, I am here to convey the message that the Unification marriage Blessing is the true road for all fallen people to take.

No matter how much persecution it may cause, we are to connect the spirit world and the physical world through this Blessing, and enter the Kingdom of God.

Other religious people think of salvation in terms of the individual. They believe that as long as their faith is strong, they can enter the Kingdom of Heaven as individuals. But from the viewpoint of God's original ideal, we were never intended to enter the Kingdom of Heaven as single people. We enter only with our loving spouse and family.

Spiritual Life as Couples

The real purpose of life is to walk forward on the road of true love. We are to grow through harmonious relationships of true love. We should carefully maintain the ideal of true love in our hearts. We are actually the representatives of the spirit world. Let us constantly strive to spread true love. Let us sow the seeds of true love throughout our lives.

When we bear the fruit of true love and enter the eternal spirit world as a loving couple, we will be embraced by God's eternal love. We then truly become one with God. Even though the physical body grows old, as long as we live as husband and wife centering on true love, our spiritual body will actually become younger! This means that the longer we live, the more handsome or beautiful our spiritual body becomes.

Our spirit is our internal self. At the proper time we simply will shed the physical body. Our physical body may feel that it does not want to retire. But with the coming of old age, it eventually must surrender its life. On the other hand, our spiritual body, like a chestnut in autumn, becomes more solid and more handsome as it becomes our physical body's successor.

Why Is Marriage Necessary?

We must love the things of the material world, which includes our physical body and the food that nourishes it. We love what is close to us before loving God directly.

By loving all things, we absorb the essence of the creation. By doing this, we love and nourish the physical body.

Your first parents, of course, are your physical parents. Your second parent is the Earth. From the Earth we receive essential elements that the body needs in order to grow. In this way the Earth is the second parent.

After being nurtured and cared for by our second parent, we prepare to meet our third parent. There is a process through which we pass in order to realize this. That process is our physical death. We do not meet our third parent free of charge. To be able to return to our third parent, we must resemble our original parent, God.

Why then do we get married? Very simply, we marry in order to resemble God. God exists as a being of dual characteristics. In God, the dual characteristics are completely harmonized as One. When God's dual characteristics manifest in our world, they do so as man and woman. Accordingly, at the proper time, a man and a woman are like a seed. They unite to become one. Thus, husband and wife return to God. Together, we are a reflection of His original nature.

We need marriage because it is the true way to develop our love. In marriage, we ripen as a seed of God. Our entire life should be centered on true love. We should be born in true love; we should grow in true love; we should live centered on true love; and we should return to true love when we die. The way of true love is life for the sake of others. This is the purpose of a holy marriage. If we take any other path, we are taking the wrong direction for eternal life.

The marriage Blessing and eternal life stem from God working through True Parents' love. Through our union with the True Parents, we can fulfill God's original hope for the individual, the family, the nation, the world and the entire cosmos. Ultimately, we can complete God's ideal of creation. Through True Parents we can find our original homeland, the starting place for the Kingdom of God on Earth and in Heaven. With this foundation in place, we can welcome an era in which God is our sovereign. The society that does so will never perish. It will continuously prosper and reach its fullest strength.

I sincerely ask that you contemplate deeply about the meaning of this sermon. If you practice it, you will find the way to receive God's abundant Blessing and eternal life.

May God truly bless you.

Thank you very much.

Understanding Life and Death

Reverend Sun Myung Moon, President, Family Federation for World Peace
This speech was presented at the International Religious Foundation for World
Peace conference, December 18, 1998, Washington, D.C.

We live in the physical world, but we know that this is not the only world that exists. There is also the spirit world. The spirit world is a definite reality. We also know that these two worlds—the physical world and spirit world—are not meant to be disconnected from each other. They should be linked together as one single world.

We human beings, who were born from the spirit world, eventually return to that world. In Korea, we commonly use an interesting idiom in reference to death. When someone dies, we say, "he has returned." To where does he return? It is not to a cemetery. We mean that we return to the point of life's origin. We return across the vast expanses of history. In the process, we shed our nationality. We return to the world that brought forth the human ancestors. If a Creator exists, then we are returning to the world of the Creator. That is where we originated, so it is there that we finally return.

The universe is engaged in circular motion everywhere. For example, when the snow melts on the mountain, it forms a small stream. As it flows down, its volume increases until it becomes a river. Eventually it reaches the ocean. From the ocean it evaporates, completing the circle by returning into the atmosphere.

The School of Life

All beings desire to reach a higher ground, a better place, through circular motion. Where, then, is the better place we go to live eternally? While in the physical world, we live in our physical body. Our mind, though, is headed toward the eternal world. We are born into this world, and we pass through our teenage years, our twenties, thirties, middle age, and we eventually reach old age. Ultimately, we come to the end of our lives, just as the sun finally sets on the horizon. Those who know that the spirit world exists, however, know very well that the time spent in our physical body is relatively short, and that the world we face after we die is eternal. They know that our life on earth is a period of preparation for the eternal world.

We are like students who must earn credits in all our classes so that we can fulfill our school's requirements. The school determines the extent to which its students meet its standard and decides whether it can recognize them. The further a student's credits fall short of the standard, the more removed that student is from the school's standard of value. In a similar way, the value of all beings is measured against a standard. Our life in the physical world is a period of preparation comparable to the time a student spends trying to earn good marks at school. In other words, we spend our entire life on earth preparing and striving to make good marks. We live each day of our life centering on a measurement. That measurement is in accord with a particular standard. We are accountable to that standard for our entire life on earth.

The Unity of the Spirit World

Most people in society do not know with certainty about the original world where we go after life in this world. They do not know whether there is life after death, or even whether God exists. Eventually, everyone goes to the spirit world. It turns out that the spirit world is a single realm. It is not divided into many countries, as is the physical world. Then, what is it like in the spirit world? We can compare it with the water that serves as the environment for fish. Water is an absolute condition for the fish to live. That doesn't mean, however, that a fish will spend its entire life in one place. A fish that lives in fresh water cannot spawn if it remains in its river. It has to leave the fresh water and come into contact with salt water in order to lay its eggs. It thus passes through two worlds. In the same way, our mind, part of spirit world, and body, part of the physical world, must be interconnected.

At the beginning of human history, a realm of global unity should have formed in honor of Adam's birthday, the anniversary of his holy marriage and the anniversary of his death. Then humanity could have united as one people by our sharing in the commemoration of those days. Instead of dividing, humanity could have lived in a single realm. If this had happened, then Adam and Eve's way of life would have passed down through human history. The culture formed would have endured as long as human beings continued to exist.

The Value of Hope

Each of us goes through life ignorant of when we will die. We do not know that we won't die in a traffic accident. I think some people will die saying, "Oh, Reverend Moon was right!" expressing regret only at that moment. We need to know that we are travelling a very serious path in life. We need to use every second of our life to prepare ourselves for the eternal world. We should be aware that we are standing on such a fateful path.

When people go to spirit world, they can be divided into two general types. The first comprises those who live out their natural life in this world, and the second comprises those who experience an untimely death. Among the latter, some die as a result of punishment and others die in order to pay indemnity for the nation or the world. Suppose God established one person in a central position with the value of a thousand people. What if God made that one person go the way of death in the place of those thousand people?

In such an instance, the grace and virtue of the one who died in their place would move the hearts of the thousand people. They would determine to live for the benefit of that person, model their lives after that person, and live as he lived. If they did this, the thousand people would enter the same realm of grace as the one who died for them. The reason we try to follow the philosophy of patriots and model our lives after wise men is that we desire to enter the same realm of grace as these people.

Some people live with hope while others live without hope. We can divide people's hope and aspiration into two general types: that centered on human beings and that centered on Heaven. A newborn infant thinks that his mother's bosom is the most wonderful place in the world. At a certain point in its development, however, the child leaves its mother's bosom. As the child grows, he or she forms friendships, thinking himself happiest when he is with his friends. Eventually, though, the young person will leave his friends behind. During our life course, we come to discover that neither loving parents, nor a loving spouse nor even loving children can completely satisfy our hopes.

People have many kinds of hopes. Eventually, all these hopes pass away. We have hopes for our family, hopes for our country and hopes for the world. But the reality is that as we grow older, our hope grows weaker. Some people boast that their hope represents the hope of all humankind, but find they lack the conviction to pursue it at the sacrifice their life. People fervently entertain many hopes during the course of their life. But when they face death, they abandon all their hopes. They desire to stay alive one more day. Day after day they wander in search of something new in which to place their hope. When they finally face death, though, all their hope fades away and they fall into despair as they set out on their final path. We know all too well that this is true.

Viewed as an individual, it may appear that a person possesses worthy aspirations. But no individual hopes live beyond death. In my view, it is important for all people on earth today to give serious consideration to one question. How can we find hope that will not collapse in front of death, but will transcend it? All things of this world will pass away. Our families, nations, and even the world itself will pass away. Ideologies and philosophies will pass away. What is it that remains? Whatever remains, that is the hope that can defeat death.

We can consider a person who does not possess such a hope or aspiration to be defeated in life. There are people who, from the time they are born, reject all the hopes and aspirations of the secular world. These people embrace aspirations not of the human world but of Heaven, hopes that are eternal. Heaven helps these people. A life of faith does not embrace any aspiration that exists on earth. Instead, it embraces the hopes that surpass even the gates of death. It dreams of the world of eternal hope.

Overcoming the Fear of Death

Someday I, too, will die. When we are young, we don't think much about death. But we become increasingly serious about death as we grow older. This is because death is a gate through which we are inevitably destined to pass. But what happens to us after we die? Do you know why I am talking about death? I talk about death in order to teach the meaning of life. Who really knows the value of life? It is not the person who is going all out to preserve his life. The only person who really knows about life is the one who goes into the valley of death. He confirms the meaning of life as he desperately cries out to Heaven at the crossroads of life and death.

Why do people fear death? It is because they do not know the purpose for which we are born. Those who do not know why we are born do not know why we die. Therefore, the first questions philosophers ask are: "What is life? Why are we born?" If we think about it, we realize that when we die we are reborn into the midst of God's love. But in the human world, people cry out, "Oh no, I'm going to die! What am I to do?" They make a big fuss. Do you think that God laughs, "Ho ho ho!" when we die? Or do you think God cries out, "Oh no!" and is overwhelmed with sorrow? The truth is, He is happy. This is because the moment of the physical body's death is the moment we experience the joy of leaving the finite realm of love in order enter the infinite realm of love. It is the moment of our second birth.

Then is God happier on the day we are born into the physical world, or at that moment we leave our physical body behind? At that moment, we are born a second time into the realm of the infinite expansion of love. We become His new children through death. Of course, God is happier at the second birth. I am telling you this because you need to know that you cannot have a relationship with God unless you are released from the fear of death.

Our Two Births

It makes God happy to watch and directly take part in our life. Consider how a baby is born and wets its diapers as it begins the process of growth. God is happy because as the child grows, the pulse of love that is in God's heart also grows. When God makes a face, babies imitate Him and make the same face. When God smiles, babies also smile, and when He is sad they also are sad. This is how babies gradually grow to resemble God. As babies grow, they also begin to resemble their parents. From their parents, they learn language and the rules for daily life. Of course, all these things have their origin in God.

So, after God has lived with us on earth and goes, whoosh, over to the other side, what are we supposed to do? If we say, "Wait, God, I want to go with You," will He reply, "Who are you? I don't know you"? Is He likely to leave us behind like that? Or will He want to take us with Him? Of course, He will want to take us with Him. But when God says, "I can't take you with me now. I'll take you with me after you have grown a little more. I want you to work a bit more on your perfection," we can reply, "Well, we can't go now, but we are certain that there will come a time when we are able to go." Then we can wait for that day.

In our physical body, we are unable to follow God wherever He goes. It is only natural that we would aspire to resemble God. On His part, God also would want His sons and daughters to resemble Him. We must conclude, then, that God designed us to be born again into a body that enables us to resemble Him. God and human beings long for that eternal day when we can soar through the heavens together. The day we are born as beings who can take wing with God, the day we are born into that body, that is the day of our physical death. On that day we cast off the physical body like an old coat. Then, should we welcome death or fear death? The answer, of course, is that we should welcome death.

For what purpose, then, should we die? We should die for the sake of God's true love. That is the love whereby we seek to sacrifice ourselves for the benefit of others. We can conclude that the reason we cast off our physical body is so that we can participate in the realm of God's work of love. We die for the sake of the world of God's love.

Wouldn't you like to be born as God's real sons and daughters, who can receive and practice true love? If we could measure God's wealth, how rich do you think He would be? Have you ever thought about that? With all those stars in the universe, isn't it likely that there is one star that is a solid diamond? How about a star of pure gold? God is truly omniscient and omnipotent. Wouldn't He want His children to have everything? What do you think? God can go from one end of the vast universe to the other in an instant. Is this something that you would find interesting to do?

To gain that ability, what do we need to do? We must keep the laws that God has established for us. Only when we do so is it possible for us to be with Him. It is impossible if we just behave any way we want. Are you confident that you can refrain from doing what God tells you not to do? Human beings have a dual structure. The mind is the subject partner and the body is the object partner. It is necessary that the two become one, with the body subordinating itself to the mind.

Three Stages of Life

We go through three realms that correspond to the stages of formation, growth and completion. We go through the realm of water in our mother's womb, then the realm of the planet earth, and finally the heavenly realm of floating in air. We go through the period in the water of the womb and are born into the world. We live in our physical body in this world for about a hundred years, until we enter the world in which we fly through the air. We pass through these three realms.

When a fetus is in the womb, it resists leaving the womb for the outside world. It fights as hard as it can to stay in the womb. The reason is that when the fetus leaves the womb, its home is destroyed. All its nourishment and everything else it had in the womb breaks apart and flows away. Also, its head and body increase in size during the birth process. Who would want to go through something like that? Every fetus cries, "No!" right up to the moment of birth. Eventually the water breaks and the infant follows soon after.

As you watch a woman give birth to a child, you really have to feel sorry for her. Women who have given birth know what I am talking about. When the mother is pushing, it makes no difference how beautiful she may be. Her face contorts into all sorts of strange shapes. She makes such terrible faces that even her husband can't stand to watch and leaves the room. She makes just about every possible face. So, the mother, too, goes through tremendous pain up to the last moment in order for the baby to be born.

After birth, is it necessary to leave the umbilical cord connected to the baby's navel? Or is the umbilical cord chopped off without a second thought? Maybe someone should object, saying, "That cord is someone's lifeline. How can you cut a lifeline that connects one human being to another?" The newborn infant, too, cries at the top of its lungs because it thinks it is about to die. As God looks on, though, He can't help but break into a happy smile. From the viewpoint of the new life that has just been born, one world has just disappeared completely. Now it must breathe the air of its new world.

A child is conceived in the depth of water. The period in the womb is a period of existence in water. As long as the fetus is in its mother's womb, it is floating in water. At first thought, you might think the time in the womb would be difficult because the fetus cannot breathe. You would think that it would need a process of taking in and sending out water. This function is fulfilled by something like a hose attached to the baby's belly. How does a fetus in the womb receive nourishment? It receives nourishment through its navel.

For the child in the womb, the navel functions as a mouth. So, we should not be disdainful of our belly buttons. Give your belly button a little rub and say, "Hey, belly button.

Thanks for working so hard back then." If you pat your belly button often, it is good for your health. No, seriously. It's a good way to exercise. It's good for your health to exercise your belly button. For example, a person sleeping in a cold room can avoid coming down with diarrhea as long as he keeps his belly button well covered.

The Breath of Love

We can refer to our belly button as our former mouth. Someone might say, "How foolish. Whoever heard of a former mouth?" There's no denying the fact, though, that your belly button once functioned as your mouth. The belly button also acted as a breathing apparatus. Your present mouth fulfills that function here on earth. The function has moved up on your body. The same function is as necessary for the spirit self as it is for the fetus in the womb.

The spirit self is attached to the physical body that lives on earth by breathing air. It lives off the physical body until the body grows old. Then the spirit self kicks the body away and tries to separate. If at that moment, the body cries out, "No, I don't want to die! I won't die!" how will God react? Will He feel sorry for the physical body, because of the pain it is enduring? Or will He quietly smile?

The child who experiences pain in order to emerge from its mother's womb grows to become the object of its parents' love. In the same way, our spirit self must leave behind our crying physical body in order to be born anew as the eternal object of the God who is a spiritual being. This is a conclusion based on the Principle. On earth, too, the baby can become the friend of its father and mother after it is born. This is because it is born into the physical world where it can share love with its father and mother. In the same way that the fetus swims around the mother's womb, life on earth is breathing and living in the swaddling clothes of air. Only when the baby shares love with its mother and father as it breathes air can we say it is alive. In the same way, we can share love with God our Parent, who exists as an eternal spiritual being, after we are born again into the spirit world.

What kind of place is the spirit world? When we enter spirit world, we begin to breathe through a hole on the top of our head and through our cells. The air in spirit world is not the air we have on earth. Instead, it is love. When a spirit person breathes, he or she inhales and exhales the nourishing elements of love. On earth, eating alone does not sustain our life. When we eat and drink, all we are doing is filling our sack with food and water. Eventually, we will die. The form we take during life on earth is our second existence. While on earth, we need to develop our character of love. Therefore on earth, the thing we need most is love. What is an orphan? Why do we call a child who cannot receive love from a father or mother an orphan? It is because such a child lacks the love by which he or she can connect eternally with spirit world. When love is absent, we are lonely. That is why we feel sorry for a person who lives without a spouse.

Death destroys our ability to breathe in the second stage, and connects us with the nourishment of love. We eventually have no choice but to leave the physical body behind. We cannot see love, but our internal structure develops centering on the love of parents, of husband and wife, and of children. Just as there is a normal development for a child in its mother's womb, there is a normal course of development on earth. We follow it by living in accordance with the laws of God. We cannot do it by living just any way we want.

Human Flight

If we examine the world of nature, we see that insignificant insects, seeds of trees and even baby birds can fly. Does it make sense that human beings, the greatest of all creations, cannot fly? Look at the dandelion. It is made so that its seeds will fly away when the wind blows. Birds fly, insects fly and the seeds of plants fly. Surely, human beings also must have been created with a way to fly. Someone might be tempted to complain, "God, why did you create us without the ability to fly when everything else in creation can fly?" God's reply probably would be, "Wait a few decades until you reach completion and then I will let you fly."

So, what should we be doing until then? We need to train ourselves to be able to adapt to the spirit world. We need to train ourselves by loving our parents, loving our spouse and loving our children. Then, when the time comes, we will enter the eternal world and live in attendance to God. For that to take place, we must put aside this physical body and die.

Look at the life cycle of the cicada. Before a cicada can fly, it goes through a larval stage. What would happen if the cicada said, "I want to go on living as a larva. I don't want to shed my skin. I don't care about land and air"? Even if it were resisting its transformation, once it shed its skin it would fly away.

A similar situation holds true with the dragonfly. First, it exists as a larva, swimming around in water. Then it crawls on land for a time. After that, it sheds its skin and flies away. It begins to eat insects that it never would have thought of eating while it was living on land. As it flies around, the entire world becomes its home. Many insects pass through three stages like this. That is why insects have wings. They develop wings through their life in the water, on land and finally in the air.

Human beings are the highest beings in creation, but do we have wings? Does living only on the earth satisfy us? Human beings have wings, but they are wings of a higher order. You may say you don't want to put aside your physical body and die. But once we die and leave our physical body behind, our spirit self passes through the blessed gates of our second birth and whoosh, we fly away.

Crossing the Finish Line

As I have already said, we cannot avoid death. We have to be prepared to suffer in order to establish the good that is in us as our second self in the eternal world. A fetus in its mother's womb must receive proper prenatal care if it is to be born healthy and strong. In the same way, we need to prepare ourselves properly while on earth. We need to grow by modeling ourselves on the image of God, the heart of God and the divinity of God.

Once we are grown, we need to invest our lives to pass over the line of life and death. We must pass over even if we have to brave the fiercest storm. It is not enough if we do well most of the way and then fall just short of the finish line. What must we do when we find ourselves approaching life's finish line? Even if we run with our mind focused totally on the goal, we can't be confident we will make it all the way. If we wander aimlessly at the end, we will be ruined. We win victory only as we dash across the finish line.

It is an effort worth making for everyone born as a human being. No matter how much opposition there may be from behind, no matter how much persecution comes from the side, you just have to push forward one step at a time. There is no time to get entangled with the opposition. You have to keep going as quickly as you can, even one step at a time, in order to traverse your path of destiny to its end and finally cross the finish line. We all must go this way.

The Value of Righteousness

We often say that a person's heart is upright. What does this mean? When a heart is firmly vertical, we say it is upright. If a tree is lying on the ground, we don't say it is upright. The same is true when we refer to a heart as upright. The expression means that the heart is standing vertically. That is why human beings walk upright. An object must be vertical in order to be upright. We must set our hearts in a completely vertical position. Then the body will be horizontal in relation to this. When the vertical and horizontal are set within us, the pulling power of the vertical and the pushing power of the horizontal will be in balance. There will arise centripetal and centrifugal forces. Thus, we need to find ourselves. When we assert ourselves, we should say that God and True Parents are also this way. On this foundation, we can expand our sphere of life through relatives, one clan and one nation.

Doctors quarantine patients who have dangerous communicable diseases. For the same reason, the time is not far off when we will send people who know the Will of God but continue to sin despite this knowledge into isolation near the North Pole or other arctic area. People thrown into such a place might not have a place to sleep or food to eat. They may go through immense suffering until they can genuinely repent.

There is one thing that makes me sad. God gave me responsibility to accomplish His will, so during my lifetime I need to accomplish His will to a level He finds acceptable. Until I have done that, I cannot die. For that reason, when I am in the valley of the shadow of death, God leads me out of danger. Whether I am eating or fasting, whether I am asleep or awake, I am always praying for the world and humankind. My suffering is not for the sake of a particular country or people. My objective is the salvation of the world. I have worked to this day and I am ready to die if necessary. I have sacrificed my life so that this objective might be achieved. You, also, should live and die for the sake of the world. If it is for the sake of world salvation, you must even be prepared to die with your wife, your family, your clan and even your entire people.

Face to Face with Death

Some day in the future, you will die. When you stand face to face with death, you will look back upon your life. You need to think what final words you will leave behind at that moment. On the path of death, your friends will not be with you. Your loving parents will not be there, nor will your loving brothers and sisters. Your spouse and children whom you love so much will not be with you. It is a path that you will take alone.

No one can go down that path twice. Once you have gone, there is no coming back. Once you take that path, you cannot return in all eternity. The heart that you have as you walk that path is important. When that moment arrives and you are face to face with death, if you do not possess the hope that can transcend death, that will be the end of you.

In history there have been many people who upheld and established God's will. They did not retreat when they faced death. Instead, they laughed in the face of death and valiantly transcended death. We know well that these people paved our way to Heaven. What kind of person is it who is joyful even when passing over the hill of death, the moment that drives most of us into heartfelt sorrow? This is the kind of person who has heartfelt hope and aspirations for Heaven. For this reason, we must not reproach the world and lament when we face death. Instead, we should feel joy as we stand before heaven with pride in the value of our death.

What happens to us when we die? Up to the moment we die, we belong to ourselves. But as soon as we die, we belong to God. This is because we are born of a fallen lineage. Until our death, we lack the ability to cut our ties with Satan. After death, though, we establish ties with God. There is no resurrection without death. It is impossible to enter into the next period without first passing through the preceding one.

To what kind of death does the Bible refer when it says that those who seek to die will live and those who seek to live will die? (Luke 17:33, John 12:25) This does not mean that we should lose the eternal life given us by Heaven. It means that we should lose the life that is connected to the satanic world, inherited through the fallen lineage. That is why those who seek to die for the sake of God will live. This seems paradoxical. But from the perspective of the fall, this is the only way restoration can come about. This is the standard for discussing the possibility of restoration.

Wisdom and Foolishness

Success or failure in life is not determined over a period of decades. Rather, it is determined in an instant. If you look at the entire course of life, it does not take very long for a baby to be born. Of course, there is a period leading up to the birth, when the fetus is in the womb. Those ten months in the womb are a time of preparation. The birth takes but an instant. The preparation may go well for the entire ten months, but if something goes wrong at the decisive moment of birth, the infant will meet a tragic end.

After living out our life on earth, we come face to face with our moment of fate. We will see our entire life flash before our eyes. The one who can say, "There was truth in my life" and "I am leaving behind something more valuable than my life," is a person who has spent his life in a worthy manner. On the other hand, the person who starts to recall the past and begins to shake his head over things he would rather not remember, is a tragic person. For some people, the more they remember, the greater the expression of joy on their face. If all their problems can be buried in the ideal, death will actually be a comfort. The moment of recalling the past will not be filled with fear. If they are leaving something behind, then that past record will not die and its reality will not die. Instead, these things will be made manifest. The people whose past allows them to do this are without a doubt people whom the nation can follow. They are the ones whom the people of the world can follow.

We need to consider whether we can stand alone before God. Truth and goodness begin with a particular individual but they do not end with that individual. Once truth and goodness have begun in a particular person, they must bear fruit in another person. Or, they can begin in another person and bear fruit in me.

If a person spends her life giving to others, then she will have no fear on the path of death. She has given everything and sacrificed herself for others. She has led a life that is close to truth; she has shed tears for others and she has invested her life for others. If a man's aspirations are for others, all the life force coming from his pulse is focused and invested for the sake of others. If this is the case, then this person's past is one of glory.

The path taken by the wise is different from that taken by the foolish. A wise person tries to live in partnership with history, in partnership with the present world and in partnership with the future. A foolish person lives for the self and tries to make the world exist for his or her own sake. There is a global environment characteristic of the spirit world, and within it are nations, clans, families and individuals. An individual cannot enter Heaven without a self-motivating character by which he or she is absolutely indispensable as an individual. The family or clan cannot enter Heaven unless they can say that they possess a self-motivating character that makes them indispensable on the family or clan level.

How to Go to Heaven

Compared with spirit world, Earth is but a speck of dust. The spirit world is an eternal world, transcending time and space. If a spirit person commands, "The person who lived in such and such an age with such and such a heart, please come forward," then that person will appear in an instant. It is a world in which feelings and intuition turn into reality. There are no factories there to produce food. There are no automobile factories. There is nothing like that.

To register yourself in spirit world, you need a certificate based upon your life on earth. How are you going to obtain it? I'm talking about a certificate of life that will let you say: "This is what I became. This is what I did." You cannot just make your own certificate. First, Satan has to write one for you. After you receive that certificate, you have to receive one from Jesus. Finally, you have to receive a certificate from God. You will need these three certificates.

When you go to spirit world, you will find that it is made up of three very large realms. Those who lived for others will go to the highest level. Those who lived for themselves, however, will find themselves on the lowest level. They will find that everyone is opposing them, whereas everyone will welcome those who lived for others.

Once you are in spirit world, your parents and spouse cannot help you. The people in the highest levels are those who lived for the sake of others. In the uppermost tiers are those who traveled throughout the world living for others with a heart that expanded their love for their mother and family. With a saintly heart, they are always looking for ways to save the people of the world from evil.

The one who lives for himself goes to Hell, and the one who lives for others goes to Heaven. People separate into these two worlds at death. Thus, we must live for the sake of the whole, for the sake of the greater good. Live for the sake of the world, for the sake of God and for the sake of human liberation. Someday competitions will take place to see who can live for the sake of others to a greater degree. In the heavenly world, the person who has lived for the sake of others will go to the higher position. Thus, you can leap to a higher position by living for the person who is higher than you are. Living for that person is the same act as God bringing forth His own object through His creative act. Thus, that person comes to stand as your object partner of love.

The Value of Living for Others

In the spirit world we live for others, centering on true love. If you encounter a person who has dedicated 100 percent of his life for the sake of others, then you have to say, "Please move past me, go ahead." It doesn't matter how great the United States seems to be. A person who dedicates his life for the people of America to a greater extent than your President does can move past the President and be welcomed.

When a person only cares about his own interests, he is everyone's enemy. It is the same way in spirit world. When a person says he will live for something greater, then he will naturally move past others. One who lives for the sake of the world does not need to worry about living for America, because America is included in the world. All countries are included in the world. The conclusion can only be that true love, by which a person lives for the sake of others, is the only content and direction that everyone can welcome.

When you die, you must take with you three accomplishments. One, that you loved God. Two, that you loved yourself and worked hard to establish your essential self. And three, that you worked hard to expand the love you shared with your spouse and your family to the entire world. This love for humanity and for God will remain forever. It will define your right to ownership in the next world. When you enter spirit world, the number of people you evangelized will determine your right to ownership.

In the spirit world, pride wells up over the extent to which you longed for people with your life. You do not need anything else in the next world. The only thing you need is the record that you loved God more than the world, more than your country, more than your spouse and more than your children. If a wife wants her husband to love her with godly love of a higher order, then she has to say, "Please love God more than you love me, and then love me."

The Family and Spirit World

I often preach about the realm of the heart. The foundation for the realm of the heart is the love of true parents, the love of true brothers and sisters and the love of true children. The world of the heart is one in which we universalize these types of love. In this original world, a person can live by the standard of husband and wife love, but theirs must be a husband and wife love that gives primacy to Heaven and earth and to the cosmos.

So, where do we go in order to establish a foundation to qualify for that world? We must lay this foundation in the physical world. We are not to spend our time here for the sake of all those things valued by this world. We are here to qualify ourselves for the next world.

That is the basis for the principle that we live as families in the spirit world. Why do we need to have children? The vertical love of God and the horizontal love of parents bring descendants into this world. This is a vertical and horizontal mixing of the blood of God and the parents. Thus, people who were unable to have descendants on earth will not be able to harmonize Heaven and earth in the spirit world. They will be unable to keep step with the rhythm of north, south, east and west. A person who has no descendants will have no place to rest or play in the next world.

Religions and Nations in Spirit World

In spirit world, there is no need for religion, much less for denominations. There is no need for entities such as the Presbyterian Church or the Catholic Church. People there are in the realm of life together with God. In that realm are people who loved the world, patriots and loyal subjects, women of virtue, and saints. As far as I am aware, however, there is as yet no one who lived his or her life in the original love of God, centering on the tradition of the realm of the heart.

Whenever you begin a task, you should begin it centering on God. Whether you go to Hell, the middle spirit world, Paradise or the Kingdom of Heaven, is determined by the extent to which you harmonize with this principle. The most precious path on earth is that which endures the greatest amount of suffering and sheds the most tears for the sake of Heaven. That is the path that will bestow the freedom to enter the next world.

In the next world, people of different nationalities cannot live together, but true followers of all religions can live together. The religious sphere is one of longing for one world and believing in one God. Thus people of true piety will be together. The uniqueness of people of faith is in their living their entire life based upon the standard of the spirit world. Religion teaches us how to relate with each other centering on the eternal world, the transcendent world, the dwelling place of the Divine Being—whether we call Him God or by some other name.

God's Call to World Leaders

There is a reason for my speaking to the participants in this gathering about the value of life in relation to issues having to do with life and death. You represent religions that are active throughout the world. I want to stress that it is religious leaders' responsibility to teach about life and death correctly.

Today, the political leaders of the world are seeking to realize peace and prosperity through the United Nations. In my judgement, however, the path to world peace will be incomplete if we build it merely upon the political, economic and military functions of the United Nations. Political, economic and military powers can deal only with that which is external, physical and material. We can reach the internal and spiritual aspects of life only through religious teaching and through the unity and united actions of the world's religions.

I would like to take this opportunity today to supplement the existing United Nations with a structure in which the UN and leaders of the major world religions can work together. I hope that the participants here today, and all the nations of the world, will seriously consider this proposal to establish a structure encompassing the world's religions and the United Nations.

My dear Leaders and Distinguished Guests, I want to again express my appreciation that you have taken time from your busy lives to attend this important meeting. May God bless you and your families. Thank you.

Unification of North and South

World Unification and North-South Unification Will Be Accomplished by True Love

Reverend Sun Myung Moon, President, Family Federation for World Peace
February 10, 2000 Olympic Gymnastic Stadium, Seoul, Korea

Distinguished guests whose fervent desire is for North-South unification, ladies and gentlemen. The new millennium that just began is a time to clean away the divisions and conflicts of the past century and to manifest the ideal of a one world family of harmony and unification. I would like to begin by thanking you for congratulating me on my eightieth birthday. Most of all, I would like to return to God all the honor and glory given to me, because it is He who has watched over me until this day.

As I look back, I am reminded that my life has never been easy. My life has been intertwined with the suffering history of our people and the numerous difficulties that our people have undergone in the midst of the great powers. As a boy of 16, I came into contact with the will of Heaven through prayer, and throughout my life after that I have devoted all my spirit and energy to accomplishing God's Will.

I came to understand that the fundamental cause of human unhappiness is that the fall severed our relationship with God. As a result, human beings fell into a state of spiritual ignorance. In an effort to resolve the fundamental problems this has caused among human beings and in the universe, I have spoken publicly on more than 10,000 occasions in many places around the world and set forth a true view of humanity, a true view of the world, and a true view of history based on Godism.

These speeches have been translated into twelve languages and published in three hundred volumes. The contents of these speeches are not the result of a comprehensive study of historical documents. My conclusions are not the result of scholarly research. Instead, I arrived at these answers to basic and fundamental questions through my communications with both the visible and invisible worlds.

The issue of unifying the Korean Peninsula is the solemn desire of our people and the final act of bringing the global Cold War to a conclusion. So today, as I express my gratitude for your having prepared this meaningful forum, I would like to share with you on the topic, "World Unification and North-South Unification Will Be Accomplished by True Love," and lay out the basic answer for how to bring about unification.

Satan's Target Is God Himself

The unification of our country involves more than the mere unification of national territory. It begins with the unification of the human mind and body which were divided against one another as a result of the fall. This is the model for the unification of a world that has been divided in two. Thus, this issue must be understood from the perspective of God's salvation providence. It must be resolved on a providential level.

What is Satan's ultimate target behind the history of struggle between good and evil? Ever since this conflict came into being as a result of the fall of the first human ancestors, Satan has had his sights set precisely on God Himself. God is eternal, unchanging, absolute and unique, and the standard of the ideal that He held at the beginning of creation must also have these qualities. If you were to ask God directly, I think He would confirm what I am saying.

How can God reply when Satan says to God, "God, when you made me an archangel in the beginning, were you acting out of a love for me that was temporary or eternal?" I think God must say that He made the archangel out of a love that was eternal. If He were to say that His love was temporary, that would make Him an ephemeral God. Unless He maintains a standard of loving Satan eternally, there will eventually come a time when He will no longer be able to exercise His authority as God with respect to Satan. Thus, no matter how much Satan may oppose Him, God has no choice other than to establish the condition of loving Satan.

Satan says to God, "I became an evil scoundrel as a result of the fall, but you and good people can't use methods that are similar to mine, can you? I may like to fight, but you're not supposed to enjoy fighting. Even when you take a blow, you have to endure, don't you?" Thus, God's philosophy is one of non-resistance. Why is that? It is because, until the world of the heavenly ideal is manifested on this Earth, God must love the archangel who became Satan, regardless of the circumstances. No matter how much trouble Satan may cause, God cannot punish him or cut him off. He must establish the condition of having loved Satan regardless of where He found Satan. God can only have complete victory when Satan confesses to Him, saying, "O, God really is God. I surrender to You." This is the problem.

Jesus Felt No Malice

Because of this, God is in the position of being tied up by Satan. Since the principle path of the providence of restoration is for God to bring about Satan's surrender by loving him, we who are His children must walk this same path. It doesn't matter if a person is persecuted around the world and is considered an enemy worldwide. This person must establish the condition of having loved those who oppose him. From this aspect, there is amazing truth in God's council to "love your enemies." In fact, this is one of God's battle strategies. These words sound simple. No one realized, though, that they have marked the boundary line between victory and defeat in the battle between God and Satan.

If God were to adopt a philosophy of looking on Satan as His enemy, and seek revenge against him, then God would never be able to stand on the pinnacle of victory. Thus, God has said, "love your enemy," and has carried out a strategy of love. The words "love your enemy" also represent the culmination of Jesus' teaching. It is remarkable that Jesus, the only begotten son of God, stood before Satan and prayed for him despite the fact that Satan was trying to kill him. If Jesus, as he hung dying on the cross, had held any feelings of malice toward his enemy, God's providence would have been turned completely around. It is because Jesus overcame death with a heart of praying that his enemies might be blessed and of loving his enemies that Satan surrendered in that instance.

This is where the qualification to be God's eternal child is fulfilled. Even Satan recognizes this qualification and gives his signature. You, too, will be able to stand before God and say, "Hey, Satan, am I not unmistakably the son of God?" and Satan will reply, "Yes, that is correct." We must conduct ourselves in a way such that if we say to Satan, "You have no problem, if people who live as I do expand God's reciprocal realm, starting from the individual and moving to the family, clan, people, nation and world," Satan's answer would be, "That is within Principle, so I can't do anything about it."

The Enemy Nation

It is under these conditions that God has pursued the providence, with the Christian cultural sphere at the center. Whether we find ourselves on the path of sacrifice, in the position of martyrdom, or in the midst of a bloody battle, we must carry out a movement of loving God and loving even our enemies. We must carry out this movement in our families, in our societies and in our nations.

The Roman Empire severely persecuted Christianity, but it was forced to surrender in the face of the love that Christianity gave even to the country that was its enemy. This is how Christianity came to be a worldwide religion. The starting point for the path to Heaven was within the country that was Christianity's enemy. Until now Christians have only thought about loving their own personal enemies, but this is not enough. We must love the country that is our enemy, and even the world that is our enemy.

The starting point on the path to Heaven is within the country that is our enemy. Unless we create the foundation of the tradition of true love and set out on the basis of this foundation, we cannot bring about the Kingdom of Heaven on Earth. There can never be a philosophy or ideology greater than the tradition that is established in this way.

When Korea was under Japanese imperial rule, the four providential countries—Korea, Japan, Germany and the United States—were enemies of one another. Given the circumstances of that time, Japanese and Koreans were enemies. Japanese and Americans were enemies. Americans and Germans were enemies. Yet, I practiced the way of the true love of Heaven by taking Japanese and Germans to America, their enemy country, and telling them that America was falling into ruin and that their help was needed to revive it.

I emphasized to the Japanese and Germans that they could not establish a new thinking capable of leading humanity into the new world that Heaven desires unless they set the condition of having loved their past enemy, America, even more than their own fatherland. I set forth this tradition of true love and created a new beginning. Unless people erect a base and tradition by which they love the countries that are their enemies, the Kingdom of Heaven cannot be realized on Earth. It is only within the true love of God that such a historic tradition can be constructed.

My Testimony

When I was humiliated by the U.S. federal government and unjustly brought before a court of law, my response was actually to work harder to give life to America by founding the conservative newspaper, *The Washington Times*, and a broadcasting station. Recently, I have been pursuing an effort to gather prominent strategic planners from around the world in order to assist China. This is one example of how all the organizations that I have founded are ready to involve themselves in any effort of Heaven that requires love.

In the future, even those with superior ability will find themselves ruled by others if they have not accumulated accomplishments in true love. Everyone here needs to bear this in mind.

I was involved in the anti-Japanese resistance movement under the Japanese imperial rule, and from that perspective the Japanese people were my enemy. This was true for the Korean people as a whole and for me individually. Yet, after Japan's defeat in World War II, I gave love to Japan. After the war, I could have reported the police who had taken me into custody and tortured me severely for my activities in the underground independence movement. Had I done this, they all would have been executed. When I came across a Japanese policeman who was running for his life, however, I packed some things for him and helped him escape to safety under the cover of darkness.

Do you know why so many young people in Japan place their eternal lives at stake and pledge their loyalty to me? This is because there is a principle of cause and effect which dictates that they must return what has been given them. It is because I planted the seeds of true love in the world, transcending national boundaries and in accordance with God's heart. It is because I planted the heartistic foundation that leads people to a life of loving the countries that were the enemies of their own country. Thus, Japan today is my prisoner. Without even realizing it, Japan is fulfilling its heavenly calling.

Under Japanese rule, I had reason to harbor resentment even toward the Emperor of Japan. But he has already been defeated. Heaven does not strike a person who is defeated. In fact, Heaven shows mercy toward those who understand their sin and apologize. Because this is Heaven's way, a person who raises a sword and strikes a defeated person will find his own descendants driven to ruin.

The United States is also a country that considered me their enemy. However, I left my family behind and diverted my attention from my Korean fatherland to bring salvation to America. I threw away everything that belonged to me in order to bring salvation to the world under Satan.

The Responsibility of Christians

Think, too, of how much hatred the established Christian denominations have directed toward the Unification Church. It might be said that we are enemies. We must not fight each other as enemies, however. We must come together in love. What would happen if we were to come together in love? The two coming together in love would lead the Republic of Korea into fulfilling the will of Heaven so as to digest North Korea. If the established denominations and the Unification Church had become one immediately after Korea's liberation from Japan, everything would have been solved.

Because that did not happen, we have had to make extraordinary sacrifices to overcome enemies of the individual, enemies of the family, enemies of the clan and enemies of the people in order to attain the position that we would have reached in the first place had there been no conflict. We have worked to overcome the path of suffering where we were not able to strike at enemies.

Distinguished ladies and gentlemen, all the people in North Korea have armed themselves with Juche thought. We must arm ourselves with the philosophy of true love that is capable of digesting them. North Korea is a part of the northern culture that has been influenced by the cold winds of the Soviet culture. We must work to naturally melt them with our warm-region civilization. Otherwise, both countries will go to ruin. Thus, we must thoroughly arm ourselves philosophically.

This philosophy must not be one that seeks the fulfillment of individual desires. Rather, it must seek the salvation of all humanity. It must not be centered on the self. Communists have the idea that everyone should work for the sake of a few top Party leaders. This is why they eliminate any person who stands out as a potential rival. We are not that way. Our idea is to unite with the reciprocal environment in order to establish a reciprocal standard of a higher level. That is Cain and Abel becoming one so as to receive their parents on a higher level.

Liberate without Fighting

I do not believe South Korea should attempt to overcome North Korea militarily. Instead, we must love our nation more than they love theirs. We must have the philosophical strength to love Heaven even more than they love communism. We must become capable men and women of character who can bring about their natural surrender. There is no other way for us to absorb North Korea. In other words, we must become able to impress them with how we live. We must be able to amaze those people armed with communist ideology in terms of our outlook on life and our standard of character.

We cannot restore the Cain-type nation unless we maintain an environment by which we are able to exert influence over them. If we cannot restore the Cain-type nation, we cannot establish the restored country capable of entering into a worldwide nation centered on the Kingdom of Heaven. Although North and South Korea are divided against one another, we must liberate North Korea without fighting them.

The Korean people in both North and South Korea fervently desire to see the country unified, but how can this be accomplished? Unification can only be accomplished when a sophisticated method for unification is put forward that will allow both sides to live together. When the South goes to the North, or the North to the South, and says, "Let's do it our way," unification will not succeed. Thus, we must find a love that will benefit both sides.

Ladies and gentlemen, at the moment North and South are going in different directions. One is trying to go south and the other trying to go north, and they are on two divergent paths. Their purposes are at odds with each other. If both sides insist on their own position, it is certain that the situation will again result in breakdown.

The question is what is to be done about this. There must be a South Korean person who loves North Korea with a greater love than any South Korean person has for his own country. Also, there must be a North Korean person who loves South Korea with a greater love than any North Korean has for his own country. There is no option or solution other than this.

If there is one person whose patriotism is greater than any South Korean's and greater than any North Korean's, then this is where the path to unification can come about. Can there be another way? No matter how hard you may think, there is no other way.

What are the Korean people to do, then? Our country straddles the boundary line between left and right centering on the 38th Parallel. We are the ones who have been placed on that line, so what are we to do? This is the question. The issue is how to resolve this problem. The answer is that we must suffer even more than North Koreans and even more than South Koreans. How are we to uphold such a standard of patriotism, established through suffering and transcending nationality? This is the way to give this country life and to solve its problems.

The Heart of Wanting to Live Together

The same principle applies to uniting the world of goodness and the world of evil. Someone must appear in the world of goodness who is a greater patriot to the world of evil than anyone in that world. A person must appear that can set a higher standard of loyalty to his nation than anyone among our ancestors who pursued goodness. This is the only way for a divided history to be resolved.

Jesus was particularly remarkable in this regard. He realized that it would do no good for both sides to fight. The only way for him to live for the sake of God and for the sake of the people of Israel was for him to die for God and for his people. This was the reasoning behind the crucifixion. Jesus' love for humanity was greater than anyone else's since the beginning of history, and his love for God was greater than anyone else's in history. Because of this, his death caused a history destined for destruction to take a new direction toward a world of purpose. This was the Christian cultural sphere. This is historical fact. Thus, the only way to unite North and South is to become a people who can die for the North and the South. There is no other path to achieve unification. There has to be a heart of truly wanting to live together in harmony with the other side.

When a person considers how to lead his life, the most basic fundamentals can be expressed as the path of a filial child, the path of a loyal patriot, the path of a saint, and the path of a son or daughter of God. Isn't this the heart of wanting to live in harmony with others eternally and of wanting to be with others without regard to whether they are higher or lower, and transcending front and back and left and right? This is the logical conclusion.

What is the common denominator among those who say, "I want to live in harmony with others"? It is not power. Power cannot transcend history. Power is limited to a specific period in time. The same is true with knowledge. The world of knowledge has an innate tendency to develop. Does knowledge give us the heart to say, "I want to live with this particular piece of knowledge forever"? Clearly, we cannot keep either knowledge or wealth with us forever.

Develop the Right Heart

What, then, is the common denominator that transcends above and below, front and back, left and right, and the time differences between past, present and future? This cannot be anything other than true love centering on God. Thus, a filial child is one who lives in his family giving profound love to his or her parents. Also, a patriot is one who lives a life of profound love for his or her country. A saint is one who lives a life of profound love for the people of the world. A son or daughter of God is one who lives a life of profound love for all humanity and God.

Thus, the problem is to develop a true foundation of heart by which a person can want to have the heart of a patriot. Such a person would want his or her life to be in concert with the fortunes of the people. Such a person would look upon any difficulties faced by the people as his or her own personal difficulties. This person would look upon any joys experienced by his people as more than temporary joys but eternal joys to be shared with everyone. The person who possesses relationships of true love and true heart is given special authority to participate in the realm of unification.

Ladies and gentlemen, even if a woman lacks any formal education, she can marry a man with a doctoral degree and suddenly become the wife of a scholar. Isn't that true? Anyone who possesses a great deal of the relationships of heart based on the desire to live with others in harmony has the right to participate today in the realm of unification. God himself is such a being. Thus, if a person attains the life content enabling him to form a unity, this person is automatically given the qualification to participate.

A Practical Movement for Unification

Where should we begin the process of unification? Where should we start in order to achieve North-South unification? What is the first step? Do we begin by using our fists or physical force? If we subjugate the other side with force, then eventually they will develop a force stronger than ours and the conflict will begin all over again. We cannot achieve unification by this method. The way to unification will open when each of us has the heart to say, "Even though I live in the South, I truly want to live in harmony with those people in the North. I truly want to become one with them."

Suppose people in the South were to look upon our compatriots in the North and shed tears to see the miserable conditions in which they live. Suppose we were to tell them, "I am living my life in a way that I can share in your difficulties." Suppose we were to promise them, "Some day soon, I will appear before you having completed the preparations for your day of liberation." Suppose, then, we were to carry out a practical movement for unification based on such a heart. If we did these things, I believe the day of unification would not be far away.

Ladies and gentlemen, we must think how we can live in harmony with our compatriots. No one can be a patriot if they do not want to live with their parents or with their compatriots. Any claim such a person might make to being patriotic would be a lie. A person must first be able to live in harmony with his own country before he or she can live in harmony with the world. Further, a person must first live in harmony with the world before he or she can live in harmony with God. Thus, a person cannot be a patriot unless he first loves his compatriots and gives love to that particular regional society.

How much do our political leaders love their country? Any politician who lacks a heart of truly wanting to share in the life of common citizens will soon disappear. It doesn't matter how well bred or educated this person may be. He will disappear like an air bubble formed on a surface of water. Any leader who does not love the citizens will not be able to escape judgment by the citizens of his country and by history.

Healing the division between North and South is not a simple process. As fellow patriots struggle to bring this about, they will need a determination of heart to work through many sleepless nights, transcending time, and overcoming all manner of difficulties. "I truly want to live with them. I don't want to die unless I can die with them. I don't want to live unless I can live with them." The movement for North-South unification begins when both sides have such a heart toward the other.

The World Will Follow

When North-South unification is accomplished, this will be the beginning point in the effort to unite the democratic and communist worlds. Each of us must consider the future of our people and of the world as a representative of the world, a representative of the six billion people of the world, a representative of the three billion people of Asia, a representative of your school, and a representative of all the students you have ever taught. We must determine ourselves to carry out a movement that will truly enable us to share in the lives of our compatriots.

When such an effort connects you to the way of the saint, then you will come to resemble a saint. If you practice this with respect to God with the loyalty of a son or daughter of God, then you will become "God's heir," and "successor to God's will." I tell you these things today because I have already confirmed their truth in my own life.

Once North-South unification is accomplished in Korea, the unification of the world will follow automatically. Do you think that political power, military force or economic wealth can bring about unification? There isn't even the slightest chance of this. That is the reason I am speaking to you in this way. Can weapons, wealth or knowledge do away with rotten philosophies? No, they cannot. Only true love can do this. This love is love that comes from God.

When a person enters into a relationship of true love with God, he or she is absolutely given special authority to have dominion, ownership and the right of inheritance. In the world of mechanics, the energy produced is less than the energy put into a system. However, in the world of true love, greater energy is produced than is put in.

What is true love? It is love that lives for the sake of others. It is love of unlimited giving and forgetting. No memory is kept of how much was given. It is a love that never tires of giving. A 90-year-old mother can turn to her 70-year-old son and say, "Be careful when you cross the street," and there is nothing strange about that. Even if the mother has repeated those same words countless times over several decades, she will always say them one more time.

If this is true with parents in the fallen world, how can we ever grow tired of giving and receiving God's love in the essential world? When we establish God's true reciprocal realm in our own lives, we will understand the unchanging glory of true love for the first time. Then we will be able to justify the ethics of eternal life centering on the true love of human beings. Who in the world is aware of such things?

The Greatest Love

In 1984, I was lying in bed in an American prison where I had been unjustly incarcerated, when God came to me. He said, "You are the only person I can trust. I want you to resolve the situation in Nicaragua." Am I really the only person to whom God can come to with such a command?

America is said to be a great country standing at the forefront of all developed countries. It had a population of 240 million people and a large number of religious leaders. How helpless God must be in that He could not go to any of those people but had to come to me. At least it is fortunate that God knows how to find a person by His love. If I had not worked for the sake of the world at that time, South America would have been completely ravaged by war by now.

North-South unification is the fervent desire of the Korean people, but it is also the earnest desire of God in this age. It is Heaven's desire that North Korea and South Korea can be united and that God's resting place will be established in your homes, in our churches, and in our worldwide church centered on God.

How, then, are we to attend God? How can we wipe everything clean? What can we use to wipe everything off so that God will say it is completely clean? This is the problem.

The answer is simple. We must clean the surroundings centering on a true love that is greater than our love for our parents, greater than our love for our spouse, and greater than our love for our children. It is only when our offerings our placed on the altar centering on such love that the ideal North-South unification will be manifested.

This is where the ideal blending of eastern and western cultures can occur. This is where the ideal unification of the divided physical and heavenly realms can occur. This is where the realm of liberation of Hell and Heaven will come about. We cannot unlock this without true love. We need the key of true love. Unification brought about by the love between a person's mind and body can always be manifested as the unification of love in the family. A loving husband and wife with a harmonious family will always see their love manifested within their clan. If a loving husband and wife unite as one, who will dare try to tear them apart and defile their relationship?

Problem Solving

A world made of the harmonious family, harmonious people, harmonious government, harmonious world, harmonious Heaven and Earth, harmonious true human love and God united as one—isn't this world the utopia of true love? In such a world, there will be no possibility of discord. Love will be the life element for all people, in the same way that plants receive life elements by absorbing the rays of the sun. Our fervent desire is to build a Kingdom of Heaven on Earth and in Heaven where we can resonate with true love eternally. How many people are there in this world, though, who are the subject partners or object partners of true love, who can stand as people of character qualified to be the master of all things, and who possess both the value of a remarkable life and the special authority that comes with such a life?

I sincerely hope that each of you here today will remember what I have said and will work to unite your mind and body. I hope that each of you become a person who lives for the sake of your spouse, and go on to become a true person who lives for the sake of your family, people, nation and world. If you do that, then North-South unification will be as good as done. Even communist ideology is easily absorbed and disappears when it is placed in the midst of God's love. The problem until now was that we did not know this. Once we develop our hearts of love, North-South unification will be no problem at all.

That is not all. Problems between East and West and the worldwide North-South problem involving differences among rich and poor nations can also be completely resolved through the true love of God. We must digest the ideal for the world centering on God's ideal that I have described, and go on to digest the ideal of the nation. Then we must move on to the boundless realm of peace of the ideal world that links the ideal of the nation to the ideals of clan, family and individual. This is, without a doubt, the way that the utopia of true love that God has desired can be built on this Earth.

Include Everyone

Distinguished guests: We cannot fight the communist world with guns and swords or any other means of physical force. We must fight them with love. Communists seek to destroy the democratic world in order to build a communist world. By contrast, we must build a structure that will bring salvation not only to the democratic world but to the communist world as well. The 38th Parallel is the deepest point and final resting place where North and South can be united by means of God's true love. When it comes to doing away with this demarcation line, the North says, "There's nothing we can do about it." Russia says the same thing. China, too, says the same thing. The government and opposition parties in Seoul say, "There's nothing we can do about it." Even the United States and Japan say there is nothing they can do about this. If this is the case, then it will be the end of everything. But if unification comes by true love, will we prosper or will we be ruined? If we can do away with the separation, it will be the end of everything evil and a new beginning for everything good. This is the reason we must unite the citizens of our country.

Millions of people in Korea, Japan and the United States have worked through the International Federation for Victory Over Communism and CAUSA to lay non-governmental foundations in each of these countries. I declared the fundamental principle for unification more than 40 years ago. Since then, I have carried out a movement of ideas, centered on Godism, both domestically and around the world. I have worked in the four major countries surrounding the Korean Peninsula to lay the international groundwork for unification. Over the years, leaders of many countries and in the philosophical world have recognized Godism as the only philosophy not only capable of uniting materialism and atheism, which are diametrical opposites, but also capable of liberating secular humanism.

My patriotic compatriots filled with passionate hope for North-South unification: let us together establish our value systems on the basis of Godism, and join forces in arming the people of this country with this new philosophy. Let us make North-South unification a matter of faith for the sake of ourselves, for the sake of the Korean people and for sake of world peace. Let us stand and answer the call of this historic age and of Heaven. Let us be leaders and people of righteousness standing at the forefront of the movement for World and North-South unification.

History took a mistaken course as a result of Eve's error at the beginning. So in the Last Days, women in particular need to take the lead in overcoming conflict and strife. Their motherly love can create a new history of reconciliation and unity. The mission of women is to educate and restore the young, who are in the position of being their children and even their husbands in order to realize the ideal of the Kingdom of Heaven.

I pray God's blessing may be with you and your families.

Thank you.

The Cosmos Is Our Hometown and Our Fatherland

*Reverend Sun Myung Moon, President, Family Federation for World Peace
This speech was delivered at the Cannon House Office Building Caucus Room,
Washington, D.C., February 2, 2000, during Reverend Moon's 80th Birthday
Celebrations.*

Respected members of the United States Senate and House of Representatives, members of the diplomatic corps, recipients of the American Century Award—whose contributions have helped make this the country most blessed by God—ladies and gentlemen:

I would like to express my heartfelt gratitude that so many leaders from a wide variety of fields in American society have gathered here today to celebrate faith, freedom and family. As founder of The Washington Times Foundation, I commend all of the award winners. All of you are champions who through your service have made significant contributions to improving the quality of life for all Americans.

I also want to thank you from the bottom of my heart for recognizing my life achievements and congratulating me on my 80th birthday. I am particularly grateful to God, who has been my constant companion and protector. To Him, I offer all glory and honor given to me.

Ending God's Sorrow

I have lived my entire life with the earnest desire to solve the many problems related to manifesting God's ideal of creation. When I came to America in 1972, I saw that this country was facing a severe crisis that affected the world. On my first evangelical tour of all 50 states, I declared that God had three major headaches: the threat of communism, the lack of cooperation among religious people against evil, and the moral crisis afflicting youth.

Our responsibility as human beings requires that we meet God halfway and fulfill what God has asked us to do in the areas of freedom, faith and family.

Because God loves America, I initiated many organizations, including *The Washington Times*, to respond to these challenges. I am grateful that God gave me the opportunity to serve America, because American-led UN forces, in the process of saving my country during the Korean War, liberated me from a communist concentration camp where I had been imprisoned for preaching the word of God.

Since receiving God's calling as a boy of 16, I have delved into the meaning of God's Will and fought against tremendous odds to fulfill the history of His restoration providence for the sake of human salvation.

I have come to realize that God does not sit on a throne of glory and grandeur. Instead, He is a God of deep sorrow and profound suffering, who has endeavored to save His children who fell into Hell. As a result of the fall, human beings fell into spiritual ignorance. This meant humanity was fundamentally ignorant regarding God's existence, the meaning of human life, and the entire universe. People did not understand how they should live their lives during their time in this world with their physical bodies. They didn't understand that there is a spiritual world after death. They didn't understand that life in this world should be lived so that it would properly prepare them for the spiritual world.

Because I have known God's Will and His heart, I have worked with single-minded determination to devote my entire heart and energy for the accomplishment of His Will, without regard to the time of day, changes in the seasons, or the environment around me. As I look back on the 80 years of my life and all the difficulties and persecution I have received, I realize I would not be here with you today were it not for the help that God has given me over the years.

I have spoken publicly on some 10,000 occasions in many places around the world. These speeches have been published in a series of more than 300 volumes. On this very significant occasion today when I am meeting some of the most distinguished leaders in the United States, I would like to share with you the essence of the guiding principles in my life and work under the theme, "The Cosmos Is Our Hometown and Our Fatherland."

Bring Balance to the World

The cosmos was created as an enormous house where human beings would live as the masters. Human beings, who are at the center of the universe, live in the context of a series of relationships, that is, the parent-child, husband-wife, and sibling relationships. The parent-child relationship can be described in terms of a vertical axis between "above" and "below." Since a husband and wife are on an equal level, their relationship can be described in terms of a horizontal axis between "left" and "right." We can say that the sibling relationship is on a third axis between "front" and "back." Every individual exists within the sphere created by these three axes. If the ultimate points on these axes are numbered 1, 2, 3, 4, 5, and 6, then God exists in the seventh position at the center of the sphere. This is how God can guide us in our daily lives, even while existing in a central position that cannot be seen.

Since the fall, human beings have existed in the satanic realm of bondage and suffering. With God's help, people can be set free. They can mature as true sons and daughters, meet their mates, and become true husbands and wives. They can go on to have children and become true parents. This is the normal course of human life. Thus, we cannot reject the concept of true children, of true husbands and wives, or of true parents. To do so would be to violate a fundamental principle of the universe, thus destroying our own existence. Each of us must participate in building a true family consisting of true parents, a true husband and wife, and true children. In fact, the family made up of true parents, true husband and wife, and true children is the model for the ideal existence.

In the context of the family, people need to fully receive the love of true parents and of a true spouse. Then, they need to fully receive the love of true children. Money, knowledge, power or physical force cannot bring such human relationships to their completed form. Only the true love of God, which brings balance to the world, can do this.

True love is a force that invests. It is a giving force, not a force that only receives. True love gives completely. It is total giving, to the degree that we ultimately reach a point where there is nothing left to give. After we reach that "zero point," we will have the capacity to receive much more than we gave. This process of giving and receiving will achieve a balance that continues forever. This is the reason that relationships of giving and receiving will produce a world where people live for the sake of others centering on true love.

Likewise, all beings in Heaven and Earth exist in mutual relationship with other beings so as to form a world of true love through relationships of giving and receiving. In mutual relationships every giving force causes a returning force, and this is what gives eternal stability to the central point. God exists in the central position of true love—a position of the "lucky" number seven—giving balance to the entire universe. Heavenly fortune develops in the process of receiving this and returning it. Within such relationships, the flow of love, air, water and light takes place in circular motion. And after going around and around, the flow returns to the original form.

Our Original Homeland

Ladies and gentlemen: What makes someone a good person? We can answer this in many ways. We could say that a bad person is someone who takes whatever he is given and keeps it for himself or herself. A good person, then, is someone who adds to whatever he or she is given and passes it on to others. This is why no parent wants his or her child to grow up to be something less than the parent. We all want our children to be better than ourselves. Also, a husband would like for his wife to be better than himself, and a wife wants her husband to be better than herself. Further, an elder brother and younger brother would each want the other to become better than themselves.

We all want to give back something more than what we receive. This is our fervent wish as parents, as husbands and wives, and as children. It is also the fervent wish of all things in nature. Ultimately, it is the fervent wish of the entire universe.

Moreover, the cosmos will welcome only those whose hearts are so wide that they can say, "The cosmos is my hometown and my fatherland." We can conclude, then, that in order to become God's true sons and daughters, we must be welcomed by individuals, by families, by nations, by the world and finally by the cosmos. That being the case, where would you most like to live? I think you would like to live in the original homeland where you were born.

Broadly speaking, "original homeland" can refer to the planet Earth within the cosmos, and our fatherland is wherever God can be found. God is the founding father of our fatherland. Our homeland is the Earth as God originally intended it to be—a place where parents, siblings and children who did not commit the fall live together. This was to be a place where black people, yellow people and white people could have lived together in harmony. Who is the parent of all these different races? There is only one parent. The God who is with us wherever we go in the universe is the Father of humankind. Thus, it would be a mistake for anyone to think that white people, black people or yellow people are the masters of America. God is the master of America.

No Racial Discrimination

Differences in skin color are nothing more than the result of our ancestors having had to adapt to different climates and environments in different parts of the globe. In areas with large amounts of snowfall, we find mainly white people living. In places such as Africa where the rays of the sun are particularly bright, we find mainly black people. Fundamentally, though, people are the same. The color of our blood is the same. Our flesh and bones look the same. We all have the capacity to love. Thus, there should be no discrimination based on race.

This is why the Unification Church has been working through the International Holy Blessing ceremonies to create unity and harmony among the races. In accordance with the natural principles of universal love and equality for all people, we have performed many inter-racial marriages. When a black person and a white person marry, it is like the North Pole and the South Pole coming together in unity. When a yellow person and a black person marry and have children, both parents contribute their good attributes and their descendants are better as a result.

Where there is love, there can be no strife. Each of us comes from a different home-town and fatherland. Yet we can all agree that the world of God's true love is the homeland of faith, peace and unity.

Nothing is more important in the human world than true love, true life and true lin-eage. True love leads to true life and true lineage. True love cannot be fulfilled unless it results in a true lineage. Further, love without true life is false love. True life is conceived within the context of true love and true lineage. Thus, true love, true life and true lineage open the way to eternal life. God's ideal for creation is for each to become true individuals and pass on true love, true life and true lineage to our descendants.

Except a Man Be Born Again

God is the ideal being and the master of eternal true love, eternal true life and eternal true lineage. Those who resemble God become His true sons and daughters living in the Kingdom of Heaven. Why do men and women get married? They do so to link together the past, present and future in the tradition of true lineage that I have described.

Before the fall, Adam and Eve could relate to God freely and directly, but this was not after the fall. Likewise, because of the fall, Cain and Abel, the children of Adam and Eve, could not inherit God's blood lineage. They inherited Satan's lineage instead. This is why Jesus said in John 3:3, "... except a man be born again, he cannot see the kingdom of God."

People need to know that they have inherited a false life through a false lineage, which originated in a false love relationship. God feels pain and sorrow when He sees the promis-cuous sex and homosexuality that are so prevalent in our world today. When they realize that they have inherited the position of the enemy of love, enemy of life and enemy of lin-eage, people will be filled with shame. God's nature, though, is to love the sons and daugh-ters of His enemy even more than His own children. He has invested Himself completely without expecting any return, and He will continue this process until He has restored all the children who were taken from Him. This is God's providence of salvation.

For God to bring a fallen human being back to life, He must provide a life force even more powerful than that of our false life. How pitiful God is, tormented by the misery of each baby brought into this world through the false seed resulting from the fall! Such children have multiplied to the point that now there are six billion fallen human beings in the world.

Human beings are created to pass through three stages of life: in the mother's womb, on Earth, and in the spirit world after death. The planet Earth, where the physical body lives, is similar to the mother's womb. In the same way that a fetus grows by receiving nutrition through its mother's womb, we grow on Earth by eating food taken from the creation. That is why we should love the Earth as our mother.

In the spirit world, light as bright as the sun shines continuously. If a person were in space somewhere in the solar system, the sun would shine on him continuously. That is the way it is in the spirit world. The light of love in the spirit world is constant and unchanging. Love does not change, whether it is day or night, at the North Pole or South Pole. The spirit world is the world of love filled with the true love of God. The spirit world is also like a storehouse in which the fruits of our hard work on Earth are stored. Our life in the spirit world will reflect our accomplishments on Earth.

Grafting into Jesus

During the course of God's providence of restoration, Jesus was the only one born with true life directly connected to God's true lineage. Accordingly, no one among fallen humanity has ever entered the direct dominion of God's love, either on Earth or in the spirit world. That is why God has been alone, leading a lonely and sorrowful existence. Hence, the world is a place where people and all of nature are often sad.

God has been searching for one person whom He could trust—one man who could purify the fallen lineage of humanity and transform it into true life. That man is the Messiah who inherits God's true love and brings liberation to all humankind. The Old Testament Age after Adam's fall is the history of the people chosen to receive the Messiah. God's will was for Jesus to come as the Messiah through the chosen people of Israel, for all people to be grafted on to Jesus' family, and for this to be expanded to encompass the world. However, due to the disbelief of his contemporaries, Jesus died on the cross, leaving this process as an ideal to be accomplished at the time of the Second Advent.

Thus the returning Lord must stand in the position of the True Parents of humankind and recover the position embodying God's true love. He must fulfill the position of the Parents of Heaven and Earth and bring God's providence of salvation for all humankind to completion. The Messiah must begin by forming a family that attends God more gloriously and with greater filial piety than that of the family that Adam and Eve would have formed had they not fallen. The Messiah is the head of the family that represents the core of the ideal for a new humanity. It must begin by linking to the lineage of true love through the life of true love. He must expand and complete the Kingdom on Earth and in Heaven by connecting blessed families together.

Therefore, as the True Parents of all humankind, the coming Messiah should renounce the love of the fallen satanic world and fallen human ways. He must establish the path and tradition of a perfected man and woman, perfected family, clan, people, nation, world and cosmos linked to God's true love. All humankind must receive the new blessing through the love of the True Parents and inherit the new family lineage. Humanity must understand that there is no way to do this except through true love. This is how the hellish world of Satan's dominion can be supplanted and overcome.

Thus, all humankind must go through an eight-stage process of restoration to recover their position as God's sons and daughters. Everyone must restore the eight stages of the womb, infant, sibling, engagement, husband-wife, parent, grandparent, and finally reach the status of king and queen. We should understand that we were born with the ultimate purpose to become princes and princesses who inherit everything in the Kingdom of Heaven.

Ladies and gentlemen, it was originally intended that each man would meet a woman as his wife to become a king, and that each woman would meet a man to become a queen. As a prince and princess of Heaven, they would inherit everything in Heaven. To restore the Kingdom of Heaven, every person must start at the bottom of hell, and work his or her way up through the eight-stage indemnity process until unity is established at every stage. This is possible only through the Blessing of the True Parents, who come as the Messiah.

More Investment, More Growth

Therefore, "blessed couples" should become "plus couples" who contribute for the sake of others in the world. To become completely reborn, we should practice absolute faith, absolute love and absolute obedience centering on God. I have personally practiced this throughout my life.

When God created the universe, He acted with absolute faith. God created us to be His absolute partners of love. Absolute obedience means that we invest ourselves completely, to the extent that we give up all self-centeredness. Furthermore, one totally forgets about the investment that one makes and invests all over again. Such a process continues until one reaches a zero point without any concept of one's own self. Since God poured out all of His faith, what is left is zero; since He poured out all of His love, what is left is zero; since He poured out all of His obedience, what is left is zero. Nevertheless, Heaven's true love is such that the more it is invested, the more it grows. We must come to resemble God in this way.

Even if our love is rejected, we should continue to love even more. Even if we invested everything that we have, we should continue to invest until we can make our enemy voluntarily surrender. Our Heavenly Father walked such a path, and the Parents of Heaven and Earth walked such a path.

The person who invests love continuously without expecting a direct return becomes a central being, the one who inherits everything, and the person of greatest filial piety. In a family of ten people, including a grandmother and grandfather, the one who lives most for the sake of others will be the central person. The same principle applies with respect to patriots in the nation or to saints in the world. The more one invests without expecting a direct return, the higher one can ascend as a patriot, a saint, and a divine son or daughter of God.

Since the beginning of human history, God has surpassed all other beings in living for the sake of others. He has continuously invested Himself without expecting direct return. And because He will continue to do so for eternity, He can be the king and ancestor of all those who live for the sake of others.

The Results of Loving One's Enemy

The reason the Unification Church that I lead could become a worldwide religious group in such a short time is that its members have worked hard according to this principle. When I reflect upon my life totally committed for the sake of humankind, I can testify that it truly has been the focus of opposition from billions of evil, satanic forces in both the invisible and visible worlds, as well as from numerous religious leaders and many governments. Yet because I lived for their sake, I eventually came to stand as their center.

As I lived for those who opposed me because of their inability to understand the truth, and as I invested myself for their children, and lived for the sake of governments that persecuted me, they eventually came to respect me. From this, we can learn God's strategy in contrast to that of Satan. God's strategy is to take the blow and initial loss, then regain everything in the end. Satan often is the first to strike, but he loses in the end.

Under this principle, I Blessed many millions of young couples from all continents in International Holy Blessing Ceremonies, as a means to save all humankind and establish one world under the one God. When the West and the East come together as one, the greatest cultural conflict in the world will be overcome. When an American and a German marry each other and become husband and wife, then perfect harmony will be created between these two nations, even though they were once enemies.

Furthermore, I gave the Blessing even to those now living in the spirit world. In order for the Kingdom of Heaven to be realized on Earth, the cosmic realms of the spirit world must also be liberated, and only the True Parents on the Earth can do that. As false parents, the first human ancestors, Adam and Eve, sowed sinful seeds. The Messiah should liberate humankind both on Earth and in the spirit world, by coming as the True Parents.

International Blessing Ceremonies

Even God, although omniscient and all-powerful, cannot by Himself untangle the problems brought about by the wrongful blood lineage of humankind. If God could have accomplished this alone, He would have saved His children a long time ago. Indeed, He would not have allowed the fall to occur in the first place. However, God is a God of Principle. This means He cannot interfere in the responsibility given to human beings. Accordingly, the returning Messiah who comes as True Parents should give rebirth through true love to humankind, whose blood lineage was defiled by the original sin.

When viewed from this perspective, the International Blessing Ceremonies are not conducted simply to bring young men and women together as husbands and wives. In fact, they are holy ceremonies in which people are reborn as God's true children through the original seed of life from God. The principle is that restoration requires indemnity, and we have passed through the stages of individual indemnity, family indemnity, tribal indemnity, people's indemnity, national indemnity, worldwide indemnity and universal indemnity. Now, finally, we have arrived at the time of liberation for both the spirit world and the physical world.

The world is divided into tens of thousands of ethnic groups. Relationships between parents and children, husbands and wives, and brothers and sisters have been divided. Even the religious world has been divided into the four great cultural spheres of Christianity, Buddhism, Islam and Confucianism. However, we have now entered the age of cosmic unification by entering the Age of the Realm of the Fourth Adam, passing the Old Testament Age, the New Testament Age, and even the Completed Testament Age, which is the era of completion.

In other words, we no longer live in an age dominated by nationalism, or even in an age of globalism. These have already passed. National purpose and global concerns still exist, of course, but we now live in an age when the universe is to be united with the one God. Moreover, by becoming the hometown of Blessed families, the planet Earth will become one with the spirit world. Then, the Kingdom of Heaven will come about on Earth and in the realm of eternal life.

The House of True Love

Ladies and gentlemen, with the arrival of a new millennium at midnight on New Year's Eve, I proclaimed a message for the new year titled, "The Cosmic Expansion of True Love Is the Completion of the New Millennium Kingdom." By "cosmic expansion of true love," I mean that Heaven and Earth should become a "house" of true love. The new millennium must be a time in which we complete the building of God's Kingdom throughout the world.

The cosmos originated from God, so families, tribes, peoples, nations and the world must work to complete a house of love that stands in a position of reciprocal relationship with God. They each can do this by each establishing their own house of love according to the principle formula and by becoming one with each other. The nation must be a house of love where all families can enter, and the cosmos must be a house of love that embraces the world. Here, the family of true love is particularly important, because it becomes the core of the cosmos, which is our enormous house in the Kingdom of Heaven.

Within the family, the husband must be the house of love for his wife and the wife must be the house of love for her husband. The parents must be the house of love for their children, and the children must be the house of love for their parents. God's Kingdom is the place where the ideal of true freedom blossoms, and where humanity's hopes are fulfilled. It is a place inhabited by true families that are the products of true love, true life and true lineage. It marks the beginning of the millennial kingdom overflowing with eternal true love and true happiness.

I have promoted true family values because the family formed by a union between a true man and true woman where God can dwell is the center of the cosmic realm where Heaven and Earth can rest. This is the reason the Garden of Eden mentioned in the Bible must be realized on Earth.

One Cosmos under God

The new millennium is the time to complete the 6,000-year history of the providence for the salvation of humanity and build the original Heavenly Kingdom centered on the ideal of creation. It is the Completed Testament Age, when the promises of the Old and the New Testaments are to be fulfilled. This means there will come a new Heaven and new Earth, where "God shall wipe away all the tears from their eyes, and there shall be no more death." (Rev. 21:4) It signifies a time of unconditional true love, when all people will be able to drink the water of life that is as clear as crystal.

It will be a time when the spirit world and physical world will be open to each other, and God's Kingdom is established. The direct dominion of the living God is to begin through restored elder-sonship, parentship and kingship, opening a new era of God's transcendence, imminence, abundance and sovereignty.

As I have mentioned, the planet Earth is the hometown of all humankind, and the spirit world is the eternal fatherland where all humanity will eventually arrive. Finally, the time has come for the global family ideal to be realized on the planet Earth centered on the Heavenly Parent, moving us beyond "One Nation under God" to "One Cosmos under God." Therefore, I request first that you understand that the fundamental relationship between God and humanity is that of parent and child. On that foundation, I ask you to take an active role to transform the "cosmos," that is, the spirit world and the physical world, into "our hometown and fatherland."

Once again, I thank all of you distinguished American leaders for your presence here. I would like to conclude by expressing God's desire that the people of the world, of all colors and races, will come to live as true brothers and sisters and build a new millennial kingdom of love, peace, freedom and righteousness. I believe that God prepared America for this very time, to help lead the world into this new era.

May God's blessing be with you and your nation.

Thank you.

Everybody Wants True Love

Reverend Sun Myung Moon, President, Family Federation for World Peace
True Family Values Awards Banquet, Chicago Westin Hotel, November 20, 1999

Respected religious leaders, I am truly grateful that so many of you have taken time out of your busy schedules to gather here for the Fourth True Family Values Ministry Awards Banquet.

We see today that people in all fields of society are doing their best to prepare for the new millennium in a variety of ways according to what they believe is right. In my opinion, however, a sober and serious examination of human life reveals that understanding the will of God, who is our eternal True Parent, is the most pressing task we face at this time, just forty days before the new millennium.

Over the past fifty years, I have communicated the Word of God in public settings nearly 7,000 times. My followers have published many of these speeches in a series of over three hundred volumes. Tens of thousands of families around the world are reading from these volumes daily.

From this vast content, I would like to share with you a sermon given to the 360 million newly blessed couples, delivered in New York on March 14, 1999. Through reading this together with you prominent religious leaders from greater Chicago, I hope we can realize that we are responsible to build the ideal world by building the ideal families that God has wanted to see for so long.

The Way of Love

Dear Ladies and Gentlemen: What is the most important thing, that which we need more than anything else? It is not money, power or knowledge. It is true love. True love is more precious than life itself and more important to us than air or water.

Why is true love so precious and important? It is because it is the means by which we can meet God. Just as human beings desire to meet God, God also wants to meet true human beings because of love. The love by which God can see, touch and share with men and women at the same time, is the love by which men and women love each other. If anything other than love were to be recognized as the most valuable thing in the universe, men and women would fight each other to try to claim it for themselves. Once we realize that love is the highest value, however, we can strive to live for each other and become one with each other, sharing the happiness of possessing love together.

Everyone desires love. Love is the only thing that can satisfy all human desires. It is humankind's, and God's, unfailing attraction to love that makes God's providence of salvation possible.

Fundamentally, love belongs to God. Yet even God cannot possess love all by Himself. Love requires a mutual relationship. A man by himself or a woman by herself cannot experience love. Women exist for the sake of men's love and men exist for the sake of women's love. Regardless of external appearance, in our heart each of us desires a mate with whom we can give and receive the highest level of love.

When we examine the universe, we see that all beings exist in pairs relating to one another as subject and object. In the mineral world, we observe the relationship of plus and minus. In the plant world, the animal world and the world of human beings, we see the relationship between masculine and feminine. This is because God created the universe in order to fulfill the expression of love. All beings desire the experience of true love through a mutual relationship. Love is the one power in the universe that absolutely no one can possess by himself. Once we have a partner, however, love gives us the power to share the entire universe. Likewise, a husband and wife need children in order to experience the profound joy of parental love.

Why Honor One's Spouse

Thus, we can say that God created human beings and the universe as His reciprocal partners in order to bring about true love. All types of love—including love of children, love of siblings, love of husband and wife, and love of parents—come about through the unity of subject and object partners. When two partners become one in true love, it is impossible to separate them. If for any reason separation occurs, true love is destroyed. Therefore, in true love there is no concept of divorce.

When a man feels love, the feeling is not generated on its own. The feeling awakens in his heart because of a particular woman. Likewise, the fire of love is kindled in the heart of a woman not by herself alone but by the man she loves. In other words, our love belongs to our partner. Thus, we should honor our partner's love as being even more precious than our love. Each person should be grateful to his or her spouse, and should live his life for the sake of the other. This basic reasoning will make it possible for the 360 million blessed couples to live together eternally. When husbands and wives live for each other, respect each other, and become completely one through true love, it will be possible for the fallen lineage of Satan to be rooted out completely.

True love comes through both horizontal and vertical reciprocal relationships. A horizontal relationship of true love is gradually elevated in a vertical direction until it eventually reaches the pinnacle. This pinnacle is the position of the "King and Queen of True Love." In this position, everything is synthesized, everything is embraced, everything is crystallized into love, and everything blooms. This is why all beings in the universe want to be transformed in love and live in the midst of love. We are born for the sake of love, live for the sake of love, and finally die for the sake of love.

The Creation Wants Love

Not only people but all beings desire true love. This is why human beings, as the highest beings in creation, should embrace and love the masterpieces of God's creation, and teach creation how to love. All creation is longing to receive and experience God's love through men and women who have become one with God at the pinnacle of true love. It is a shame that we have not yet realized this degree of love.

All beings exist at a certain level in mutual attraction with another. At the same time, all beings want to be absorbed into higher levels of love. Thus, minerals want to be absorbed into plants, plants want to be absorbed into animals, and finally all of creation wants to be absorbed into human beings. Through this process they ultimately reach the position where they can experience the essence of true love, which is the love that is nearest to God—the origin of love. God created everything with an intrinsic nature to provide value to a higher level. For example, creatures such as eels, and worms which fish like to eat also provide ingredients for natural medicines for humans. Creatures on a higher level are meant to consume beings on a lower level. Without this process, the universe could not exist.

Darwin's theory regarding the survival of the fittest needs to be reexamined in the context of this logic of love. Even ants and microorganisms want true love so much that they will die to become part of an entity of greater love. Because of this principle, human beings, created as the highest partners of God's love, can consume all creatures. We can enjoy everything we desire, on one condition: that we do so with a heart that represents the love of God, the Creator.

God's ideal was for one couple, Adam and Eve, centering on true love, to become the seed from which all the world's families, clans, nations and, finally, the multitudinous citizenry of the Kingdom of Heaven would be descended. Citizens of the Kingdom of Heaven can be created only in accordance with God's tradition of true love.

The view I'm sharing is very different from the theories of Charles Darwin. Yet it is through this perspective, and not Darwin's theories, that we will achieve a world of peace. This is because my words witness to the fundamental principles of creation.

Darwin proposed in his theory of evolution that species evolve through a process of natural selection based on random mutations. Such a theory implies that there is no fundamental meaning, order or goal in the development of the natural world. Today scientists and others debate the theory of evolution vs. the creation theory. The word "creation" acknowledges the existence of God the Creator and that there is purpose embodied in God's act of creation. Each subject and object partner unites to achieve a higher purpose.

Together with Darwinism, communist theory, based on materialism, also lacks the element of purpose. God's creation embodies the purpose of true love, whereas Communism posits only struggle and destruction. Thus, it is destined eventually to disappear.

Have Only One Partner

In all creation, the most precious entities are human beings—men and women. Furthermore, the most precious part of the human body is not the nose, the eyes, the hands, or even the brain. It is the sexual organs, the main organs of love. Everything in the universe can be recreated through the sexual parts.

Most living things—whether plants or animals—multiply through sex. The most precious and outstanding family begins with a husband and wife who are one with each other. Our love organs are the main sanctuary of life, occupying a position of incredible value where blood lineage and history are connected.

God's fundamental principle is to create through male and female. For a man and woman to share absolute love, however, they should have only one partner. We must not have two or more partners, but only one, eternally. There is absolutely only one man for each woman and one woman for each man. That is why God did not create two Adams or two Eves. Tragically, in the world today we see children who have had as many as ten stepfathers. How false and degraded love has become!

When men and women uphold and preserve chastity, they are protecting the universe. The discipline of love between men and women is the foundation of the universe. We must not abuse our love as if we were animals. Our love can only have one owner. The word "true" in "true love" does not allow for the possibility of more than one partner. There can be only one. This is an absolute law.

Not just anyone can say they have "true love." Only God can really love with true love, and only God absolutely owns true love. God's true life, God's true lineage, and God's true conscience emerge from true love. In this way, the most fundamental essence of God is true love.

Therefore, to connect with true love, we must first relate with God. A child might say, "My mother and father don't fight and we live well," but that doesn't necessarily mean that this is a family of true love. A young man and woman may say, "We are so much in love that we could die," but that doesn't mean this love is true love. If God is not present, then it is not true love. True love always centers on God. To become God's son or daughter, we first need to connect with God's love, life and lineage.

God Harvests True Love

Power, knowledge, money and military might cannot ensure that a person will be welcome in the world of true love. Everyone wants true love, but such love is only possible when we live for others. We need to sacrifice for and serve our partner. Everyone avoids a person who relates to others with the mindset that says, "You should live for me." This kind of selfish individualism is Satan's strategy, purpose and tool. The result can only be hell. We must live for the whole. If a person lives for others, sacrificing himself or herself and serving the whole, then everyone and everything will come to love him.

We are created as God's children. As we grow in love, relating to brothers and sisters, becoming husbands and wives, giving birth and raising children, God is present each step of the way, harvesting true love. God observes and guides us as we develop, and He becomes the owner of love at each stage. In this sense, it can be said that human beings, through whom God comes to own all love, are more precious to God than He is to Himself. In the same way, we attach a thousand times more value to the person we love than to ourselves.

God invests Himself for those He loves and then forgets this investment. Then He invests again. He invests Himself one hundred percent and then forgets one hundred percent. That is why He can continue to invest.

In the same way, a wife who wants her husband to be a success invests herself in her husband and then forgets this investment. By investing herself and forgetting, she enables him to achieve his full potential in life. When we as partners continue to invest in each other and forget, the level of our love is elevated, and we will ultimately find ourselves connected to God. This is how we can fulfill our parent-child relationship with God and have eternal life.

Everyone wants to go to heaven, but those who have the attitude that "Everyone should live for me," will not get there. True love begins with embracing and living for the sake of all God's masterpieces of creation. The way we can reach heaven is to live for all humankind and ultimately for God.

During our lives, each of us should have at least three experiences in which we dedicate our lives to someone or to some higher purpose. This is how we can indemnify the selfish acts involved in the fall of Adam's family, the crucifixion of Jesus, and in the persecution directed against the family of the Lord of the Second Advent.

And then even after we figuratively pass through death and resurrection three times, we should not ask for God's praise but instead pledge our lives to Him even more. This is how we can meet God. When such people populate the world, this will be the Kingdom of Heaven on Earth. This is the path that I am teaching, and this is the kind of world that I am building.

Family: The Form of Love

Children are the fruit of the love of the mother and father. We need to understand that children embody their parents' love, life and lineage. Little children often say "This is mine," but parents are the origin of everything that children refer to as their own. Parents are the root and the trunk. Without parents, we would all be orphans. We cannot live if we break the ladder of love that connects us to our parents. We are the sons and daughters of God, the parent who is the origin of true love. Parents are the highest masters of love for children.

The parent-child relationship is vertical, and the husband-wife relationship is horizontal. The lines of these two relationships should cross at right angles. The relationship among siblings forms a third dimension, a front-to-back axis. When all are equidistant from the center, and are freely circulating in love, their relationships form a sphere. That is why all beings existing in love, and the universe as a whole, are spherical. The entire universe achieves balance centering on these relationships.

All love is united and achieves a peaceful dynamic harmony in the central point of this sphere of love relationships. This center, where all these relationships intersect, is where God resides. If we picture this three-dimensionally, we see that God is the ultimate origin of love, life, lineage and conscience. In the God-centered family, vertical and horizontal loves are united as one. Such a family will multiply to become a clan, society, nation, world and cosmos of love. The fundamental center, though, is always the one God.

If Adam and Eve had not fallen, they would have realized the ideal of the God-centered family and become the True Parents of humankind. As True Parents, Adam and Eve would have provided a model of true husband-wife love and true parental love. God's providence of salvation has been a providence of restoration. Throughout human history, God has been working to restore True Parents who can establish, as a model for all humanity, the ideal of true love, true life and true lineage.

The Tradition of Marriage

After Adam and Eve had children, who would have overseen the marriage of these children? Adam and Eve, as their parents, would have done this. We need to look seriously at the deficiency of parental involvement in their children's marriages in today's society.

The Unification Church, which has True Parents, is standing in the position of parents to give the marriage blessing to all the peoples of the world. These marriages transcend not only racial, religious and ethnic differences. By knowing True Parents and being engrafted to them, even saints and evil persons are being blessed in marriage with each other. The True Parents reject evil love, evil life and evil lineage, but they do not cast out Cain, who murdered Abel. Everyone, including Cain, receives the same blessing.

In the ocean, there is a point during the changing of the tides when the forces of outgoing and incoming tide are at equilibrium. There is a similar turning point in the Providence of Salvation in the balance between the forces of good and evil. By blessing good and evil people at the time of this turning point, Satan can be expelled completely.

The human fall occurred when there was an error in the Garden of Eden that involved marriage. Now, the True Parents have corrected that error and are Blessing marriages with the original foundation restored. By clearing up the problems created by Adam and Eve as fallen parents, the True Parents are eradicating hell and giving the blessing to tens of billions of ancestors in the spirit world. In other words, by centering on true love and restoring the original true love, true life and true lineage, we restore the true parent-child relationship.

In this way, we come to perfect the master of love, the model of true love in the eight stages of God's ideal of creation. That is, we establish the eternal, unchanging true love tradition by going through life in the womb, infancy, life as brother and sister, as an adolescent, which is the engagement period, as newlyweds enjoying conjugal love, as parents, as true parents and finally as true king and true queen. Upon this foundation, we can perfect the true love model, the parent-child relationship.

True Family Values

In God, love, life and lineage are absolute, unique, unchanging and eternal. Humankind is to inherit this as the model of true love. This model will not change through tens of thousands of generations. Centering on true love, we can reach oneness between parent and child, between husband and wife, and between brothers and sisters.

A father becomes the owner or master of love through his son. A husband becomes the owner of love through his wife. An elder brother becomes the owner of love through his younger brother. On the other hand, children without parents, women without husbands and elder brothers without younger brothers cannot find the central position, the position of the owner of love.

In order to become the owner of true love, we must serve and honor our parents. By doing so, we will attain mind-body unity as individuals, conjugal unity as husband and wife, fraternal unity as brother and sister, and world peace as nations. In this way, we can perfect the realms of love defined in the eight-stage ideal model.

Again, the ideal family and ideal nation are the places where all of us—as parents, children, couples, brothers and sisters, and nations—want to establish ownership of the eight-stage model, centering on true love. From there, eternal world peace will emerge, the Kingdom of God on Earth will dawn, and the Kingdom of God in Heaven will blossom.

Beginning from the year 2000, in every corner of the globe, countless Blessed families united with the Parents of Heaven and Earth will initiate a new family revolution and world-wide moral revolution, centering on true love. God is longing to see the eternal ideal Kingdom of God built on Earth as well as in Heaven. Let us join in this holy task. I pray that all of you will become the owners of God's true love. May God's blessing be abundant upon you and your family.

Thank you very much.

The Course of Life for the Princes and Princesses of God

Reverend Sun Myung Moon, President, Family Federation for World Peace
This speech was delivered on March 12, 2000 at the Olympic Main Stadium,
Seoul. It was first given on March 9 in Taegu, as part of a speaking tour of Korea.

Distinguished international guests, fellow compatriots, ladies and gentlemen—you who are gathered here for the sake of the unification of North and South! The new millennium we have just begun is the time for us to wipe away the residue of division and struggle left over from the previous century, and realize the ideal of one family, one global village of peace and unity. I pray that the blessings of the new millennium will be with each and every one of your families represented here today.

First, allow me to thank you for coming from around the world to congratulate me on my 80th birthday. However, more than anything, I would like to offer this glory to God; He has been my constant companion and protector, and it is He who has made this day possible.

Looking back on my life, at no time have things ever been calm and quiet. I have walked a path of suffering side by side with the people of this nation, a nation whose history has seen much strife and tribulation, nestled as it is, here, in the midst of the world's great powers. Ever since I suddenly came into contact with the will of Heaven while in prayer at the age of fifteen, I have devoted my life and given all my thought and all my effort to bringing about the fulfillment of the will of God. I have found that the root cause of human suffering is that the ancestors of humankind fell into a state of spiritual ignorance due to corruption, and that this resulted in the relationship between them and God being cut off.

The result of this fall is that humankind became ignorant of such basic issues as the facts relating to God, life and the universe. Throughout my life, I have spoken in public more than 10,000 times, and presented a true world-view, life-view and history-view based on the principles of Godism. This content in its entirety has been translated into twelve different languages and published in a series of some 300 volumes. It was not brought to light as a result of some kind of comprehensive literary research or academic study, but is comprised of the fundamental and essential answers I found while freely traversing both the visible and the invisible worlds.

Today I would like to gratefully take this opportunity and talk about a fundamental solution to the problem of the unification of the Korean peninsula—the unification that is our nation's most cherished desire as well as the last issue in the Cold War that awaits settlement. I would like to entitle this talk *"The Course of Life for the Princes and Princesses of God."*

Distinguished guests! What nation are you citizens of? Many of you are citizens of Korea. For you, Korea is your fatherland, your homeland, isn't it? Then where is God's homeland? At present, God has no homeland. Where is it that all the nations of the world have their origin? Do they have their origin in God, or is their origin somewhere else? The historical origin of the world's nations is a big question.

The Historical Roots of Conflict

All the nations of this world were cut up or formed as the results of conflicts. In many instances, where two nations are divided by a border, that border is one of intensely painful resentment. We all know the historical reality that the fiercest fights and the most blood has been shed over adjacent borders, rather than, for example, the borders of a third or fourth nation. This shows us that the walls between two nations, and the walls between two ethnic groups, are the highest kind of walls. Conflicts' are not always fought by traveling thousands of miles. From ancient times, wars have been fought over the borders between two neighboring countries. This is the reason why even you yourselves will find that you get into fights with those neighbors and people closest to you. Why? Because humankind has fallen. It is a result of the human fall that fights tend to start with one's neighbors.

What is the fall? It is the discordance between God and humankind. It is the eruption of conflict between God and Satan, and eruption of conflict between humankind and Satan. We can therefore conclude that the fact that there have been numerous nations in the history of this small planet is evidence that there have also been numerous conflicts.

Where will the nations that were formed from this go? All nations seek a world of peace, but are they capable of getting there? This question points to the one common task that remains before all humankind today. Looking at things this way we can understand that if we continue to harbor enmity towards a neighboring nation under the justification that it is our historical enemy, we can never achieve a world of peace. No matter how much we long for our ideal, and say how much we are marching towards our ideal, it is impossible to reach that goal. In order to negate the motives that give impetus to these conflicts, and wipe away our malformed dysfunctional history, we need a movement that will lead the way and embody the substantial content of the opposite direction.

Distinguished guests! You yourselves are exactly the same as a people without a nation. Did you have a nation in the past? Has there ever, in history been the kind of nation we could call "our nation"? We have never had that kind of nation. Is that because nobody ever tried to build such a nation? No. The reason we have never had such a nation is that the people who desired it in history were never in a position to build it. They couldn't build such a nation because the ages in which they lived didn't allow a fully developed and complete standard by which that nation could be built. The homeland that we need to build is not a nation with a certain history and tradition that exists in the world today. Rather, it is of a dimension essentially different from the nations that exist in today's world.

If we want to inherit this different kind of nation, we must become a people who possess the ideological consciousness that makes it possible. If an absolute creator exists, that ideology and thought would need to be one with the Creator's ideology and thought. If the absolute being wanted a nation, he would want a nation where the citizens can be completely united centering on the national sovereignty. We need to have that kind of national character, and we need to have that kind of national pattern.

Sovereignty

In order to form a nation, there needs to be sovereignty, a people, and a national soil. God's nation is the same. The parents represent the sovereignty, the sons and daughters represent the people, and the country represents the national soil. This is an unbreakable rule; none of these elements can be omitted. What, then, is the most precious thing? It is living for the sake of the nation and the world. As long as you live like that, you cannot fall into ruin. That place where ruin cannot occur is the ultimate point.

A person who dies while working for the sake of that nation will become a citizen of that nation even though he or she dies. He or she will remain as long as that nation exists. For a nation to be formed, you need a national soil, a people and sovereignty.

What, then, is sovereignty? It is a connection and link with God, the root and origin. The people who govern the nation must create their connection with God and then govern. In this way, the rulers need to be one with the people. They need to become one with the people, and think that everything that they possess exists not for their own sake, but for the sake of the nation. If they can do this, then that nation will prosper.

From this point of view, when you consider the issue of realizing the kingdom of heaven on earth, who is the owner of heaven? Who is the ruler? Without a doubt, God is the ruler. Then who are the people? The people are all the people of the world. And where is the national soil? The national soil is the planet Earth. Who, then, does the Kingdom of Heaven on Earth resemble? It resembles "me." If you look at any one nation, what does it consist of? Sovereignty, people and national soil. This is the same as a single human being.

Who did you say that the Kingdom of Heaven on Earth resembles? "Me." It resembles "me." Individuals such as myself are gathered together, and that forms the nation. Just as I have my own mind, the nation has to have sovereignty. Just as I have a personal identity, there must be a national people. And just as humans interact with the created universe, so a nation must have the national soil.

Within this basic principle, the people control the national soil, and the sovereignty governs the people. That is how things are. This national soil, people and sovereignty are the three essential elements that form a nation. If you look at humans, the basic principle is that our mind controls our body, and our body controls nature. Because of this principle, if you look at the entire world, the definitive conclusion is Ch'eon Ji In (Heaven, earth, humankind—Translator's Note: a concept also found in Neo-confucianism that says these are the three essential elements of the cosmos). What did you say that Heaven is? It is the same as the human mind, so it is also the same as the sovereignty. Humankind is the nation's citizenry, and the earth is the created world. In the end, whom does the nation resemble? It all resembles my individual self.

No matter how big the society, no matter how great the nation, they need to resemble a human being. That is because God likes those things that resemble His image. Then what is the thing that humans like the most? Things that resemble their own image. So what does an ideal nation need to resemble? It has to resemble a human being, and it has to resembles *Ch'eon Ji In (heaven, earth, humankind)*.

In Unification Church terminology, the homeland doesn't refer to a single nation like the Republic of Korea, but to a global nation. Actually, the word "global" is a word used in this corrupted, fallen world, and I really don't like it. The ism or teaching that seeks for this homeland is called *Ch'eonju jui ("Cosmos-ism")*.

That homeland is not the Republic of Korea. God does not want the Republic of Korea, nor the United States, nor the communist nations. That homeland is the fatherland that God wants, and because this is so, we have to create the culture of that new fatherland, and create the history of that new fatherland. We have to define a new standard so that we are able to establish a new and ideal homeland. So we have to change our way of life, because that world is completely different from the world we have now. The words and language are different. Do the people of the world today understand the meaning of such important phrases as *"the realm of dominion of the Principle," "reciprocal base," "common base," and "providence for the foundation of restoration"*? This means that the language is different. If and when the nation that the Unification Church desires is established, we will have to take down and dismantle the Unification Church signboard. And when the world that the Unification Church desires is realized, then we will have to dismantle the nation the Unification Church established. We have to be able to discard the kind of religion that exists only for the sake of the culture and character of the people in the Republic of Korea. Only a religion that exists for the sake of the world will be able to continue into the future.

Love of Others and the Will of God

Distinguished guests, ladies and gentlemen! What do you suppose a person who seeks to inherit the Will of God must advocate? There is absolutely no way he or she could tell the people of this world to just go the way they enjoy. In fact, he or she would have to tell the people of this world to go in the opposite direction. A saying that expresses this fact is the motto "Love your enemies with the heart of true love." "Love your enemies!" These words can turn around our false history; they are the same as an anchor, and an anchor chain for a ship being blown before a howling typhoon. However, throughout the history of the providence of restoration, there has been no one who has actually practiced these words. If there were people who could love their enemies, we would have to raise them up to the world stage using some form of systematic organization. Because this is the logical conclusion, each of you needs to understand that God actually has to present this kind of movement to the world, and that the religious movements that have arisen in history are a reflection of this.

Who is the person God has been able to love the most in history? It is Jesus. Jesus presented a new direction for this conflict-ridden world. High walls are created between oppressor nations and oppressed nations, such as between Rome and Israel, by them viewing each other as enemies. Jesus' philosophy is that these walls need to be demolished. Jesus thought, You in Rome want to conquer me by force, but I will conquer you in the opposite way—with love. That is why he even sought blessing for his enemies when he was hanging on the cross.

We need to recognize that when Jesus said of the Roman soldiers, "Forgive them for they know not what they do," he was expressing this kind of amazing philosophy. Because Jesus made this plea, he became a model and archetype for all nations of the world to transcend the way they see each other as enemies, and also a model for transcending the borders between any two nations.

Jesus knew that individual enemies were not the only enemies. He knew that family enemies, clan enemies, ethnic enemies, national enemies and global enemies surrounded him on all four sides. This means that there are many enemies awaiting those who want to follow his path. It also means that if you go the family path, there are family enemies waiting, and if you go the clan path, there are clan enemies waiting. You can expect fierce battles, but you must love those enemies whenever you encounter them. If you possess this kind of spirit, someday victory can be yours.

From what point will God's ideal nation be realized? Where will the restoration of the fatherland take place? It starts from the individuals who live by the philosophy to love their enemies. Therefore, as long as God exists, there is no way Christianity can avoid becoming a global religion, because Christianity offers a movement to break down national borders with love, to transcend all environments and cultural barriers, and to embrace even one's enemies. If you plant beans, you get beans, because kidney beans come from kidney bean seeds, and red flowers bloom from red flower seeds. In the same way, if you plant a satanic seed, a seed of paying back your enemies, you will get a tree of evil—a tree of paying back enemies. But if you plant the seeds of goodness, the seeds of loving your enemies, you will get a tree of goodness, a tree of love for the enemies. This is just a natural principle.

Where did I say God's fatherland starts from? By what path does it come? It comes by the path of loving one's enemies. It comes by the path of leaving behind a tradition of loving the individual's enemies, loving the family's enemies, loving the clan enemies, loving the national and global enemies. You all need to understand that God's homeland cannot appear except by this path.

Take a look. Because the U.S. opposed me, because the State Department opposed me, because the Congress opposed me, some day I will get a certificate of recognition, saying that I was victorious in the Congress, that I was victorious in the State Department, that I was victorious in the United States. Even in the State Department, which opposes me, I am winning friends. In the Congress I am winning many friends. It has already been determined that the victory will come to me in the end.

And even if I don't have any such friends, I have the conviction that I can overcome any kind of opposition and lead the way to victory. The more anyone opposes me, the greater will become my love for my enemy, so I do not need to be worried about greater opposition.

The laws of nature dictate that if low pressure occurs in one place, high pressure will appear somewhere else. If one area develops high pressure, another area develops low pressure. When a high place like the U.S. State Department opposes me, then it will have to surrender to me if I develop a field of low pressure, just as a high-pressure area is absorbed by a low-pressure area in nature.

Even though I had to take all sorts of abuse in the past, when I didn't fight and instead loved them, they became my friends in the end. Families that became friends appeared, clans that became friends appeared, nations that became friends appeared.

If a nation composed of people who have this spirit of loving one's enemies appears, that nation can be the ideal that God desires, and it can be the ideal that all humankind can enter. You have to understand this. There is nothing good-looking about me, Reverend Moon. Isn't that true? You people here don't say so, but the people of the world think I am pretty ugly. But God loves me the best. Even if the world thinks that I am a terrible fellow, God recognizes me, so I can go at this world from a bold and open position.

There is nothing you can't say if in your heart you love your enemies. Why? If God says the man is a good-looking chap, then he is a good-looking chap. If He says he's a really cool fellow, he's a really cool fellow. If He says that the man is brave and fierce, then he's brave and fierce. So if I think like that .I take it as glory and I can take on the world in confidence. When I get intoxicated like this and work alone, do you know what happens? Young people, young men and women, a family of all races, an entire people appears, a people that God can truly take joy in appears, and the dawning of God's homeland becomes possible.

Because Jesus said we must love our enemies, that means we have to love even the worst person. Even if the most handsome man is matched with the ugliest woman, he has to love her even more than he loves his enemies. When it comes to loving the enemies in this world, that kind of person is a candidate for marching ahead and carrying the flag of the highest prince. Just think how noble that kind of person is. That kind of person can just leap over national and racial boundaries.

You have to understand that on the day you live with nothing but a loving heart, all the walls will be brought down, the history of the providence of restoration will be shortened, and Heaven will come that much closer. My philosophy is simple. There is nothing I haven't done. I've been a farmer, I've been a laborer; I've tried everything that can be done. I've been a fisherman and caught tuna. Living my whole life in this way, I thought I was all alone, but when I turned around, I found British people following me, Americans following me; people from all over the world are following me. Even if I tell them to get lost and kick them away with my feet and try to go over there, they still come back and follow me. I go this way, I go that way, but they still follow me. That is how it is, so no matter how much you might research the Unification Church, there is always something more to learn.

The Way to Go

Distinguished guests, ladies and gentlemen! What is the path we need to go now? No matter what kind of clan you establish, if the sovereignty of Satan's nation continues to exist, all of you are nationless people. Is this your country here? You do not have a country! No matter what kind of clan you have, if the sovereignty is not a sovereignty centered on Heaven, the clan can be killed off just like that. Isn't that so? Therefore, we have to go out in search of the nation that Heaven can welcome with open arms. What it means when we talk about the realm of the first Israel in this world today is that the land needs to become one that all of Heaven can welcome, a land that the individual can welcome, that the family can welcome, that the clan, race and church can welcome. But whether you look at this issue centering on the Unification Church or centering on Christianity or centering on the Republic of Korea, did they ever stand in a position that can be welcomed by the whole? They couldn't. The direction is different. Different. The path that the Republic of Korea is going is external. Isn't that so? It is moving ahead, not centered on God, but centered on the worldly society. This country has no mainstream thought or philosophy.

Thus if we can't connect this nation with God centering on a national mainstream ideology to form a new national concept equipped with new three-dimensional, or two-dimensional content, and take that national concept and stand forth with it as the ideal content centering on the nations of the world today, we will be unable to see the dawning of the fatherland.

The liberation that we have today is the first liberation. Now, in the Unification Church, we need a second liberation. The Republic of Korea also needs a second liberation. Here, the people and the nation may achieve their full desire if the Republic of Korea undergoes the second liberation, but the Unification Church also needs a third liberation. That is how things will go. The Republic of Korea obtained its current national pattern by the first liberation, but now the time has come when it requires a second liberation. North and South need to be united.

What kind of country is that nation? That country has to be a nation whose people have passed through a suffering course in its history, whose national character is capable of becoming one with the principles of restoration through indemnity, and which has inherited a historical tradition. What kind of country does it need to be? It needs to be a nation completely unified. So, how does today's Republic of Korea need to act if it wants to become this kind of nation?

To rise to the standard of that nation, it needs to unite the north and the south. Just like the divided northern dynasty of Israel and southern dynasty of Judah, the divided north and south of Korea need to be united into one. Just like Cain and Abel nations, North and South were divided, and if these are not united, a single victorious Israelite nation will not appear.

Unification Based on a New Global-Level Ideology

Therefore, in this country, centering on the Republic of Korea, how must North Korea and South Korea be united? They cannot be united without a new global-level ideology. The Unification Ideology being advocated by the Unification Church has been prepared for this very time. Do you understand? Now we are in the position where we have to do two things. We have to form a united people that no nation of the world can match, and then we have to create a united nation with a single faith so indomitable that no other religion in the world can match it. Centering on this kind of ideology, North and South need to become a unified nation. Without doing that, God's nation, namely the sovereignty of a heavenly nation that we can proudly proclaim to all the world, will not be born. You have to understand that this is the priority purpose on earth for us today.

If we cannot establish the fatherland, we will not be able to have a nation that can center on God and surpass the nations of Satan's world. Without that nation, we cannot chastise the satanic nations of the world. We cannot push them away. We cannot do that with just a religion, with the Unification Church. A nation has to establish its direction centering on the ideology of Unificationism, and then move forward. You have to understand that this issue still remains to be resolved.

From this point of view, if we see that the Unification Church is like Judaism in Korea today, the thought of the Unification Church will become the mainstream thought of Korea, just as Judaism was the spiritual pillar of the Israelite nation. In the future, there will be a time when it must become the national religion. That is what some people say. Even members of the National Assembly say that. If the thought of the Unification Church becomes the state religion, the communist party won't be a problem. Ladies and Gentlemen! The people who live for the sake of Heaven today are the emmisaries of Heaven sent into the satanic world. Each one may be different, a milsa may be big or small, broad or thin, high or low, but the lifestyle he maintains must not deviate from the lifestyle of an emissary because there is always a life and death danger involved. He is always placed in a situation where even the smallest mistake can determine the issue of eternal life.

Therefore, if the emissary's spirit of working for the homeland, the homeland that can support and protect eternal life, if his spirit is not hundreds of times stronger than the environment, he cannot live as a secret emissary. He needs to be able to ignore his current situation by thinking of how all the people of the world will rejoice when all resentments have been erased. He has to look to the fatherland's glory, and while creating a new history, think that all his efforts will be known and recognized on the one day when he sees the birth of the fatherland. Without having that kind of mind, he can't carry out an emissary's secret mission. In other words, his mind must contain a hope for the dawning of a homeland that is a thousand times, ten thousand times greater than his hopes for the present reality, in order to be able to overcome all resentments and execute his secret mission.

Even if by some chance he was to die in an unfortunate accident while executing his responsibility, God can dispatch, to the same place, a new emissary, who can carry out that responsibility. Even though he has already passed on, people will appear who can become his friends and become his allies. Because he dies in a situation where he can be a model, people who can become his allies will remain even though he becomes a sacrifice himself. As long as these people remain, God can send someone in his place on that foundation. However, if he does not die in that situation, no matter what he may have achieved, it all stops there.

The One-Time-Only Mission

From this viewpoint, what kind of stance do you all need to take in meeting this new age? Your conviction for the dawning of the fatherland must be burning in your chest more passionately than any other thing. In other words, you have to feel pride in becoming a flag bearer who builds the fatherland that God has longed for for 6,000 years. You have to take pride in bearing the responsibility for this incredible pioneering mission as a member of the crack troops standing on the front line. Many people in the past hoped for this mission, but even so, it was not available to them. You have to have a very solemn sense of responsibility for having taken on this one-time-only privileged mission.

Thus every aspect of your lifestyle, eating and sleeping, coming and going, has to be for the establishment of the fatherland. How much do you think God has been longing for you to step forward and cheerfully, coolly declare you will carry out this mission as an emissary dispatched especially by God Himself? Up until now, God has been mercilessly pushed aside, heartlessly chased away. He needs to establish the will of Heaven, the will He has never been able to unfold, a will that presents its entire contents on the basis of a complete national foundation, the will that can establish the fatherland. He has never been able to fulfill this will even once.

Now, however, it is possible to establish this homeland. That fatherland has a sovereignty, it has a national soil, and it has a people. Moreover, there is the lineage of a homogenous ethnic group connected to that land, and there is a history that no other people can possess. For this kind of fatherland, we need to carry out our mission as emissaries. If you can fulfill that mission at an earlier date by your own volition, then the foundation for the dawning of the homeland will be that much closer, thanks to you. Paying the price of sweat and tears today creates the foundation for meeting the dawn of the fatherland that much earlier. Thinking of this fact, you people have to go out into the world with the determination to live and carry out an emissary's secret mission. If not, we will be unable to receive the unprecedented blessing and fortune that God is preparing to give to us.

We have to construct Heaven on this earth. What I am saying and, surely it makes sense is that, to be able to hold up our heads before our Father, we have to found that nation on this earth, become one with the center of that nation, and in that heavenly nation, live and then die with the standard that Heaven hopes for.

But then, do you people have a nation? When you think about the fact that you don't, then you can't die even if you want to. Where are you going to go if you die? If you go, how are you going to avoid that sense of shame or self-consciousness, that feeling of pain? The length of my life is limited, and to get everything done in that period, how busy do you think I am? On top of that, the evil satanic environment opposes us; don't you think our enemies will try to block our way? To pierce through that and forge ahead, we cannot avoid the unsettled lifestyle of a special emissary.

My comings and goings are all for the sake of building that nation. I take up the mission to become a true founding citizen for the sake of the dawn of the homeland. I receive my orders as Heaven's emissary and enter the evil world of today to carry out my work accordingly. We have to live with these thoughts uppermost in our minds.

Without doing this, you will not be able to establish your dignity and authority as citizens of the nation that is on its way here. Do you people want to make a difference individually? Do you want to influence things as a family? Nationally? Globally? How do you want to make a difference? You'd like to make a difference globally, wouldn't you? However, if you want to rise to the global stage, you will not be able to do that on your own. You'll need a nation. But what I'm asking you is, where is your nation?

The Lifestyle of Love

Right. So we eat, we sleep for the sake of that nation, day and night for the cause of the nation. Do you understand that you have to live your life pledging before heaven and earth that this is the reason you were born? When you're sleeping, you've got to imagine that you have gathered together all the beds of millions of people around the world and that you are sleeping there positioned on the top. Even when you look at a dinner table, you've got to have that kind of thought. Wherever you go, you've got to think that you are not sitting alone, but that all the different races of the world are gathered together, piled up together, and that you have climbed to the top and are sitting on your seat there. The sons of heaven have to do things like that.

Each of you needs to understand that the lifestyle of the sons and daughters of Heaven requires being able to stand in the position to surpass the authority of the satanic world, that it requires attaining and preserving the position of glory in the course of life. If God wants to love His sons and daughters, that is the kind of son and daughter He should love, don't you think? If He loves sons and daughters who don't even match up to Satan, He can't really preserve the dignity of His fatherhood, can he? I want you all to keep that conviction in mind and make a new determination that you will live every single day of your life marching ahead, hand in hand with the entire world. The way I see it, that is where the foundation for the unification battlefront is determined.

"Even though I live in the midst of the satanic world, I am a secret agent for Heaven. I am the one ambassador of Heaven." That is what you have to think. The emmisary's route of contact allows him to contact the king of the nation directly. Other people do not know his situation, but he has to push ahead with the conviction that he is living with the mission and authority of an emissary. Each of you has to understand this clearly. Even the nation's king is waiting for a report from the emissary. In the same way, when we are fulfilling this mission on the earth, God is waiting for our reports and also for our requests.

So if I, in this position, send a request that I urgently need such and such, don't you think He would brave troubles and difficulties from every sector to send it to me? In the same way, if you have that conviction and recognize that you are sons and daughters of God's special glory and ask, saying "This is what I need, Father; please make it possible," then it will come into being. In this way, you can discover God as He lives, and see God working.

You have to be able to do this to become a leader. If there are sick people, you can heal them; if you encounter difficulty, God can help you directly. You have to learn about many things through this kind of lifestyle so that you can have confidence, have convictions, and breakthrough everything that lies across your path.

Respected guests! Where is it that we have to go? Our purpose is not to go and find the individual. Also, our current purpose is not to go and find the family. The path we have to go is to find the nation. Do you understand? Whether you're a dad or a mom or someone's child, we have no choice but to do this. But then, the followers of the Unification Church today, the families who have been blessed, the people in the clan realm, they all say "Whew! The nation? The church? Don't ask me!" If it gets like this, then everyone's a failure; they've flunked out. That is how it is from the Principle view.

Establish God's Nation

You seek for the nation until the day you die, and give all your heartfelt effort. Only then can the day arrive when you can celebrate and sing a triumphant song for the dawning of the Heavenly nation. Among all of Jesus' teachings, this is what you need to know. The direction being shown to you is not two, just one. If he were to say "Let's go," you'd have to go. That is how it is. Isn't that how it is? So if he says, "Sacrifice being with your husband, sacrifice being with your family and go," do you have to go or not? You don't do that for the sake of the Unification Church, but you have to be able to do that for the sake of the nation. Then things will work out.

Currently in North Korea, they are tearing up the family registers and re-doing them. Do you know why? Satan's world does things first. You have to be able to step forward and put aside your husband, or wife, or parents, or children, or whatever, for the sake of the nation. Otherwise, we cannot establish the nation that embodies our hope. When that nation is established, you will find your parents at the same time. If you can't establish that nation, you will have to sit and see your parents shedding their blood, your wife shedding her blood, your children spilling their blood. Is there anything worse than that kind of situation? Therefore, before we find that nation, we cannot love our wives, we cannot love our parents, we cannot love our children. This is the path that Christians need to go, the path that the Unification Church needs to go.

The Person Who Can Build God's Country

You people have to become those who can deny themselves and live for the nation and that purpose. No matter what kind of difficult situation you find yourselves in, you have to be people who can fight and overcome it thinking of the hope that your father has in you. You have to become that kind of person before you can be called God's true son or daughter. So, what kind of person, then, can build God's country? Someone who can deny himself or herself and value Heaven with an aching heart. Someone who denies his or herself and lives for the sake of society and the people, for the sake of the nation and the world is the person who can build God's country.

Going one step further, the person who lives for the sake of Heaven, even if it means he or she must deny the nation and the world, is someone who can build the kingdom of Heaven. Also, the person who feels sorrow for society and the nation, for the world, and even for Heaven, rather than sorrow for himself or herself, no matter what kind of sorrowful and painful situation he or she encounters, that is the person who can build God's country.

Not only that, you people have to be able to be victorious, and not lose in the fight with Satan during the course of establishing God's nation and God's purpose. Then, starting from the individual, you have to connect the family, society, people, nation and world into one. In other words, you have to be able to fight and win over Satan in whatever situation you are put. If you go into society, you have to be able to fight and win over Satan in any environment that society presents you with. If you go out into the nation, you have to be able to step forward, take responsibility for that nation's worst problem, then fight and win over the satanic forces involved.

Do you think that Satan, who has given God such a hard time for six thousand years, is just going to quietly say "Oh boy, I've had it. I think I'll just give up," then lower his eyes and crawl away? Don't you yourselves value even a wash cloth too much to just throw it away? Before you throw it out, you'll probably turn it over, inspect it, even smell it. What I'm saying is that Satan will not just give up and go away like that. That is why he keeps on putting up such a stubborn fight.

Never Give Up

We have to fit with and match up with the center. Even Reverend Moon of the Unification Church will be snapped off and ejected the day he deviates from the center. If the direction isn't right, then you can't make any progress. The reason we seek that nation is to be able to find the world, and the reason we seek the world is for the sake of the spiritual world. And after we do that, then what do we do next? Then we attend Heavenly Father and return to the earth, grab our spot, our position, and with all nations of the world attending God, we march forward to dedicate and return the glory of victory to Him. To do everything right, you have to understand that the mission of the Unification Church connotes us having to fight this kind of fight.

We have to step forward in bare feet to build the eternal homeland. Can we save this nation just with what is left over after we have had our fill? Can you spend your energy worrying about what you wear, when you'll eat, what you get around on? We have to clear the path and pioneer the way with our bare feet and bare hands. This is the kind of thing that we do in the Unification Church.

Are you folk *"Yeongsa"* (brave courageous people, heroes) who should stand forward for the establishment of the homeland, or are you failures who bring it down? When we say *yeongsa*, we mean someone who can represent the nation and carry out the things that other people cannot do. We do not use the word hero for the people who do what just anyone can do. Such people are called soldiers. If, when his comrades can't do the job and they have to retreat, a person can carry the job out, then he's what we call a hero. The Chinese character *Yeong* means swift, quick. He's got to run faster than anyone else, even to be able to dodge bullets. We can't use the word hero for someone who does what anyone else can do.

Who is the vanguard general who must be the hero to lead and pioneer the building of that nation? Then, where is the site where that nation can be established? If you want to establish a nation, you need a sovereignty, a citizenry and a national soil. Then looking at the problem centering on the Kingdom of Heaven, what is the site that can fulfill the role of the national soil? That can only be the church's assets, right?

And next, who can become the people, the citizens of the Kingdom of Heaven? That is the congregation, the followers. Then who are the rulers? You are. You are the representatives of the village head, the representatives of the tribal head, the representatives of the county head and the representatives of the provincial governor. People, have you become the subjects, the centers? When someone comes along with a bomb from the satanic world, you have to be the first to jump forward. Do you understand? Do you feel like you can do that? And if you have money, even if it is only a penny, you use it to develop the church. You use it to expand the domain of the nation and to bring the people together. A church director is the representative of the ruler. He or she represents the village chief; he or she represents a father and mother. You have to leave this kind of tradition and philosophy behind. We ourselves don't have anything.

How We Approach the Future

What kind of nation are we going to establish here, in Korea? When we start distributing goods and communicating, will we set up a communist nation, or will we just keep going along as the Republic of Korea is today or will we pursue a new nation that is neither of these? Considering things in light of this issue, one comes to feel that our time is getting closer and closer. If you people are the Unificationists who have to keep things steady and take responsibility for this, how much of a sense of responsibility do you feel for this situation, and to what extent are you determined to sacrifice for this? That is what I'm asking. Do you have the confidence? We will need to go up north, cross over the 38th parallel and prepare our bases in the towns and counties of the North's five provinces. You have to think about who is going be responsible for Jeongju up in the North, now, at this time, when we are short of people. Have you become the people who invest their heartfelt effort and who can prepare for 10 or 20 years to take responsibility, centering on the Jeongju area, and if it can't be done, then when you die leave instructions telling your descendants to study hard, train hard and prepare hard, and to become those who take responsibility in place of Heaven at Jeongju? That is what I have been thinking about and preparing for up to this day.

Thinking of this, is it okay for young fellows to just return to their hometowns, smiling and chuckling and taking their wives and their kids along? Is that okay or not? Even though you may die, you've got to establish that nation, and then go; even though you may die, you've got to build that nation for your children, and then go. What I'm telling you is that, for things to go right, you've got to make a new determination. You have to determine, "I will go up there to the Russian and Manchurian frontiers and lock horns with the Communist Party. In the midst of gunshots day and night, I'll take responsibility; I'll be a sentry for the national border detachment. Even if my country doesn't know, no matter if no one knows, even if I have to give my life in the process, my heart, my loyalty for that nation will not change." That sort of thing is exactly what we need.

God Trusts Each One of Us

It doesn't matter if the world ignores you. Everything will come out when you get to the spirit world. That is how the universe is set up. When we think of this, to get things right, you have to understand that we are short of people. Do you understand? You've got to understand that we need more people. Even if some guy is a scraggly old scarecrow, we can set him up with a trumpet, or construct some robots and have them go around the North blowing on trumpets. That is what I wish I could do, and that is what God wants to do. It just doesn't make sense to say that you can't teach the Principle when you were born as a man, with a mouth and everything, with feelings, and with a mind and body of 20 or 30 years of age as well. You have to study hard, even if you get so little sleep your eyeballs fester and pop. You have to prepare even if you are so hungry that you are nothing but skin and bones. Then, that haggard, skinny bag of bones will be thoroughly capable of receiving the love of Heaven. What I'm saying is, don't you think that God can place all His expectations in that one man, even if he's slender and frail?

Jesus also came to establish the nation. If there is no homeland, then the situation is pitiful. Religious people were always in a pitiful situation because they had no fatherland. If the judgment is to come, the individual, family, clan, people, nation and world must conform to an unchanging standard, and then the judgment will be made on the basis of that standard. The fatherland is the final hope. The people, the clan, the family and the individual are all included within the fatherland.

Has this three thousand li (the length of the Korean peninsula) become the Fatherland? It hasn't, and we need to settle this matter. Every one of us needs to work with single-minded devotion to create the homeland that God wants, that Jesus and the Holy Spirit want.

What is goodness? Goodness is sacrificing the individual for the family, the family for the clan, the clan for the dawning of the fatherland. All are sacrificed for the restoration of the homeland, and when the homeland is restored, all become loyal and beloved patriots. If loyal devotion is offered on the national level, and the national standard is established, then you are also recognized as having built the foundation for the family and the clan as well. The standard of the path is absolute loyal devotion for the sake of God. Then all the contents of that course are given recognition.

How do we have to do it to get things right? Jesus said, "Father, not as I will, but as thou wilt." Here, "as I will" is the will of the world, and "as thou wilt" is the will of God. You Unification Church members, what did you do? Have you established the path of loyal patriots, and stepped forward with the actual results in hand? You have to fulfill the path of filial children, then present yourselves with actual accomplishments and be resolved to fight on the individual, family, clan, national and world level. Jesus came with the mission of an offering. You all have to build the ethnic foundation while moving ahead, fighting on the global level. You've got to be endowed with a value tantamount to that of the Messiah. While the leader is pioneering the global path, the ones who are being led, you, have to prepare the ethnic-group path. Many people died while hoping for the path to liberation. They passed away believing that it would be achieved one day, although they did not know when.

The Unificationists have prepared the foundation from the individual, through the ethnic, up to the national level. Now we have to mobilize all humankind and all the nations of the world. We have to seek the day when our fatherland is established, the day of freedom, peace and happiness, and we have to go, even though the path is difficult. That is the way that I look at things, and that is the standard that God has. Jesus died while pursuing this standard. We have to suffer and forge ahead on the course to establish the homeland. We have to take responsibility for Korea. We've got to relieve the built-up pain and anguish that surrounds the fact that Jesus' homeland, the Holy Spirit's homeland, the homeland of all the saints and 'sages, God's own homeland has never been built. If we do not, there is no way we can hold up our heads.

Living for the Homeland

What we have to do is to find our homeland. In order to find it, we've got to live for it. If we do not live for our homeland, we will not be able to build it. Then how do we have to live to be living for our homeland? Set the world up as your own homeland, and live for the sake of the world. That kind of person is capable of creating the homeland. Eating and sleeping, walking the street, your entire lifestyle and all your actions have to be for the sake of creating the homeland.

That is why we fight, prepared even to receive a sword attack from the communists in broad daylight. When the people of Korea can't do the job, we are the ones that have to. Because the people can't go, we have to go. And to be able to do that, we have to love our fatherland more than anyone else. What I'm saying is, if you have to eat, eat for the sake of the homeland. When you get married and go to join your husband, do it for the homeland. It is for the sake of our homeland. Now there is a group that can rise up when I give the word, a group that can mobilize when I present the direction, but I am not the sort of man to be satisfied with that. I will continue to develop and build a foundation that will guarantee the dawning of the homeland, even if I have to sacrifice the Unification Church foundation to do it. There has to be a religious order, a people and a nation that can receive the family that has been established as the central goal of the six-thousand-year providence.

The foundation to receive God was prepared, and God's desire was for it all to be connected at once, but it was broken and shattered, so the task of rebinding things together remains. To connect everything together again, we have to stand on the front line and run. When it gets dark and it is time to go to bed, you have to fall asleep together with that nation of hope. What I'm saying is that, of course, that nation does not exist at present, but as a member of its citizenry, go to sleep for the sake of that nation, and when you wake up, wake up as one of the workers who is working to create that nation. And all your senses, such as seeing, hearing and touching, don't use them if you can't do it thinking of that nation.

Until that day arrives, don't even die. Until that day arrives, time is pressing. To accomplish this task, we have to overcome every kind of suffering and adversity.

If you have something to do, you have to get it done, even if it means staying up late at night. I mean, when the only way to establish the homeland is to add the weight of a sacrificial lamb based on the providential timeline, and you have the responsibility to use this time to add, even if it is one more drop, the sacrificial lamb of tears and sweat, do you think it is okay for you to just sleep comfortably and wake up stretching and yawning? In fact, as soon as you wake, you've got to bow down and pray: "Father, I cannot help but feel the sorrow of this lonely, miserable path that I am walking, the path towards the foundation for our victorious nation, the path towards that place of rest and security that you have always looked for, the path towards that nation through which you can make that world you have always wanted to realize. Father, if I feel this kind of sorrow, how must You and heaven feel?"

You can't just lie down because you're tired, and even if you die, you've got to die for the sake of that nation. Because of that, when I get old and start to feel tired, the one thing I want to be able to leave behind me is the last will and testament that "I did all I could for the sake of Heaven. I did everything I could for the sake of that nation."

Jesus said, "Worry not what you will wear or what you will eat, for the Gentiles seek after these. Seek ye first the Kingdom of God, and His righteousness." As this shows, the central stream of thought in the Bible is that Kingdom (nation). This philosophy says to seek that nation. It doesn't say to seek your own happiness. If you are born as a citizen of that nation and you have a husband, then that husband represents that nation, so you have to love that nation before you can love your husband. And the wife also represents the nation; you have to love that nation before you can love your wife. You have to be able to ask him or her to die in the position of being able to say, "I did everything I could; there is nothing more I could have done." It is no good if you die having said, "I should have tried such and such." For this reason, we are busy even though we may have accomplished a certain amount. If you walk the path a ways, you've got to go even further. When everyone else is sleeping, we have to go one step further. "Hey Satan's world! Take it easy! You guys, rest the whole day if you like! We are going off to seek that nation." That is what you've got to say.

Fellow compatriots, all you who seek the unification of the North and South! I especially want to say the mission of you women is to restore the young men and women, and the mission of the students is to be true children through true education. That is what you must do.

And beyond that, mothers and children have to unite to set the standard, so that the husbands can be raised and educated to be the true sons of Heaven. Then following True Parents, and attending God, restore the ideal of the Kingdom of Heaven on Earth.

In closing, let me say that it is my fervent hope that these words today will help you build a nationwide movement to bring closer the day when North and South meet in true love.

May God's blessing be with both you and your families.

Thank you.

The Way of the World and the United Nations

The Way to World Peace

Reverend Sun Myung Moon, President, Federation for World Peace
This address was given on August 28, 1991 at the founding of the Federation for
World Peace, Seoul, Korea.

Since the Fall of Man, there has been a constant war going on within each of us. It is an inevitable consequence of the Fall of Man that there is continuous struggle and conflict going on within ourselves between mind and body, and between the desire for good and the desire for evil. Originally, mind and body were to be one. The human mind represents God's mind. The human body is to be a container to accommodate the mind, or a dwelling place for the mind. Separation came between these two when the Fall of Man occurred.

The Fall of Man resulted in the body coming under the domain of Satan or selfishness. Thus, tragically, the human body has become the servant of Satan.

On the other hand, the human conscience is the agent of God in the individual person. One's conscience does not exist for the benefit of oneself. The conscience is planted by God for the sake of righteousness. Yet the body rebels against this conscience. The body only seeks after comforts and tends to act selfishly, going after carnal desires. The conscience in turn is trying to chastise the body and direct it toward the mind. This is why there is always inevitable conflict and struggle within one's self.

This is the reason why the traditional religions of the world unanimously teach the principle of chastisement of the body through fasting, prayer, and other disciplines—doing things the body does not want to do. Religion is the training ground where the desire of the body is suppressed, thus bringing the body to the will of the mind. For this reason religion has been the instrument of God to bring men back into the original ideal.

However, no one is capable of dominating his body without uniting with God within himself. The only power that enables the mind to have dominion over the body is that generated by the unity of the mind with God's truth and love. Mind is subject and body is object. God's love and truth have the power to bring them together into one harmonious person. This is what religion defines as a man of perfection or a holy man.

God-centered men and women in perfection are called men and women of goodness. These good men and women may receive God's blessing of marriage and be united into a couple, husband and wife. This will be the beginning of one ideal family of man on the face of the earth. This model family is what God wanted to have as a building block of the society, nation and world.

The Family Is the Foundation of Peace

There is an old saying in the Orient that "once peace is dwelling in the family, everything goes right." A happy and harmonious family is a family of peace and the foundation of the heavenly kingdom.

The dynamic of the family is true love. You must love God first, then love your husband or wife and your children with truly pure and sacrificial love. This is the manifestation of true love. God created love as the supreme force in the universe. He has created nothing greater in this universe. True love is supreme.

True love, of course, originates from God. God has invested everything, every ounce of His energy, for the creation of all things and mankind. Love is the only thing that when invested fully, returns fully; When you invest true love, no attrition occurs. It will multiply and prosper. Investing 100 percent of true love will yield or return 120 percent. One might think that those who practice true love would become poor and miserable, yet the end result is to the contrary. By practicing true love you will acquire prosperity and eternal life.

This kind of family of true love becomes the foundation for creating a society, nation and world. That society, nation and world shall be true-love centered, and shall become ideal and peaceful. There you will find understanding instead of misunderstanding. You will find unity instead of division. You will find unselfishness instead of selfishness. This is the society, nation and world where sacrifices and good service become the dominant virtues. The realization of the ideal of God is the way to achieve the ideal of true peace in the world.

The Ideal of True Parents for True World Peace

When the Bible says that God sought to create human beings in "His own image," this means that the invisible God wanted to manifest Himself into a visible form. In other words, men and women would have become the personifications of God.

If the first man and woman had realized the ideal of God, they would have become the first visible form of God and created the first family of man. Then God-centered children and grandchildren would have formed an ideal society, nation and world. In this case the invisible God would become the vertical True Parents of man centering upon true love, and the first man and woman, Adam and Eve, would have become the horizontal True Parents of mankind centering upon that same true love. Centered upon these True Parents of man, humanity would have become one family eternally fulfilling true brotherhood.

However, the fall of Adam and Eve meant that humanity lost True Parents. That day we became orphans. Brothers turned into enemies. As a result, nations came to develop antagonistic relationships rather than friendly ones. Accusations abound on every level.

In the final fulfillment of human history, therefore, God's work of restoration is the restoration of True Parents first, liberating humanity from its orphan status. Today this is the central dispensational work of God—to bestow True Parents upon mankind, to create the original family of man centering on God and true love.

Ladies and gentlemen, today's creation of the Federation for World Peace must be different from that of the League of Nations and the United Nations. Most important is that we must found this organization upon the true ideal and philosophy of lasting peace as well as the ideal of True Parents. In the final analysis, peace in God and with God is the newest level of awakening. This is therefore a refreshing new beginning toward the attainment of peace. The exclusion of God from human efforts for peace is the core reason for their failure. Therefore, we shall make God the center of this movement and the dynamics of this movement will be true love.

Historical Gathering

For men and women who are fervently longing for world peace, today's gathering is an historic gathering. There are many presidents and former presidents here today, as well as prominent religious leaders and leaders from every walk of life. This is truly a rare and extraordinary assembly. Furthermore, there are leaders from the East bloc and the West bloc. Until recently, those leaders were mired in the Cold War and locked in a chilling confrontation. In this auditorium, however, there is no East or West. Everyone is gathered together in one spirit of cooperation and reconciliation.

On November 9, 1989 the Berlin Wall finally came tumbling down. Ever since that event we have been living in a different world. The world is moving quickly toward reformation, change, mutual understanding and friendship. Everyone today feels acutely that the mood of the world is opening up to the blossoming opportunity of peace.

If you agree that the principles I have expounded are the fundamental criteria for peace, then true peace is reachable and achievable. The industrialized North must reach out to help liberate the South from pervasive impoverishment. The developed nations must reach out with a helping hand toward the developing countries and the new democracies. Each nation's attitude must be changed from a selfish one to an unselfish one. That in itself is a revolution. Nations can do this when leaders see from the position of parents. The most unselfish and sacrificial love of all is the love of parents. From that perspective one can see that all nations are brother and sister nations. Then a fresh new vision emerges and new opportunities will open up in front of us.

It has already been announced that in September North Korea and South Korea together will become member nations of the United Nations. This is another significant positive development toward the achievement of world peace. Then the number of member nations of the UN will reach 163. What should be the priority of those 163 countries in the days to come?

The time of colonialism is over, where the powerful nations exploited the weakest ones. The law of the jungle and Herbert Spencer's "survival of the fittest" do not apply in our world. The age of the superpower arms race that drove the world and humanity into fear and uncertainty has also passed; humanity ought to be liberated from the devastating threat of nuclear arms. What time is it in God's timetable? This is the time that the Holy Scriptures refer to as that of "beating our swords into plowshares."

This is the time for developing mutual trust based on a high moral standard. It is a time when all the member nations of the United Nations, in a relationship of mutual respect and love, should jointly declare one final war against our common enemies—the scourges of hunger, ignorance, disease and crime.

This is in God's plan. From this time on, the definition of "my country" will expand. Although everyone has their home country where their family lives, in a larger sense, the world now becomes "my country" because it is where God, my Father, and my brothers and sisters—all the people of the world—live.

From this point of view, advanced nations should seek to share high technology with the developing nations and new democracies. To do otherwise would be a moral crime. Things that are good and beneficial must be shared among all nations. When a new discovery is made, it should benefit all nations. If something is good for humanity and the world, we must fulfill it, transcendent of national boundaries. For a long time, I have been fighting for equal opportunity in the use of high technology by all developing nations.

A Century of Peace

Ladies and gentlemen, your coming to this place is not an accident. Nothing happens by accident. I feel you are ordained to be here. You are chosen by God as champions of peace.

Within our lifetime we shall commemorate the year 2000. That year will be history's new turning point. A new era is unfolding. With the cooperation of God and man together the twenty-first century will be a century of peace. In order to make that happen we shall work tirelessly together for the next nine years. If we do, we shall be able to eliminate all obstacles that might hinder the attainment of peace.

The twenty-first century shall be a righteous century. In the twenty-first century, wealth will not be the dominating factor. Instead, the human spirit and human soul shall be dominant. The twenty-first century shall be the era of unity between God and man. It shall be the era where a new awakening will come to every man—a realization that he shall benefit himself more when he genuinely lives for the sake of others. In the twenty-first century, selfishness will decline. Life, honor and glory based on unselfishness shall be triumphant. These are the characteristics of the coming twenty-first century.

The era for peace is approaching. Even the opportunity for the Kingdom of Heaven on earth is closer. The twenty-first century shall be a hopeful and glorious century. To make this happen, the Federation for World Peace will provide the ideal and philosophy to educate the world's population. The Federation will assist spiritually, mentally and financially in the development of needy nations. The Federation will set a high moral standard and take a dynamic role in building a world of peace.

Ladies and gentlemen, you are the apostles of peace. A bright new hope as well as an exciting new future is awaiting us. Today we should fervently feel the desire to fulfill the great mission that is being bestowed upon us.

In order to achieve this sacred duty and the historic responsibility of building lasting peace, we should dedicate our lives, our fortunes and our sacred honor with total commitment. The very first item on our agenda shall be to invite God into our individual hearts, and those of our family, society, nation and world. When God is with us, who shall be against us?

Respected friends, my beloved brothers and sisters, we are called to this sacred mission—the building of world peace. Our noble march shall begin today toward that glorious future. Let us build a true world of peace together with God.

Thank you very much.

Leaders Building a World of Peace

Reverend Sun Myung Moon, President, Federation for World Peace
This address was given on August 24, 1992, to the assembled leaders attending the
World Culture and Sports Festival, Seoul, Korea.

Distinguished chairpersons of the First World Culture and Sports Festival, distinguished guests and participants from Korea and around the world:

As founder of the World Culture and Sports Festival, I would like to express my deepest gratitude to you for having gathered here in such a large number to pray for the success of this festival.

I would like to speak to you this evening on the topic, "Becoming the Leaders in Building a World of Peace." During the mid-1930s, when I was sixteen years old and the Korean peninsula was under the forced occupation of Japan, I received a special mission from Heaven through Jesus. I am seventy-two now, and in the intervening years there has not been even a single second when I did not think of God's will and His commands.

I lived my boyhood and youth under the colonial rule of imperial Japan, so I know only too well the excruciating pain and tragic circumstances suffered by the weaker and smaller nations of the world. Because I possess a certain degree of discernment into God's heart, it was with unspeakable pain and sorrow that I witnessed, first, the cruelty of the more powerful nation as it plundered the weaker nation of Korea and, later, the terrible carnage of the Second World War.

Then immediately following World War II, in a development that compounded our already difficult situation, the Korean peninsula was divided between north and south. In 1950, the Korean War broke out and Koreans found themselves in a fratricidal conflict. Various countries of the world on the left and right chose to support one or the other of the opposing sides. I witnessed this tragic history directly, and I know from my heart of hearts how much pain and sorrow has been brought to God and humanity by the loss of a world of peace.

How do you imagine God has felt since the time of creation as He had to watch while time and time again brothers set themselves against each other, with Cain, the older brother, taking the life of Abel, the younger? All wars since the beginning of human history have been, in their essence, struggles among brothers. The Bible teaches us this through its record of the murder of Abel by Cain in the family of Adam. Why do such conflicts among brothers occur over and over on the levels of family, tribe, society, nation and world?

Original Sin

The reason lies in the sin committed by Adam and Eve, the parents of Cain and Abel. Adam and Eve were the original ancestors of humankind, placed in a position to represent all the men and women who would come after them. As such, they should have brought God's ideal of creation into reality. By breaking God's commandment, however, they forfeited their position as the true parents of goodness for all of humanity who would be born after them. Instead, they became fallen parents of evil. It is this evil that is the original sin, the fundamental root of all crime and unhappiness in human society.

The original sin of the first human ancestors was that Adam and Eve broke God's commandment and engaged in an illicit sexual relationship. In this way, they formed a blood relationship with the devil, and became fallen false parents, passing on false love, false life and a false lineage to the entire human race. There is only one way for humanity to escape this world of evil and struggle, and that is to be reunited with their true parents and be reborn through them. Only when this is accomplished can the true way to cast off original sin be revealed.

After I received my calling at the age of sixteen, I spent the years searching for the answer to precisely this problem of how to bring salvation to humankind. The result of that lonely search for truth is the new expression of God's truth that we refer to today as the Unification Principle, Godism and Headwing philosophy. On August 15, 1945, the day Korea was liberated from imperial Japan, I began proclaiming this truth on the earth. Because I have proclaimed these teachings, I have had to undergo tremendous persecution and attack.

Think for a moment about the fact that I have been imprisoned as many as six times in my life. This alone is enough to tell you how harsh the attacks against me have been. The First World Culture and Sports Festival, being held during this forty-seventh year since I began proclaiming the Divine Principle, is a holy celebration. It is an occasion to let the entire world see, and to offer to God, the harvest reaped from the seeds I have sown and nurtured for the liberation of God and humanity and for the realization of a world of peace. Everything I have striven to achieve during my life has been for the purpose of confirming the fact that all people in the world are brothers and sisters before God, our common Parent. Our common ties as members of the global family centered on God transcend our differences based on race, nationality and international boundaries.

Organizations

The primary institution in which my teachings are being practiced is the Holy Spirit Association for the Unification of World Christianity, that is, the Unification Church. There is now no country in the world where the Unification Church does not exist. The Unification Church has put its roots down in all races, nationalities and countries. The International Marriage Blessing of 30,000 couples that will be held tomorrow in Seoul's Olympic Main Stadium is certain to be a testimony to the fact that humanity is one great family centered on God.

With the Unification Church as the root organization, I have founded many other organizations for projects in a wide variety of fields. These organizations are for the purpose of building a world of peace in which we, the human family, centered on God, can rejoice in our freedom, ideals and happiness. For the World Culture and Sports Festival, I have gathered the most prominent of these organizations here in Seoul. During the festival, a new unified structure will be founded to facilitate stronger mutual ties and closer cooperation among these organizations.

The International Conference on the Unity of the Sciences, the Professors World Peace Academy, the World Media Conference, the Summit Council for World Peace, the Assembly of the World's Religions, the Inter-Religious Federation for World Peace, the Women's Federation for World Peace, the international performing arts groups and International CARP will meet during this time of the International Marriage Blessing and provide forums for us to enlighten our intellects and reaffirm our determination in devoting ourselves to the cause of building a world of peace.

The International Marriage Blessing of the Unification Church, which I will be conferring during this time, is the blessing of resurrection. Through this ceremony, humanity is able to cut itself clear from original sin and recover true love, true life and true lineage of God. It is within the context of this ceremony that we can give birth to peace that enables us to realize the ideal of the great brotherhood of humanity which transcends race, nationality and international boundaries.

As the founder of these organizations and groups, I wish to reaffirm here this evening that their purpose is to bring about world peace, according to the ideal of God and humanity. They are not created for the benefit of any particular group or political faction. They do not serve the narrow interests of any particular nation or state. Rather, they exist to bring happiness, peace and freedom to God, the Creator of the universe, and to all humanity.

Family Salvation

Our movement, thus, must bring salvation to all families, all nations, all states and, finally, to the entire world. It must be a family-saving, nation-saving, world-saving movement.

Our families are being destroyed by the debasement of sexual ethics through illicit relationships and decadent lifestyles. Every nation is suffering the agony of the destruction of its moral standards and the accompanying increase in crime. There is no solution in sight to the conflicts between political factions. Poverty and ignorance continue to plague us. There is no sign that we may be nearing solutions to the world's international border disputes, to the attitudes of prejudice between religious groups, or to the conflicts between the various races and ethnic groups. World peace is under constant threat from the selfish actions of the world's countries and peoples.

Environmental pollution also is destroying our planet to the degree that we are approaching a serious crisis for the future of humankind. We may all find ourselves on a common path of destruction, unless we are able to resolve the crisis we face through a love which transcends all national boundaries and ethnic differences and encompasses all the world's people. Let me emphasize again: any successful resolution of this crisis must be based on an effort to build a unified world through a movement of true love rooted in the Divine Principle, or Godism.

In early July, I spoke in five cities around Korea at rallies held by the Women's Federation for World Peace. There, I declared that my wife, WFWP President Hak Ja Han Moon, and

I are the True Parents of all humanity. I declared that we are the Savior, the Lord of the Second Advent, the Messiah.

Why would I stand before women leaders of Korea and make such an astonishing and fearful announcement? The reason is that God has been carrying out His providence to send the Messiah as the second perfected Adam who has subjugated Satan, in order to establish a perfected Eve who will represent all women. God has done this because it was when Satan caused Eve to fall that human history came to be permeated with sin.

Also, women are the central point for the love, peace and spirit of service that protect our families, and it is the healthy family that must be the starting point in our work to build world peace. The establishment of God-centered family ethics and the education of our children lie at the innermost core of my teachings as the person who has declared for himself the responsibilities of the Messiah. The family is the holy sanctuary that must cleanse this defiled world.

House of Unification

That is the reason it was necessary that I, as the Messiah, make my declaration to women leaders gathered around President Hak Ja Han Moon, my wife, who stands in the position of perfected Eve. This declaration is an exhortation and notice to all who follow my teachings to join Mrs. Moon and me in our attendance to God on the path of sacrifice and service for the salvation of this world.

As I conclude my remarks this evening, I would like to propose, so that all of our activities for world salvation can be carried out more effectively, that we establish "The House of Unification for World Peace" as a structure for the peaceful unification of the world.

To avoid any possible misunderstanding, particularly regarding the title of this structure as rendered in the Korean language, let me state clearly that I am not proposing to create a political party. The House of Unification for World Peace that I propose is not a political party. It will not have the function commonly associated with political parties, that is, to seek the executive powers of government in a given country. It is, rather, a "house" to reinforce the concerted actions of the world's countries, and foster a unified foundation and common effort for world peace.

If we say that heaven is a symbol of man, then earth is a symbol of woman. The house is the stage on which a woman's life is played out. The mother is the center of a nest filled with love for all the members of the family. The family, with the mother at its center, is the basic unit making up the nation and the world. I use the word "House" in the title of the structure I am proposing, because this word contains the meaning of "exalting the earth, centering on the mother." It also signifies "to teach." The word "House" in this title, therefore, signifies a center for the education of women.

Through this structure, we can provide new impetus to the work of giving opportunities for meaningful exchanges and education on a God- centered vision for world peace to people of all countries and all walks of life, including political leaders, scholars, religious leaders, journalists and educators, as well as leaders of women and youth. This vision of world peace will be centered on families in which mothers, representing all women of the world, accomplish mind-body unity through love.

If you will embrace my proposal and join me in this task, then our efforts are certain to bring the world of peace which is the object of God's desire to all of humanity within the remaining eight years of the twentieth century. We who are gathered here this evening will be the leaders in opening the gates to a world of peace in the coming twenty-first century.

I pray you may have a pleasant visit during the time of the festival and that God will bestow His boundless blessings and protection upon your work.

Peace and the 21st Century— The Fundamental Principle of True Peace

Reverend Sun Myung Moon, President, Federation for World Peace
Founder's Address, March 27, 1994, at the Second Federation for World Peace
Conference

My dear President Mikhail Gorbachev, distinguished Co-Chairmen, honored heads of state and government, respected ladies and gentlemen:

To all of you I express my deep gratitude that you have been able to come here in such large numbers to take part in the Second World Peace Conference. As we enter the age of internationalization and globalization of the 21st century, we are confronted with the urgent task of overcoming a large number of difficult obstacles to world peace. I have an absolute conviction about our global problems, and it presents a solution that addresses the fundamental root of all these problems. I have dedicated my entire life to the pursuit of the Will of Heaven based on this persuasion. Please allow me to share with you a few elements of my conviction. Our world today has become evil, filled with conflict, confusion and hatred. This is true of individuals, families, societies and countries. The root cause of so much wickedness is a conflict between the mind and body of individual human beings, a conflict that started at the beginning of human history and has dragged on throughout the ages. As embodiments of discord, such individuals naturally produce families fraught with conflict, which compose countries torn by strife and a world divided by struggle. What is the result? An evil world of hell. For Heaven, it is the most abominable of all possible worlds.

The origin of this ongoing conflict lies in the relationship between two individuals, man and woman, who are themselves torn by conflict within. Therefore, the solution to our complex global difficulties lies in creating unity between mind and body and in harmonizing the relationship between man and woman. If we accomplish these two goals, we will have found the solution to the problems of the entire world. Why have mind and body come into conflict with each other? Why have man and woman not been able to establish harmony and unity? The reason is that something in our history went wrong. It is my firm conviction that the original fall took place at the dawn of human history. It was then that the mind and body of individual people became divided, and strife emerged between man and woman. The human world became evil, centered upon Satan.

The Solution to the World's Problems

The first step in solving the world's problems, then, is to find God. The second, expel the evil Satan from this world. The third would be to establish men and women who have accomplished the unity of mind and body. God expelled fallen Adam and Eve from the Garden of Eden. They had become husband and wife centering on Satan instead of God, and because they bore children while in that state, all the ancestors of humankind came to inherit the lineage of Satan. Their blood lineage was corrupted. Through adultery, the archangel who became Satan stole the intended bride of Heaven. It is a principle of Heaven that whenever a relationship of love is established (whether false love or true love), ownership becomes established from that point. According to this principle, the human ancestors came under the ownership of Satan. Originally, the mind and body were to become one, centering on God's true love. As it turned out, however, before God's true love had a chance to be perfected within the human mind, the mind became bound by false love from Satan. That enabled Satan to take root in the body. Originally the mind was to exert a positive polarity over the body, but due to the Fall the body formed another positive pole, repelling the original mind and finally coming to dominate it. For that reason, God has been working to project the power of true love into the human mind in order to bring about the absolute subjugation of the body now engulfed in false love. Only when unified through true love can mind and body return to the state where God dwells within them.

The fallen ancestors became false ancestors. This is what created the need for religion and for a Messiah. The tasks of religion and the purpose of the coming of the Messiah are to break down the hell of false love, false life and false lineage, which have given rise to false individuals, false families, false societies, false states and a false world. Religion and the Messiah must guide us back to the original world of true love, true life and true lineage. It is the world of the true parents centering on God. God, too, feels loneliness when He is alone. He created the heavens and the earth centering on a relational ideal, and his reason was to find true love. Look at the created world. You will see that it is structured in pairs: The mineral world, the plant world and the animal world are all arranged in subject-object relationships as a way of providing ideal models for true love between human beings. True love is the reason why women are born for the sake of men, and men for the sake of women. Solutions to global problems become possible only when our minds and bodies—and when men and women—come to live for the very purpose of becoming one centering upon true love. True love can be found only in a situation where a person exists for the sake of his or her relational complement. Satan's love is centered on the self, whereas God's love is centered on others. These two kinds of love are diametrically opposite. For our fallen bodies to be free from the world of Satan, we need to know absolutely that we have achieved the position of a second, visible God, that the invisible God is our ideal subject of true love and we are in the position of His absolute objects. Our minds and bodies must be united by means of the invisible God and by means of true love, and we must honor and respect our heart and conscience just as we honor and respect God Himself.

Three-Subject Thought

We can recover our "original selves" only when we submit absolutely to the commands of our conscience. God is the Parent of parents, the Teacher of teachers, and the Master of masters. This forms the basis for the "Three-Subject Thought" encompassing heaven and earth. It is only through the conscience that these three can form an absolute unity and to fulfill the Three-Subject Thought. Thus, the conscience is more important to us than our parents who gave us birth, more important than any teacher, and more important than the king of any country. Only when elevated to such a position can the conscience become an object of God's love. The conscience needs no education about right and wrong. We must give it absolute honor and obedience, just as we would honor and obey God.

There is nothing I do that my conscience does not know about; it sees everything. The conscience objects whenever the body schemes to do something wrong. Yet, because the power of fallen love was stronger than the power of the conscience at the time of the fall, the body is able to drag the mind around wherever it chooses. This kind of problem would not exist if the human conscience had achieved perfection and had formed a relationship of true love with God in the Garden of Eden.

Adam's family in the Garden of Eden was to be a family of true love, in accordance with God's ideal. God created them so they would give visible expression to every kind of invisible existence. God and man were in a subject-object relationship centering on true love. He created the two ancestral human beings, Adam and Eve, with the expectation that they would become the substantial perfection of the invisible children, invisible brother and sister, invisible husband and wife, and invisible parents that exists within God's heart. God wanted the true love of children to be perfected in substantial form; he wanted to see His objects of true love perfected as actual brothers and sisters in a family, as actual husband and wife, and then as actual parents.

True love in a father-son relationship is vertical; in a husband-wife relationship it is horizontal; in a brother-sister relationship it is on the front-and-back axis. God wanted such a spherical ideal of true love.

Unification, then, is accomplished at one central point, where there is a convergence of the upper and lower hemispheres on the vertical axis, the right and left hemispheres on the horizontal axis, and the front and back hemispheres on the third axis. This point becomes the focus of centripetal force. The Four Great Realms of the Heart--that is, the realms of love of the child, brother-sister, husband-and-wife, and parents--reach their perfection when human beings who are centered on God are married and enter their first relationships of love. This is the central place where all perfection bears fruit.

Marriage thus represents the synthesis of the virtues of heaven, earth, and humankind and the perfection of all things vertical and horizontal, left and right, and front and back. Accordingly, Adam and Eve as husband and wife, as God's most beloved substantial objects, were meant to be the second ancestors. From that position they would stand as the second creators and would inherit all of God's feelings. They would feel the joy of God in the positions of children, brother and sister, husband and wife, and parents. Their joy as the second creators would be in the experience of bearing children, by which they could experience the position of the First Creator.

From this perspective, God was the first Creator; Adam and Eve were to be the second creators; and the children of Adam and Eve were to be the third creators. The first, second, and third creators—that is, God, Adam and Eve, and the children of Adam and Eve—would have established a formal pattern, a pattern that would have been the fundamental principle that all humanity would have to follow.

From the perspective of Adam and Eve, there would be connection between upper and lower (the parent-child relationship), left and right (the husband-wife relationship), and front and back (the brother-sister relationship). It would have led them to the perfection of their family. It would have been the unified foundation of God, Adam and Eve, and their children. As people approached God, they would accomplish the unification of mind and body and the unification of man and woman, and they would form a stable foundation where peace, freedom, happiness, and hope would converge to form the basis of fundamental peace.

The Family is the Base of True Love

Through Adam and Eve's having children, God would have enabled Adam and Eve, who were the second creators and who were visible and substantial, to take part in the creation of the third creators.

Through this process, the family becomes the foundation on which the Four Great Realms of Heart can be experienced generation after generation. The family is the base where each form of true love can be brought to perfection. In this way, the family achieves the unity of God and man through love, and it serves as the starting point toward the perfection that enables us to establish true ownership in heaven and earth. This is another way of saying that the family is the origin from which we come to have children, brothers and sisters, husband or wife, and parents.

Only in such families can we find men and women who have accomplished mind-body unity. Only in such families can we find husbands and wives who have achieved the ideal unity between man and woman. Such families are the starting point for ideal parents. Here, too, we can see the creation of a model, centering upon true love, for the perfection of children, brothers and sisters, husband and wife, and parents.

It was God's ideal of creation that this model be expanded not just to the level of country and world but to the entire cosmos. Thus, it is possible for a country to become a family-patterned unit that is larger than the family; the world can become a family-patterned unit that is larger than a country; and the cosmos can become a family-patterned unit larger than the world.

Accordingly, the models for children, brothers and sisters, husbands and wives, and parents—which represent the Four Great Realms of Heart—can be found in the family, in the nation, in the world and in the cosmos. Since a country contains many families and is larger than a family, families should exist for the sake of the country. Since the world contains many countries, countries should exist for the sake of other countries in the world. In similar fashion, the world must exist for the sake of the larger cosmos. Finally, the cosmos must exist for the sake of God, who is the greatest and most central existence.

Thus, when the standard of the perfected Four Great Realms of Heart within the family is projected onto higher and higher levels, the ideal of unity becomes a reality. On that basis, we can enter a cosmos of peace, happiness, and freedom. This is why we need, and need vitally, the unity of mind and body and family harmony centering on man and woman.

God Is Also Growing

God, too, you see, has been growing. He created Adam and Eve as the substantiation of the inner son and daughter, brother and sister, husband and wife, and father and mother, who are all within His invisible heart. With Adam and Eve, God becomes a growing child, a brother and a sister, a husband and a wife, and finally a parent. By experiencing His second self, God establishes children, brothers and sisters, husbands and wives, and parents. He unites them in true love, and that brings to Him boundless joy.

As well as to God, humans are designed to give joy to other humans. We are all in the position of someone else's child, sibling, spouse, or parent. All human beings are members of families centering on the Four Great Realms of Heart, which make the family an underpinning to experience the ideal realm of heart. We all have a longing to form families, and the reason is that only those persons embodying the Four Great Realms of Heart can become ideal human beings, capable of making heartistic oneness with anyone in the Kingdom of Heaven, on earth or in the spiritual realm.

This explains the consummate human desire to achieve mind-body unity and husband-wife unity. Unless we achieve this all-important mind-body unity, we are unqualified in all other aspects and can develop no unity in the family either. We will fall away from our families, from our nation, from the world, from the universe, and from God Himself. Only through an utmost effort to accomplish mind-body unity and family unity can we achieve perfection.

We need to know that we ourselves are God's representatives. We are in the position of a second God. All people, need to be working together to restore the family to a position of goodness and happiness.

We must become aware that the position of husband and wife is the union between a son of God and a daughter of God, the union of a brother and a sister within God's family, and the union of a father and a mother. From the perspective of the Four Great Realms of Heart, the position of husband and wife is the absolute goal of human life, through which we can actually achieve the perfection of our individual selves.

The husband, therefore, stands in the position that enables the wife to receive an ideal son of God, to receive an older brother of heaven, to receive a husband of heaven, and to receive a father of heaven. The corresponding case is true of the wife in relation to her husband. Such husbands and wives bear children in a manner analogous to God's creative act. They feel joy through experiencing their own growth in a substantial manner, through their children.

Achieving a World of Peace

God's love is absolute. Accordingly, it is a principle of heaven that the relationship of husband and wife cannot be broken. Fallen human society has lost sight of this principle and must be restored so that we may return to the original homeland. When such a restoration is accomplished, the Federation for World Peace will have fulfilled its purpose. At that point, the family-level heaven will become a country-level heaven; the country-level heaven will become a world-level heaven; and the world-level heaven will become the Kingdom of Heaven in the spirit world. This will be the point at which, at last, we will have achieved a world of peace.

The position at which a husband and wife marry and love each other with true love is the heavenly palace, which is the origin of the love, life, and lineage of God and humankind. It is the starting point for the ideal of the Kingdom of Heaven on earth and in the spirit world. When children who are the fruit of such true love achieve perfect unity as husbands and wives, they form families living in attendance to God. They constitute the base upon which peace and all ideals can be established. Then men and women, each representing one side, will perfect

Centering on true love, God perfects humankind as an existence of unlimited value. When that is done, God, too, will see the perfection of true love, the fulfillment of the family ideal, the fulfillment of His own ideal for the creation, and the cradle of eternal, ideal love. From the perspective of Adam and Eve's family, God is the first ancestor; Adam and Eve, the second ancestors; and their children, the third ancestors. A royalty centering on God. Adam and Eve's family forms a royalty centering on God. God is in the position of grandparents; Adam and Eve, in the position of parents; and Adam and Eve's offspring, in the position of children. In this manner, the original pattern of three generations within the family comes to be established. According to this original pattern, the grandparents are in the position of king and queen of the spirit world, representing God and the Kingdom of Heaven in the spirit world. They should be honored and respected just as we would respect God.

The parents are in the central position of king and queen of the family, representing the Kingdom of Heaven in the present world. They should be honored and respected just as we would the king and queen of the present world. The children are in the position of princes and princesses within the family. They should be loved as the ones standing to inherit the future Kingdom of Heaven on earth and in the spirit world. In this way, the members of Adam and Eve's family were to form a royalty centering on God and were to live peacefully on earth until they moved into the heavenly, eternal world. Only in that heavenly world can human desire, freedom, aspiration, peace, and happiness attain complete fulfillment. This is the purpose which humankind must fulfill.

A Philosophy and Conviction of Peace

As respected representatives from countries around the world, each of you has devoted an important period in your life to tireless efforts for the sake of your individual country and the world as a whole. As a result of your sacrificial efforts, humankind today enjoys conditions much improved over what existed in the past. Still, the ideal world of freedom and peace, which is the fervent desire of all the people of the world, has not yet been achieved. Even at this hour, countless people in many places around the world are dying from hunger and pain as a result of conflicts and struggles among peoples, races, and religions.

I have responded as a religious leader to God's calling. I have lived my life for the purpose of saving humankind from war and sin, and of establishing a world of peace. Out of this calling, I have acquired a conviction and daily philosophy regarding peace, which is the Headwing Philosophy. In my address to you today, I have expressed a few elements of that conviction. The perspective of Godism and Headwing Philosophy is that world peace will be achieved neither by means of political ideologies oriented toward power nor by any argument based on physical force. Peace will only be accomplished when all men and women share in God's love and truth and put these into practice—starting with the individual and expanding to the family, to the society, to the country, and to the world, thus forming one global, extended family.

From this perspective, the founding purpose of the Federation for World Peace is to promote education and practices related to true peace as a means to realize peace in various societies, nations, and the world. May all of us here perfect the family-level heaven and go on to play major roles in the accomplishment of world peace.

I pray that God's blessing be upon each and every one of you.

Realization of a Peaceful World by the Ideal of True Family

Reverend Sun Myung Moon, President, Federation for World Peace
Founder's Address at the Fourth World Peace Conference,
November 27, 1997, Washington, D.C.

I welcome you and extend my heartfelt thanks for your participation in this Fourth World Peace Conference of the Federation for World Peace to address the theme "A World Vision for the 21st Century." I would like to personally invite you to a very special event at RFK Stadium on Saturday morning. Along with representative leaders of the world's religions, my wife and I will officiate at the blessing of 39.6 million couples in 185 countries around the world. The goal for this ceremony was 3.6 million couples, but we went far beyond that to more than 36 million couples. Many couples from your countries will be participating. More than 30,000 couples will be at the stadium, and ceremonies worldwide will be connected via satellite and video. These couples are dedicating their marriages to God, promising to remain eternally faithful to their spouses and to raise their children with commitment, fidelity and strong moral values. These couples are of different religious backgrounds, languages, races and national origins, but what draws all of them together is a love of God and a belief that world peace begins with stable, healthy and God-centered families. I would like you all to observe this history-making ceremony but, more than that, I strongly encourage all of you gathered here to also participate and renew your own wedding vows before God.

For Mankind's Common Vision

Today I would like to share with you about the course that I have gone over the past 50 years in search of a common vision for humankind. After the devastating experience of World War II, all nations were searching for peace. God gave me the direction to build a global movement and help establish God's Kingdom on the foundation of 2,000 years of Christianity. The central message of this revelation is to find the formula course for "True Parents" and "True Family," which means those who live for the sake of others. But the failure of Korean Christian leaders to receive this message brought great disappointment to God, and I had to go a suffering course of rejection and humiliation, which led to my being imprisoned many times even though I was innocent. This providential mistake by the established religions provided the spiritual foundation for evil to run rampant in Korea, beginning with the division of that nation, and for the other calamities that have plagued the world this past half-century.

To understand why all this happened, we must understand the mission that God gave me 50 years ago to bring a special message to Christian leaders. That message is essentially the same today—but today the message is not just for Christians, but for Jews, Muslims, Buddhists, Hindus, and all religions and denominations. The message is that the ideal of the true family, centered on God, is the basis for true relationships and peace among individuals, societies and nations. As a young man, I desperately searched for the answers to the mysteries of human sin and suffering. I shed many tears and spent many years in lonely prayer fighting spiritual battles that most would never comprehend. After many years of searching through the Bible and the vast spiritual world, God revealed the true purpose of human life and the root cause of human suffering that originated in the Garden of Eden with the first human ancestors.

Ideal of True Love and True Family

Esteemed leaders! You need to know that God created all things for the sake of "True Love" and "True People." All creation is structured in pairs. Animals, plants, and minerals are arranged in subject-object relationships, and the harmonious give and take between them forms the base for all existence, for all energy for productivity, and for love and goodness. Humans were also created with this duality between the mind and body within the individual and between man and woman. God's ideal was for an individual's mind and body to be united, centered on His love, and then for perfected men and woman to unite in the family unit. In this way, Adam and Eve could become a true reflection of God's divine nature and become an object of God's love. Then they could bequeath to their descendants true love, true life and true blood lineage emanating from God. Adam's family was to be a family of true love, in accordance with God's ideal. The two ancestral human beings, Adam and Eve, were created with the expectation that they would transfer God's will and love to the world and all creation. Adam and Eve and their children were to establish a pattern that would have been the fundamental principle for all humanity to follow. Adam and Eve's descendants should have become one with God, accomplishing the unification of mind and body, and man and woman. They would create a stable foundation for peace, freedom, happiness and hope to fill the world. It was God's ideal that this model be expanded not just to the level of country and world, but to the entire cosmos. Thus, it would be possible for a country to become patterned after the family unit which would expand God's family-level to the country level, and the country level could expand to the world level centered on God. This would be called the Kingdom of Heaven on Earth.

The fundamental character and personality of an individual is formed in the family. Family is the starting point and foundation of love, personality and life. The Principle of Creation teaches us that we are born in the cradle of our family through the love of our parents. We come to perfect ourselves as beings of love beginning as children who gradually grow to positions of spouse, parent and grandparent. Ultimately, we pass to the spiritual world in the midst of love from our descendants. Family, therefore, is the most precious hearth of human love and life. It is more important than all value systems and ideologies as well as all policies and social systems. Through the family, history and country come into being and the ideal world starts. If there is no family, then there is no meaning in individual existence and there will be no passing of love through the generations. Therefore, family takes precedence over all value, ideology, system and structure. Family is the most precious and fundamental base for the love and life of men and women.

Origin of Man's Sin and Restoration of the Ideal of True Family

But, tragically, God's ideal of true family was never realized. The serpent tempted Eve in the Garden of Eden, and then Eve tempted Adam. Instead of God's true love, selfish false love was planted in the human race. Human history became one of sin and misery because our ancestors, Adam and Eve, entered into an illicit relationship with Satan. Because of the fall, the progenitors of the human race did not become good ancestors but, rather, evil ancestors corrupted by the root of evil life and evil blood lineage. The first family started with false love and did not establish the perfected true love character of a true person, a true couple and true parents. The fruit of false love, fallen mankind's selfishness, destroys the true order, beginning with the discord of mind and body and expanding into division and struggle in the family, nation and world.

The solution and cure for humankind's affliction, therefore, is to return to God through the principle of restoration by indemnity. Through true love for others, you can stop the struggle between your mind and body and be restored into your original character of true love. Humankind needs to receive the blessing and create an ideal family from true parents who are the model of true love character. We need to restore the individual and true family and expand true love and goodness to the world level. Fifty years ago, I tried to bring this revelation to my fellow Christians, believing that this truth could unite the conflicting denominations and bring about the Kingdom of Heaven on Earth. I never intended to form a separate church. However, God's message was met with denial and persecution by the established churches, and I was left with no choice but to make another foundation that has taken me 43 years to build! Starting in Korea with the Holy Spirit Association for the Unification of World Christianity in 1954, I sent missionaries to Japan, the United States, Europe and all over the world. On that foundation we have built many organizations to expand the principles of the true family in the media, arts, academia, economy and industry, and to create examples and models through which the world could be restored and indemnified.

God's Three Headaches

The strategy of Satan, who originated sin, is always to destroy the ideal of true family and to prevent true family from taking root and becoming substantialized. This led to God's three headaches during the past 50 years. The first headache was communism, which denies God's existence. The second is corruption and immorality. The third is the division and disunity among denominations and world religions. Think about it. How many innocent people died because of communism? Over 100 million were killed as a result of communism, and millions more were enslaved, starved, abused and wounded, and spent their whole life in suffering. But in addition to deaths and physical suffering, the crime of communism is even bigger: spreading false truth to deny God and make men and women unable to find their ultimate value.

Immorality, the second headache of God, is destroying families and countries and taking lives just as surely as an invading army. Moral corruption is one of the main causes of divorce, teenage pregnancies, crime and drug addiction. The decline of morality is not limited to any single nation's borders but is becoming the world's common problem. The worldwide AIDS plague is a direct consequence of sexual promiscuity and moral decay. If AIDS continues to spread, tens of millions of people will die and humankind's existence will be threatened.

How about God's third headache—the division and disunity within Christianity and between the world religions? For God, religious people are the conscience of the world. Religious people should have traditions and values and practical power to overcome evil. Instead they are divided. They antagonize and fight with each other. They have became incompetent and have lost the power to overcome evil and educate the world about the true way of life.

Importance of Man's Portion of Responsibility

These three fundamental headaches are the direct result of the failure 50 years ago of those chosen to receive God's message. Distinguished world leaders! From God's point of view, all of that suffering was totally unnecessary. All the misery, death and destruction were not inevitable. It could have been avoided. If in the late 1940s, the religious world centering on Christianity had followed God's revelation and become one with the true family ideal, then communism would have naturally declined. Also, through the influential leadership and example of each religion, the degeneration of youth, broken families, and AIDS would never have grown into a worldwide plague.

Confronting God's three headaches, particularly communism, made me unpopular and controversial. I was labeled a fascist and a religious charlatan. I was even jailed in the United States on trumped-up charges of tax evasion. Nevertheless, for 25 years I have been pouring out my soul, heart and energy to make the United States understand its global providential responsibilities. Through my work in the Western hemisphere and around the world, I was able to help the United States overcome communism. Now communism has almost disappeared. But immorality and social decay are systematically attacking the family. Modern thinking holds that the traditional family is only one kind of family and that even homosexuals can form a family and have children through adoption or artificial insemination. This is being done without any thought of the dire consequences of undermining and destroying a fundamental biological, social and spiritual unit that has been vital to human survival for tens of thousands of years. It is ironic that scientists warn of the threat to endangered species of plants and animals, but do not study far more seriously the consequences of family destruction.

Today God is asking us these questions: Will it be necessary to lose one-third of humanity before it is saved? Will we destroy the earth's natural resources and environment before we learn to live in harmony with the creation as God originally intended? God will never give up! He will save this world, no matter what, and He will save it through the ideal and structure of the true family. The question is, at what price, not only in terms of human lives, but financial and environmental. The social problems brought about by corruption and immorality are leaving a toll of economic collapse and environmental degradation. The leaders of the world need to reflect on these points. God's desire is to end human suffering and build a world of true, peaceful families. God needs for us to take care of our portion of responsibility. If humankind receives and acts decisively upon God's message, the achievement of God's Kingdom will be relatively swift and joyful. If not, God's and humanity's suffering will be prolonged, and the misery and needless deaths will continue.

Blessing of Marriage by True Love

Then how can God's headache be solved? How can families become fundamentally healthy? How can divided religions reconcile and cooperate under God? That answer is in the international Marriage Blessing Ceremony. My wife and I began officiating blessing of marriage ceremonies starting with three couples in 1960. If I had said at that time that many millions of people will receive God's blessing, who would have believed it? But today, with God's help and going beyond nation, race, and religion, the blessing ceremony of 39.6 million couples, promising purity and fidelity, is being carried out right in front of you.

Respected leaders! I only want to stress once again that, through the Marriage Blessing, the world's families can stabilize and finally fulfill their original role. For true family to be restored, we have to establish true love character, we have to attend God, and we have to seriously pledge to become true couples and true parents. Those harmonious families that are restored to the ideal through the Marriage Blessing Ceremony can create a peaceful society, nations, and world. This Marriage Blessing that encompasses all nations, races, and religions and goes beyond all boundaries is itself the foundation for world peace. Is this not God's desire? That this miraculous number of families – almost 40 million! – can participate in this blessing of marriage is because of the active support of the world's religious leaders. It was also made possible because many national leaders agreed that this true family movement can cure the fundamental teenage problems and the breakdown of families, and they have actively supported it. I would like once again to thank all the volunteers.

The Marriage Blessing Ceremony can awaken people, especially young people, to the value of true love, and it can become the motive and catalyst for them to realize the necessity of absolute purity. All the world's good young men and women who are awakened through this movement should gather together to stand up for a true love revolution, establishing themselves as eternal couples under God's blessing. All these new families can receive support from already married couples who have renewed their vows before God and practice right ethics, and they can all become examples of moral citizens and build an ideal family, society, nation, and world – the fruit of true love.

The Marriage Blessing Ceremony eradicates the connection to false love and brings to life the holy content and value of marriage centered on absoluteness. This ceremony recovers true couples' love, true parents' love, and true children's love. Therefore, those who participate in the Marriage Blessing Ceremony value purity and trust as highly as they do their lives and promise unchanging couple's love. On the foundation of that true love, they can establish a true family, raise true children, and pledge to sacrifice themselves to build a true nation and peaceful world. In the world of the future, God, humankind, and creation are in harmony, living in a new culture of heart, a culture of love centered on true family. In the world of the future, true love means living for the sake of others in a world of interdependence, mutual prosperity, universally shared values, and cooperation. In the future, the natural desire of young people to live in a world of true brothers and sisters, one family of mankind, will be realized by centering on true love, true parents, and true family.

Esteemed world leaders, the Marriage Blessing is the most precious gift that God is giving to us. My wife and I devoutly hope that you will participate in this historic ceremony to receive God's blessing of marriage. From now on, the Family Federation for World Peace and Unification will expand the true family movement. By the year 2001 we will carry out the 360 million couples blessing in three different events. Because of immorality and the loss of values, our young people are falling into moral decadence, and the family is being utterly destroyed.

Is there anything more important than saving humanity from plunging into ruin? My effort to globalize and universalize the True Family Movement and the Marriage Blessing Ceremony, which are the fundamental solutions to save humanity, needs the active support from respected leaders like you. Those who understand the fundamental problem and the solution God is offering should band together within their country and form a True Family Marriage Blessing support group and create a movement to save your nation. I ask that you put yourselves at the center of this great work to restore humankind to its original ideal. We have to quickly educate all men and women so they can establish true families and enter into the age of God-centered kingship on earth and heaven, centered on true love, and live in the victorious world of freedom, peace, and unity.

May God's love fill you and your family and your country.

Thank you very much.

True Unification and One World

Reverend Sun Myung Moon, President, Federation for World Peace
This address was given on April 10, 1990 at the Eleventh World Media
Conference in Moscow, Russia.

It is a great honor and pleasure to convene with you this historic 11th World Media Conference in the city of Moscow, the capital of the Soviet Union. The theme of this conference is "The Advancement of Global Communication and Cooperation," and I feel there is no place more appropriate to gather for these discussions than right here in the Soviet Union.

Furthermore, it is an added pleasure for me to open these proceedings because we are simultaneously conducting the Third Conference of the Summit Council for World Peace, and a gathering of the Association for the Unity of Latin America. Both of these excellent organizations are also committed to the quest for world peace.

For me to come to Moscow is an emotional experience. I would like to express my appreciation to the Soviet government, especially the officials of Novosti Press Agency. You have welcomed us to your great capital in a most hospitable manner. My wife and I, and our entire family, are moved by your kindness. I am sure that all of the guests in this room who have come from every corner of the world, including former heads of state and government, will join with me in expressing our deep gratitude to our hosts in this country. Would you join with me in giving them a round of applause?

I was recently asked by members of the Soviet media regarding my views on the importance of a spiritual renaissance as a precondition to social, economic and political progress. I would like to take this opportunity to elaborate on some of those views. I believe that such a spiritual renaissance is vitally important. To achieve it, a deeper understanding of the human situation is necessary. This calls for some reflection on philosophical and religious topics. It may not directly concern either communications or media, but for me it is the fundamental understanding necessary to secure true peace in our world. Furthermore, it is the essence of my lifelong search, discovery and teaching.

God's Original Ideal

When we observe our universe, we recognize that every being exists through the union of paired elements. This is true on all levels, beginning even with the mineral realm. Molecules are made from the union of a positive ion and a negative ion. On the level of plants, existence and reproduction require the union of stamen and pistil, representing the male and female aspects.

The pair system is even more obvious on the level of animals. Fish, birds, mammals and all animals exist as male and female. Finally, the supreme creations of God, human beings, are either men or women. The first man, Adam, and the first woman, Eve, were the original ancestors of mankind. What is the purpose of the pair system? Why did God create in this way?

The Creator made all things male and female so that they might unite through their give and take of love. Through the action of love, each species multiplies and extends its lineage.

Human ambition is limitless and infinite. Then, what is the true goal of this infinite desire of man? For woman, it is man. For man, it is woman. Man and woman can find true love only through each other. In history, differing views of life, the universe and God have presented unresolved problems. The solution to these problems is to be found when true man and true woman unite with God in true love, creating absolute oneness. This is the source of absolute value.

Man exists for the sake of woman. Woman exists for the sake of man. Each is to be the object of love of the other. God is a being of absolute love. He wanted to create objects of love, human beings, upon which He can pour out his love. In doing so, He would naturally look forward to the return of that love from men and women. In this way, God would feel infinite joy. Adam and Eve must be united in love themselves first, in order to become perfect objects of the love of God. Therefore, a period of growth and maturity was necessary before Adam and Eve could stand as the mature human couple resembling God and receiving and returning His love.

The pattern of true love is not that of being served; it is to serve others. When God Himself initially created His object of love, He invested every ounce of His energy—100 percent of His being. This established the pattern of true love. In other words, the tradition of true love as total investment was established by God. At that point, true love became the center of the universe. And even almighty God chooses to be obedient to it.

When God created, He totally spent Himself. He made of Himself a vacuum. In the atmosphere, when a low pressure area comes into being, high pressure air is automatically attracted. Whenever someone serves others to the absolute degree, energy rushes in to fill that person up. Therefore, all the love that God has given to create His perfect object must ultimately be returned to Him by men and women.

Only love transcends all barriers. When you are united with God in true love, you have dominion over all of God's creation, both physical and spiritual. When you live completely for others, you are reaching the very essence of God's own being. God's vibrations become your vibrations. God's feelings are naturally transmitted to you. Living this way, you become a resonant body of God's heart and love. As much as two tuning forks resonate together, you and God always resonate together.

That is the ultimate, original state of the human being. When you achieve that state, the love of God becomes your love, the life of God becomes your life, and the blood lineage of God becomes your blood lineage. The world that God created becomes your world. We are to share the love of God with all things in heaven and earth. We are to be citizens of the Kingdom of Heaven with the heart of parents.

Man's Separation from God

The law of cause and effect is clearly evident in history. Whatever you have sown, you will surely reap. Adam and Eve, the first human ancestors, engaged in sexual immorality and the abuse of love while they were still growing. This was the fall of man. God wanted them to grow in purity until He blessed them in heavenly matrimony, becoming the foundation of God's true love, true life and true blood lineage. Humanity, descending from this perfected and blessed Adam and Eve, would naturally become the sons and daughters of God, enjoying the love of the Creator, and living in the Kingdom of Heaven on earth and in the spirit world.

However, before Adam and Eve matured and received the blessing from God, while they were still teenagers, the archangel tempted Eve and engaged in fornication with her. In this way, the archangel became Satan. By engaging in relations with fallen Eve, Adam also fell. This is how the beginning of human history was sown. Today, we are reaping the consequences: immorality is rampant. Teenagers, in particular, are the victims of widespread sexual degradation. Modern society in the advanced nations is little different from Sodom and Gomorrah of biblical times. God abhors this immoral behavior. We must fear the wrath of God. His punishment is imminent.

The Struggle of Good and Evil

God is the center of goodness. Satan is the center of evil. The history of humanity has been the history of struggle between good and evil—between God and Satan—working through men and women. But the respective strategies used by God and Satan have been exactly opposite. Satan, being arrogant and greedy, always attacks the side of goodness. God's camp is always hit and suffers, but this gives God the opportunity to bring justice. The side of good is vindicated and occupies new territory. Satan's side must withdraw and decline.

For example, in World War I, the belligerent nations were ultimately defeated. The same was true in World War II, where the Axis powers, after initially attacking, were finally defeated by the Allies. Every exploiting power will ultimately decline, while whoever suffers persecution for the sake of good will ultimately be raised up by God.

My own life is representative of this. I have been struggling for the sake of good and the cause of God, but the opposition has been relentless. Years ago, I was tortured and beaten, and I have been imprisoned numerous times. One would think that my movement would die out and be forgotten, but the opposite has occurred. I have built a worldwide foundation, and have continuously advanced and prospered.

Conscience: Teacher and Parent

Every human being, throughout his life, has a most precious teacher within himself. Nevertheless, that teacher has been mistreated, trampled upon, and abused. That teacher is the human conscience. Your conscience always speaks out for your own benefit, trying to connect you to true love. Like a parent, your conscience urges you to be a good, unselfish individual, and guides you to do the will of God. But within each person there is also a rebel who always goes against the conscience. That rebel is the physical body.

The body has trampled and abused the conscience miserably. When one becomes aware of this, can he take the side of the body which has been the enemy of his own conscience, and which has greatly damaged his own life and personality?

Your conscience should be your constant internal teacher and parent, leading you to complete unity with the ultimate parent of mankind, God. The conscience, then, is the agent of God within you, and may even be called a "second God." Do you think you should be sympathetic and protective of your body, the enemy of the conscience? Or do you think you should control and confine your body and vindicate your conscience? Your body only goes after carnal desire. When it is hungry, it steals and satisfies itself. It always seeks for comfort, and wants to take advantage of others. The body has its own realm. To conquer the realm of the body is an awesome responsibility which every person must undertake.

When this is achieved, the mind as the vertical self and the body as the horizontal self are completely harmonized into oneness, and a person reaches perfection, united in love with God for eternity.

The Role of Religion

God is the source of true love, true life and true blood lineage. Since we human beings originate from this source, we must also have true love, true life and true blood lineage. However, because of the fall of man, tragically, man never achieved the position of being the child of God. Instead, men and women have received love, life and lineage from Satan.

Due to the fall of man, love today is basically self-centered. That self-centered love does not originate from the mind, but is centered upon the body. The body is where Satan's activities are conducted. The body is Satan's dancing place, the mooring post of Satan. The mind represents God's position, the plus position. But the body, which should assume the object or minus position, tries to make itself another plus, and continuously teases or fools the mind. In human life, it is crucial to correct this relationship.

Therefore, God established religion to rehabilitate fallen man. Through religion, God is teaching people how to strengthen their God-centered mind, and reverse the body's domination of their life and personality. That is why religion oftentimes demands fasting, sacrificial service and a meek and humble attitude. These are methods for reducing the power of the body and causing the body to submit to the mind. Normally, in religious life, it takes about 3 to 5 years to change from the habit of a body-centered life, and create a new spirit-centered way of life.

Furthermore, the Bible says, you must pray without ceasing. This is vitally important because Satan controls the environment of the fallen world. Satan tempts and distracts fallen man from all directions 24 hours a day, while God is only able to work from one direction, the vertical direction of the mind.

The Restoration of God's Ideal

In the eyes of God, the fallen world is the world of spiritual death. His will is the restoration of that world of death into the world of life. Restoration is another way of saying salvation. When the original ideal state has been lost, it must be restored. When a healthy man becomes sick, a physician must come and bring him back to his original health. By the same token, the God-intended original ideal was lost. Therefore, the work of God is to restore this fallen world to the original sinless state.

In order to accomplish that task, God sends the Messiah. But before the Messiah comes, God prepares a certain chosen group of people to be ready for the Messiah. This is what the Bible calls the orchard of wild olive trees.

The orchard of wild olive trees represents a certain sphere in the fallen realm that God can still direct and control. After this has been prepared, the Messiah comes. The Messiah then cuts all the wild olive trees in the orchard of God, and grafts into them the true branch of life. In this way, the wild olive trees all become true olive trees. They are returned to the original state of man.

The religious people of today are these wild olive trees in God's orchard, but even the most devout religious person must still seek the Messiah because he has not yet received the true lineage of God. The Messiah comes as the True Parents of mankind, restoring the position of Adam and Eve. Therefore, in order to be connected to the true lineage of God, each person must unite with the True Parents, and become a recipient of true love. By doing so, each person can become a true son or daughter of God. In this way, the Messiah brings salvation to humankind.

The Messiah, in the position of True Parents, must root out the trees that have grown from false seeds, subjugate Satan and connect mankind into oneness with God in true love, making all people true sons and daughters of God. In this way, the Kingdom of Heaven on earth can be created, where men and women will finally be able to enjoy true freedom.

What is the way of unification? Let us consider the first human family. First of all, there is God. Second, there is Adam and Eve. Adam is masculine, and Eve is feminine. They compete with one another to secure the love of God first. If they are selfishly motivated, there will be no unity. However, if they are unselfishly motivated, Adam will say, "I want to reach God first solely for you, Eve." The woman will be overjoyed. She, in turn, will say, "I only want to reach God for your sake, Adam." Then the husband will be fully satisfied. There is no struggle; there is unity even in their competition.

This is not only the way husband and wife can be happily united; it is more than that. It is the very key to the unification of all people.

God-Centered World View

Throughout history, God has been working through the human conscience. In spite of God's efforts, however, every attempt made thus far to restore man into the original starting point—the heart of God—has failed. It still remains for someone to liberate humankind from this satanic environment and lead a successful search for truth and true love. That is the mission of the Unification movement.

Godism is a God-centered world view, whose essence is the ideal of true love. Godism has two distinct missions: Bring unity between God and man, and bring unity between mind and body.

Since I have discovered the solution to these two fundamental problems—the unity of mind and body, and the unity of man and God—I must proclaim this truth as clearly and effectively as possible without any hesitation.

When you follow this teaching, I assure you that you can definitely conquer the carnal desires of your body. You can become 100 percent united with your mind. Then you are eligible to become the true object of God and establish a true love partnership with God.

Whenever two people are bound together by true love, they are entitled to three important rights: First, the right of inheritance. Second, the right of dwelling together. Third, the right of participation.

Take for example the relationship of husband and wife. The husband might be the president of a great nation, while his wife might be a woman of very humble origin and very little education. If they truly love each other, however, they are equals. They own all things in common, live together, and participate on an equal level.

In the same way, when man and woman are connected to God through true love, they will also enjoy the rights of inheritance, participation and living together eternally with God. When you reach this depth of heart, you will constantly experience the presence of God, and God will truly dwell among men.

True Parents

True love always travels the shortest distance at the greatest speed. Therefore, true love coming from God to the earth travels the shortest distance—a vertical line. The love between man and woman also travels the shortest distance, forming a horizontal line. When the vertical true love meets with the horizontal true love, the crossing point must absolutely be 90 degrees. There is no other way these love lines can intersect.

Who is God? God is the vertical True Parents centered on true love. He is intimately close to each of us because He is our vertical parents. When we welcome the perfected human ancestors—perfected Adam and Eve—as True Parents, we create a 90-degree crossing point between the vertical true love of God and the horizontal true love of True Parents. We have two sets of True Parents. From them we receive true love, true life and true blood lineage. This creates one world totally resonating with true love.

The Soviet Union

Ladies and gentlemen, I am very grateful to have the opportunity to share with you these reflections on the nature of God and humanity. I am also very happy to be here in the Soviet Union. My heart truly goes out to the people of the Soviet Union. Many of you have gone through unbearable suffering, and that saddens me. I love your country and your people very much. I clearly envision a moral and economic renaissance for the Soviet Union that will dramatically affect the entire world. I will do all I can to encourage and support that renaissance.

You are undertaking a new Soviet revolution, but this should be a revolution without blood or bullets—a revolution of the heart and soul.

I have been speaking about the importance of the family. But I want to tell you that in the depths of my heart, I feel that the Soviet people are a part of my family. I assure you that my wife and children feel the same. Also, I assure you that members of the Unification movement worldwide will do their utmost to work together with you for the future prosperity and well-being of all humanity.

I believe the Soviet Union will play a key role in God's plan to build a world of lasting true peace. This vast union of nations, which stretches from the Far East, with its border on my country of Korea, to the very heart of Europe birthplace of Western civilization, has a natural destiny to be a bridge between Europe and Asia. We must regard ourselves as being members of one global family living in one global house.

May God bless the Soviet Union and all its people.

World Unification and North-South Unification Will Be Accomplished by True Love

Reverend Sun Myung Moon, President, Family Federation for World Peace
This is the text of the speech given at the Opening Banquet of the WCSF
Convocation on Feb. 10, 2000.

Distinguished guests whose fervent desire is for North-South unification, ladies and gentlemen.

The new millennium that just began is a time to clean away the divisions and conflicts of the past century and to manifest the ideal of a one world family of harmony and unification. I would like to begin by thanking you for congratulating me on my eightieth birthday. Most of all, I would like to return to God all the honor and glory given to me, because it is He who has watched over me until this day.

As I look back, I am reminded that my life has never been easy. My life has been intertwined with the suffering history of our people and the numerous difficulties that our people have undergone in the midst of the great powers. As a boy of 16, I came into contact with the will of Heaven through prayer, and throughout my life after that I have devoted all my spirit and energy to accomplishing God's Will. I came to understand that the fundamental cause of human unhappiness is that the relationship with God was severed by the fall. As a result of the fall, human beings fell into a state of spiritual ignorance. In an effort to resolve the fundamental problems this has caused among humans and in the universe, I have spoken publicly on more than 10,000 occasions in many places around the world and set forth a true view of humanity, a true view of the world, and a true view of history based on Godism.

These speeches have been translated into twelve languages and published in three hundred volumes. The contents of these speeches are not the result of a comprehensive study of historical documents. My conclusions are not the result of scholarly research. Instead, I arrived at these answers to basic and fundamental questions through my communications with both the visible and invisible worlds.

The issue of unifying the Korean Peninsula is the solemn desire of our people and the final act of bringing the global Cold War to a conclusion. So today, as I express my gratitude for your having prepared this meaningful forum, I would like to share with you on the topic, "North-South Unification and World Unification Will Be Accomplished by True Love," and lay out the basic answer for how to bring about unification. The unification of our country involves more than the mere unification of national territory. It begins with the unification of the human mind and body which were divided against one another as a result of the fall, and it is the model for the unification of the world that has been divided in two. Thus, this issue must be understood from the perspective of God's salvation providence. It must be resolved on a providential level.

Satan's Target

What is Satan's ultimate target behind the history of struggle between good and evil ever since this conflict was brought into being as a result of the fall of the first human ancestors? Satan has his sights set precisely on God Himself. God is eternal, unchanging, absolute and unique, and the standard of the ideal that He held at the beginning of creation must also have these qualities.

If you were to ask God directly, I think He will confirm what I am saying. How can God reply when Satan says to God, "God, when you made me an archangel in the beginning, were you acting out of a love for me that was temporary or eternal?"

I think God will say that He made him, the archangel, out of a love that was eternal. If he were to say that His love was temporary, that would make Him an ephemeral God. Unless He maintains a standard of loving Satan eternally, there will eventually come a time when He will no longer be able to exercise His authority as God with respect to Satan. Thus, no matter how much Satan may oppose Him, God has no choice other than to establish the condition of loving Satan.

Satan says to God, "I became an evil scoundrel as a result of the fall, but you and good people can't use methods that are similar to mine, can you? I may like to fight, but you're not supposed to enjoy fighting. Even when you take a blow, you have to endure, don't you?" Thus, God's philosophy is one of non-resistance. Why is that? It is because, until the world of the heavenly ideal is manifested on this Earth, God must love the archangel who has become Satan, regardless of the circumstances.

No matter how much trouble Satan may cause, God cannot punish him or cut him off. He must establish the condition of having loved Satan regardless of where he found Satan. God can only have complete victory when Satan confesses to Him, saying, "Oh, God really is God. I surrender to You." This is the problem. Because of this, God is in the position of being tied up by Satan. Since the principle path of the providence of restoration is for God to bring about Satan's surrender by loving him, we who are His children must walk this same path. It doesn't matter if a person is persecuted around the world and is considered a worldwide enemy. This person must establish the condition of having loved those who oppose him. From this aspect, there is amazing truth in God's words to "love your enemies." In fact, this is one of God's battle strategies.

These words sound simple. No one realized, though, that they have marked the boundary line between victory and defeat in the battle between God and Satan. If God were to adopt a philosophy of looking on Satan as His enemy and seek revenge against him, then God would never be able to stand on the pinnacle of victory. Thus, God has said, "love your enemy," and has carried out a strategy of love. The words "love your enemy" also represent the culmination of Jesus' teaching.

It is remarkable that Jesus, the only begotten son of God, stood before Satan and prayed for him despite the fact that Satan was trying to kill him. If Jesus, as he hung dying on the cross, had held any feelings of malice toward his enemy, God's Providence would have been turned completely around. It is because Jesus overcame death with a heart of praying that his enemies might be blessed and of loving his enemies that Satan surrendered in that instance.

This is where the qualification to be God's eternal child comes about. Even Satan recognizes this qualification, and gives his signature. You, too, will be able to stand before God and say, "Hey, Satan, am I not unmistakably the son of God?" and Satan will reply, "Yes, that is correct." We must conduct ourselves in such a way that if we say to Satan, "You have no problem, then, if people who live like me expand God's reciprocal realm, starting from the individual and moving to the family, clan, people, nation and world," Satan's answer will be, "That is the Principle, so I can't do anything about it."

It is under these conditions that God has pursued the providence, with the Christian cultural sphere at the center. Whether we find ourselves on the path of sacrifice, in the position of martyrdom, or in the midst of bloody battle, we must carry out a movement of loving God and loving even our enemies. We must carry out this movement in our families, in our societies, and in our nations.

The Roman Empire severely persecuted Christianity, but it was forced to surrender in the face of the love by which Christianity loved even the country that was its enemy. This is how Christianity came to be a worldwide religion. The starting point for the path to heaven was within the country that was Christianity's enemy. Until now Christians have only thought about loving their own personal enemies, but this is not correct. We must love the country that is our enemy, and even the world that is our enemy.

Where Do We Start

The starting point on the path to Heaven is within the country that is our enemy. Unless we create the foundation of the tradition of true love and set out on the basis of this foundation, we cannot bring about the Kingdom of Heaven on Earth. When the tradition is established in this way, there can never be a philosophy or ideology greater than this.

When Korea was under Japanese imperial rule, the four providential countries—Korea, Japan, Germany and the United States—were enemies of one another. Given the circumstances of that time, Japanese and Koreans were enemies. Japanese and Americans were enemies. Americans and Germans were enemies. Yet, I practiced the way of true love of Heaven by taking Japanese and Germans to America, their enemy country, and telling them that America was falling into ruin and their help was needed to revive it. I emphasized to the Japanese and Germans that they could not establish a new thinking capable of leading humanity into a new world that Heaven desires unless they set the condition of having loved their past enemy, America, even more than their own fatherland. I set forth this tradition of true love, and created a new beginning.

Unless people erect a base and tradition by which they are able to love the countries that are enemies of their own, the Kingdom of Heaven cannot be realized on Earth. It is only within the true love of God that such a historic tradition can be constructed.

When I was humiliated by the U.S. federal government and unjustly brought before a court of law, my response was actually to work harder to give life to America by founding the conservative newspaper *The Washington Times* and a broadcasting station.

Recently, I am pursuing an effort to gather prominent strategic planners from around the world in order to assist China. This is one example of how all the organizations that I have founded are ready to involve themselves in any effort of Heaven that requires love. In the future, even those with superior ability will find themselves ruled by others if they have not accumulated accomplishments in true love. Everyone here needs to bear this in mind. I was involved in the anti-Japanese resistance movement under the Japanese imperial rule, and from that perspective the Japanese people were my enemy. This was true for the Korean people as a whole and for me individually. Yet, after Japan's defeat in World War II, I gave love to Japan. After the war, I could have reported the police who had taken me into custody for my activities in the underground independence movement and tortured me severely. Had I done this, they would all have been executed. When I came across a Japanese policeman who was running for his life, however, I packed some things for him and helped him escape to safety under the cover of darkness.

Planting the Foundation

Do you know why so many young people in Japan place their eternal lives at stake and pledge their loyalty to me? This is because there is a principle of cause and effect which dictates that they must return what has been given them. It is because I planted the seeds of true love in the world, transcending national boundaries and in accordance with God's heart. It is because I planted the heartistic foundation that leads people to a life of loving the countries that were the enemies of their own country. Thus, Japan today is my prisoner. Without even realizing it, Japan is fulfilling its heavenly calling.

Under Japanese rule, I had reason to harbor resentment even toward the Emperor of Japan. But he has already been defeated. Heaven does not strike a person who is defeated. In fact, Heaven shows mercy toward those who understand their sin and apologize. Because this is Heaven's way, a person who raises a sword and strikes a defeated person will find his own descendants driven to ruin.

The United States is also a country that considered me their enemy. However, I left my family behind and diverted my attention from my Korean fatherland to bring salvation to that country. I threw away everything that belonged to me in order to bring salvation to the world under Satan.

Think, too, of how much hatred the established Christian denominations have directed toward the Unification Church. It might be said that we are enemies. We must not fight each other as enemies, however. We must come together in love. What happens when we come together in love? The two come together in love and lead the Republic of Korea into fulfilling the will of Heaven so as to digest North Korea. If the established denominations and the Unification Church had become one immediately after Korea's liberation from Japan, everything would have been solved. Because that did not happen, we have had to make extraordinary sacrifices to fight enemies of the individual, enemies of the family, enemies of the clan, and enemies of the people in order to attain the position that we would have reached in the first place had there been no conflict. We have worked to overcome the path of suffering where we were not able to strike at enemies.

Distinguished ladies and gentlemen, all the people in North Korea have armed themselves with *Juche* Thought. We must arm ourselves with the philosophy of true love that is capable of digesting them. North Korea is a part of the Northern Culture that has been influenced by the cold winds of the Soviet Culture. We must work to naturally melt them with our warm region civilization. Otherwise, both countries will go to ruin. Thus, we must thoroughly arm ourselves philosophically.

This philosophy must not be one that seeks the fulfillment of individual desires. Rather, it must seek the salvation of all humanity. It must not be centered on the self. Communists have the idea that everyone should work for the sake of a few top Party leaders. This is why they eliminate any person who stands out as a potential rival. We are not that way. Our idea is to unite with the reciprocal environment in order to establish a reciprocal standard of a higher level. That is, for Cain and Abel to become one so as to receive their parents on a higher level. I do not believe South Korea should attempt to overcome North Korea militarily. Instead, we must love our nation more than they love theirs. We must have the philosophical strength to love Heaven even more than they love communism. We must become capable men and women of character who can bring about their natural surrender. There is no other way for us to absorb North Korea. In other words, we must become able to impress them with how we live. We must be able to amaze those people armed with communist ideology in terms of our outlook on life and our standard of character.

We cannot restore the Cain-type nation unless we maintain an environment by which we are able to exert influence over them. If we cannot restore the Cain-type nation, we cannot establish the restored country capable of entering into a worldwide nation centered on the Kingdom of Heaven. Although North and South Korea are divided against one another, we must liberate North Korea without fighting them.

The Korean people in both North and South Korea fervently desire to see the country unified, but how can this be accomplished? Unification can only be accomplished when a sophisticated method for unification is put forward that will allow both sides to live together. When the South goes to the North, or the North to the South, and says, "Let's do it our way," unification will not succeed. Thus, we must find a love that will benefit both sides.

A Greater Love

Ladies and gentlemen, at the moment North and South are going in different directions. One is trying to go south and the other trying to go north, and they are on two divergent paths. Their purposes are at odds with each other. If both sides insist on their own position, it is certain that the situation will again result in breakdown.

The question is what is to be done about this. There must be a South Korean person who loves North Korea with a greater love than any South Korean person has for his own country.

Also, there must be a North Korean person who loves South Korea with a greater love than any North Korean has for his own country. There is no option or solution other than this.

If there is one person whose patriotism is greater than any South Korean's and greater than any North Korean's, then this is where the path to unification can come about. Can there be another way? No matter how hard you may think, there is no other way.

What are the Korean people to do, then? Our country straddles the boundary line between left and right centering on the 38th Parallel. We are the ones who have been placed on that line, so what are we to do? This is the question. The issue is how to resolve this problem. The answer is that we must suffer even more than North Koreans, and even more than South Koreans. How are we to uphold such a standard of patriotism, established through suffering and transcending nationality? This is the way to give this country life and to solve its problems. The same principle applies to uniting the world of goodness and the world of evil. Someone must appear in the world of goodness that is a greater patriot to the world of evil than anyone in that world. A person must appear who can set a higher standard of loyalty to his nation than anyone among our ancestors who pursued goodness. This is the only way for a divided history to be resolved.

Jesus was particularly remarkable in this regard. He realized it would do no good for both sides to fight. The only way for him to live for the sake of God and for the sake of the people of Israel was for him to die for God and for his people. This was the reasoning behind the crucifixion. Jesus' love for humanity was greater than anyone else's since the beginning of history, and his love for God was greater than anyone else's in history. Because of this, his death caused a history destined for destruction to take a new direction toward a world of purpose. This was the Christian cultural sphere. This is historical fact.

Thus, the only way to unite North and South is to become a people who can die for the North and the South. There is no other path to achieve unification. There has to be a heart of truly wanting to live together in harmony with the other side.

When a person considers how to lead his life, the most basic fundamentals can be expressed as: the path of a filial child, the path of a loyal patriot, the path of a saint, and the path of a son or daughter of God. Isn't it the heart of wanting to live in harmony with others eternally and of wanting to be with others without regard to whether they are higher or lower, and transcending front and back and left and right? This is the logical conclusion.

What is the common denominator among those who say, "I want to live in harmony with others"? It is not power. Power cannot transcend history. Power is limited to a specific period in time. The same is true with knowledge. The world of knowledge has an innate tendency to develop. Does knowledge give us the heart to say, "I want to live with this particular piece of knowledge forever"? Clearly, we cannot keep either knowledge or wealth with us forever.

What then is the common denominator that transcends above and below, front and back, left and right, and the time differences between past, present and future? This cannot be anything other than true love centering on God. Thus, a filial child is one who lives in his family giving profound love to his or her parents. Also, a patriot is one who lives a life of profound love for his or her country. A saint is one who lives a life of profound love for the people of the world. A son or daughter of God is one who lives a life of profound love for all humanity and God. Thus, the problem is to develop a true foundation of heart by which a person can want to have the heart of a patriot. Such a person would want his or her life to be in concert with the fortunes of the people. Such a person would look upon any difficulties faced by the people as his or her own personal difficulties. This person would look upon any joys experienced by his people as more than temporary joys but eternal joys to be shared with everyone.

The person who possesses relationships of true love and true heart is given special authority to participate in the realm of unification.

Ladies and gentlemen, even if a woman lacks any formal education, she can marry a man with a doctoral degree and suddenly become the wife of a scholar. Isn't that true? Anyone who possesses a great deal of the relationships of heart desiring to live with others in harmony has the right to participate today in the realm of unification.

God himself is such a being. Thus, if a person attains the life content enabling him to form a unity, this person is automatically given the qualification to participate.

What is the First Step?

Where should we begin the process of unification? Where should we start in order to achieve North-South unification? What is the first step? Do we begin by using our fists or physical force? If we subjugate the other side with force, then eventually they will develop a force stronger than ours and the conflict will begin all over again. We cannot achieve unification by this method. The way to unification will open when each of us has the heart to say, "Even though I live in the South, I truly want to live in harmony with those people in the North. I truly want to become one with them."

Suppose people in the South were to look upon our compatriots in the North and shed tears to see the miserable conditions in which they live. Suppose we were to tell them, "I am living my life in a way that I can share in your difficulties." Suppose we were to promise them, "Some day soon, I will appear before you having completed the preparations for your day of liberation." Suppose, then, we were to carry out a practical movement for unification based on such a heart. If we did these things, I believe the day of unification would not be far off.

Ladies and gentlemen, we must think how we can live in harmony with our compatriots. No one can be a patriot if they do not want to live with their parents or with their compatriots. Any claim such a person might make to being patriotic would be a lie. A person must first be able to live in harmony with his own country before he or she can live in harmony with the world. Further, a person must first live in harmony with the world before he or she can live in harmony with God. Thus, a person cannot be a patriot unless he first loves his compatriots and gives love to that particular regional society.

How much do our political leaders love their country? Any politician who lacks a heart of truly wanting to share in the life of common citizens will soon disappear. It doesn't matter how well bred or educated this person may be. He will disappear like an air bubble formed on a surface of water. Any leader who does not love the citizens will not be able to escape judgment by the citizens of his country and by history.

Healing the division between North and South is not a simple process. As fellow patriots struggle to bring this about, they will need a determination of heart to work through many sleepless nights, transcending time, and overcoming all manner of difficulties.

"I truly want to live with them. I don't want to die unless I can die with them. I don't want to live unless I can live with them." The movement for North-South unification begins when both sides have such a heart toward the other.

When North-South unification is accomplished, this will be the beginning point in the effort to unite the democratic and communist worlds. Each of us must consider the future of our people and of the world as a representative of the world, a representative of the six billion humankind, a representative of the three billion people of Asia, a representative of your school, and a representative of all the students you have ever taught. We must determine ourselves to carry out a movement that will truly enable us to share in the lives of our compatriots.

When such an effort connects you to the way of the saint, then you will come to resemble a saint. If you practice this with respect to God with the loyalty of a son or daughter of God, then you will become "God's heir," and "successor to God's will." I tell you these things today because I have already confirmed their truth in my own life.

Once North-South unification is accomplished in Korea, the unification of the world will follow automatically. Do you think that political power, military force or economic wealth can bring about unification? There isn't even the slightest chance of this. That is the reason I am speaking to you in this way. Can weapons, wealth or knowledge do away with rotten philosophies? No, they cannot. Only true love can do this. This love is love that comes from God.

When a person enters into a relationship of true love with God, he or she is absolutely given special authority to have dominion, ownership and the right of inheritance. In the world of mechanics, the energy produced is less than the energy put into a system. However, in the world of true love, greater energy is produced than is put in.

What is true love? It is love that lives for the sake of others. It is love of unlimited giving and forgetting. No memory is kept of how much was given. It is a love that never tires of giving. A 90-year-old mother can turn to her 70-year-old son and say, "Be careful when you cross the street," and there is nothing strange about that. Even if the mother has repeated those same words countless times over several decades, she will always say them one more time. If this is true with parents in the fallen world, how can we ever grow tired of giving and receiving God's love in the essential world? When we establish God's true reciprocal realm in our own lives, we will understand the unchanging glory of true love for the first time. Then we will be able to justify the ethics of eternal life centering on the true love of human beings. Who in the world is aware of such things?

In 1984, I was lying in bed in an American prison where I had been unjustly incarcerated, when God came to me. He said, "You are the only person I can trust. I want you to resolve the situation in Nicaragua." Am I really the only person God can come to with such a command? America is said to be a great country standing at the forefront of all developed countries. It has a population of 240 million people and a large number of religious leaders. How helpless God must be that he could not go to any of those people but had to come to me. At least it is fortunate that God knows how to find a person by his love. If I had not worked for the sake of the world at that time, South America would have been completely ravaged by war by now.

North-South unification is the fervent desire of the Korean people, but it is also the earnest desire of God in this age. It is Heaven's desire that North Korea and South Korea can be united and that God's resting place will be established in your homes, in our churches, and in our worldwide church centered on God.

How, then, are we to attend God? How can we wipe everything clean? What can we use to wipe everything off so that God will say it is completely clean? This is the problem.

The answer is simple. We must clean the surroundings centering on a true love that is greater than our love for our parents, greater than our love for our spouses, and greater than our love for our children. It is only when our offerings our placed on the altar centering on such love that the ideal North-South unification will be manifested. This is where the ideal blending of Eastern and Western cultures can occur. This is where the ideal unification of the divided physical and heavenly realms can occur.

This is where the realm of liberation of Hell and Heaven will come about. We cannot unlock this without true love. We need the key of true love.

Unification brought about by the love between a person's mind and body can always be manifested as the unification of love in the family. A loving husband and wife with a harmonious family will always see their love manifested within their clan.

If a loving husband and wife unite as one, who will dare try to tear them apart and defile their relationship? A world made of the harmonious family, harmonious people, harmonious government, harmonious world, harmonious Heaven and Earth, harmonious true human love and God united as one—isn't this world the utopia of true love? In such a world, there will be no possibility of discord. Love will be the life element for all people, in the same way that plants receive life elements by absorbing the rays of the sun. Our fervent desire is to build a Kingdom of Heaven on Earth and in Heaven where we can resonate with true love eternally. How many people are there in this world, though, who are the subject partners or object partners of true love, who can stand as people of character qualified to the be master of all things, and who possess both the value of a remarkable life and the special authority that comes with such a life?

Solving Everything Through God's True Love

I sincerely hope that each person participating today will remember what I have said, and will work to unite your mind and body. I hope that you will start by becoming a person who lives for the sake of your spouse, and go on to become a true person who lives for the sake of your family, people, nation and world. If you do that, then North-South unification will be as good as done. Even communist ideology is easily absorbed and disappears when it is placed in the midst of God's love. The problem until now was that we did not know this. Once we develop our hearts of love, North-South unification will be no problem at all. That is not all. Problems between East and West and the worldwide North-South problem involving differences among rich and poor nations can also be completely resolved through the true love of God.

We must digest the ideal for the world centering on God's ideal that I have described, and go on to digest the ideal of the nation. Then we must move on to the boundless realm of peace of the ideal world that links the ideal of the nation to the ideals of clan, family, and individual. This is, without a doubt, the way that the utopia of true love that God has desired can be built on this Earth.

Distinguished guests: We cannot fight the communist world with guns and swords or any other means of physical force. We must fight them with love. Communists seek to destroy the democratic world in order to build a communist world. By contrast, we must build a structure that will bring salvation not only to the democratic world but to the communist world as well.

The 38th Parallel is the deepest point and final resting place where North and South can be united by means of God's true love. When it comes to doing away with this demarcation line between North and South, the North says, "There's nothing we can do about it." Russia says the same thing. China, too, says the same thing. The government and opposition parties in Seoul say, "There's nothing we can do about it." Even the United States and Japan say there is nothing they can do about this. If this is the case, then it will be the end of everything. If that happens, will we prosper or will we be ruined? It will be the end of everything evil and a new beginning for everything good. This is the reason we must unite the citizens of our country.

Millions of people in Korea, Japan and the United States have worked through the International Federation for Victory Over Communism and CAUSA to lay non-governmental foundations in each of these countries.

I declared the fundamental principle for unification more than 40 years ago. Since then, I have carried out a movement of ideas, centered on Godism, both domestically and around the world. I have worked in the four major countries surrounding the Korean Peninsula to lay the international groundwork for unification.

Over the years, leaders of many countries and the philosophical world have recognized Godism as the only philosophy capable not only of uniting with materialism and atheism, which are its diametrical opposites, but also as the only philosophy capable of liberating secular humanism.

My patriotic compatriots filled with passionate hope for North-South unification: let us together establish our value systems on the basis of Godism, and join forces in arming the people of this country with this new philosophy. Let us make North-South unification a matter of faith for the sake of ourselves, for the sake of the Korean people and for sake of world peace. Let us stand and answer the calling of historic age and of Heaven. Let us be leaders and people of righteousness standing at the forefront of the movement for North-South unification.

In particular, history took a mistaken course as a result of Eve's error at the beginning, so in the Last Days women need to take the lead in overcoming conflict and strife in the age of division with their motherly love and create a new history of reconciliation and unity. The mission of women is to educate and restore young men and women, who are in the position of being their children, and even their husbands in order to realize the ideal of the Kingdom of Heaven.

I pray God's blessing may be with your families.

Thank you.

The Path for America and Humanity in the Last Days

Reverend Sun Myung Moon, President, Family Federation for World Peace
The Washington Hilton and Towers, Washington, D.C. January 22, 2000

Distinguished and honorable guests, ladies and gentlemen:

I want to express my heartfelt gratitude to all of you, as world leaders representing many walks of life, for gathering to congratulate and celebrate my 80th birthday. In particular, I would like to express my deepest gratitude to God who has been my constant companion throughout my life. To Him I offer all the glory and honor given me.

During the course of my life, I have totally committed myself to the salvation of humankind centered on God's Will. As a result, I came to realize that God is not sitting in the throne of glory and honor, but is a God of suffering, grief and lamentation, endeavoring to save His children suffering in hell as a result of the fall.

Ever since I understood the Will of God and His heart, I have lived my life with a single-minded goal to accomplish God's Will, transcending time and space and forgetting everything else.

When I reflect upon the 80 years of my life, filled with misunderstandings and persecution, it is just amazing that I can be with you today. I believe that it is entirely thanks to God. On this day of such great significance, in order to understand human history and the world from the perspective of God's providence, I would like to speak on the topic, "The Path for America and Humanity in the Last Days."

Search for a True Nation

When viewing human history as God's providence of salvation, the "last days" is a turning point when the evil history of Satan concludes and God's good sovereignty begins. Accordingly, the last days are the time when everything is brought to fulfillment.

Thus in the last days, individual perfection is to be realized, family perfection is to be realized, the perfection of a people, of a nation, of the world and finally, the complete fulfillment of the cosmos is to be realized.

Whenever the time of the last days was heralded in God's providence, God led humankind to a God-centered ideology, but we failed to fulfill our responsibility to stand in the position of goodness and eradicate evil history. However, God is eternal, unchanging, absolute and unique, and God's Will is also eternal, unchanging and absolute. Therefore, through the true individual, true family, true society, true nation, true world and true sovereignty, God will surely build the world in which He can live, freely traveling and acting both in Heaven and on Earth.

Then, what is the original world for which God is seeking? It is a world that is centered on the True Parents. However, due to the fall, we lost the True Parents of humanity and the true world from the very beginning. Therefore, nothing in the world, not the land where we are living, human ideology or anything else, can connect us directly to the True Parents. Therefore, we ourselves should first be restored to trueness. By so doing, when true parents, true husband and wife, true children, true people, the true creation, the true sovereignty and the true cosmos are born and can communicate with God in heart, the evil world will eventually come to an end.

The last days is the time when such an ideal will be realized. It is the time when the Second Advent will occur. Accordingly, in the last days, there will be no external catastrophic phenomena such as judgment by fire, the destruction of the earth or people levitating into the air. Instead, it is a time when the history of evil entangled with countless tragedies will be sorted out.

This is established through sacrificial conditions offered on every level, those of the individual, family, society, people, nation, world and ultimately, cosmos. Thus, it is the time when all of these levels that lost their vertical connection with God will be restored. We have been longing for such a day, and that is the final destination at which we all should arrive.

However, the individual, the family and the nation have been estranged. Moreover, all kinds of problems such as air pollution, food shortage, religious struggles and racial conflicts are constantly arising throughout the world, causing disputes and even wars. Who, then, is going to take responsibility for this world? This is a serious question. Communist countries in the past could not transcend their own nationalism. Nor can today's super-power nation, America, transcend the idea of Americanizing the world. When a nation places its self-interest first, it will not be able to lead the world. Therefore, we need a people or a nation who are willing to sacrifice for a higher purpose and strive to build or become an ideal nation that embraces the entire world.

My Message to Youth

With this view, in response to the call of God, I came to this country, the United States of America. I have been making my utmost effort to revive America, by educating the youth in a country that is faced with a moral crisis and declining Christianity.

You might be curious about what I am teaching them. It is actually simple. First, it is "to live for the sake of others." More specifically, my teaching is that the individual lives for the family, the family for the society, the society for a people, a people for the nation, the nation for the world and the world for God. Then, God will come to us.

In the family, the parents are to live for the children, the children for the parents, the husband for his wife and the wife for her husband. Anyone who lives for others more than his or her own self will become a central person on the side of goodness.

Second, I am teaching people to "love your enemy." God Himself sacrificed Jesus, His own begotten and beloved son, for the salvation of humankind. Since God did this in order to save the children of His enemy, Satan could not exercise his full authority and power before God. Even Satan cannot help but voluntarily surrender before the God who loves

Satan's children more than His own. Satan's pattern is always to strike first but he loses in the end, and God's strategy is to win in the end by taking the first blow and initial loss. Living with faith in such a heavenly law is the very secret explaining the foundation that I could lay, dispatching missionaries to 185 nations throughout the world despite fierce persecution and misunderstanding.

Christian Sacrifice

Even when looking into the history of Christian missionary activities, we can discover that theirs was a path of persecution and martyrdom, hindered by enemies. On such a way, during the course of a 2,000-year history, the lives offered on this trail of blood became the fertilizer in the foundation for a powerful democracy to develop. Today, however, Christianity, which once was the source of power and strength for democracy, is facing a crisis. Christian nations have lost the right direction; they deny God, Jesus and God's providence. Now, we even hear voices asserting, "God is dead" or "God does not exist." Looking at them, how does God feel? God's heart has been searching for His children, sacrificing everything that He has, with hope to see a great day like today.

Ladies and gentlemen: for whom has God been sacrificing Himself so far? It is not for America, nor is it for Christianity. But it is for each of us, in other words, for "you" and "me" as individuals. Likewise, the reason why Jesus was crucified was also not to save the Messiah, himself, but was to save each one of us, "you" and "me." Since the fall began on the individual level, salvation should also begin on the individual level. Accordingly, a representative of humankind should come and proclaim, "I will take full responsibility as a representative of all humankind. I will pay off all the debt that man has incurred during the entire course of history and I will become a person who will make God indebted to me instead." Without such a realization and determination, restoration is impossible.

This should not be only conceptual or theoretical. On behalf of God, unless we are willing to experience miseries more than the one who is undergoing suffering in the world, we cannot reach God's heart. Have you ever prayed in desperation for the 6 billion population of the world, with a feeling that your own children are dying? How much heart have you invested to save a family, a tribe, a people, a nation and the world, with the willingness to sacrifice yourself for them? I believe few people are confident to give a positive answer to that question. The Lord of the Second Advent comes to the world with such an absolute standard as the representative of all humanity.

The Bride of the Messiah

God, who has been leading the providence of salvation, found Abraham 2,000 years after the fall of the first human ancestors. God made his descendants the chosen people, Israel, by multiplying them on every level, as a new family, a new tribe and a new people. Based on the victorious foundation, the Israelites were called as the chosen people to receive the Messiah. They became the central people to receive the substantial Messiah who was to come in the future.

If you go to the central core, you can understand that we need to restore the standard and ideology that the first human ancestors, Adam and Eve, should have reached and fulfilled. This is the thought of the Messiah. In it, the believers stand as the "bride." Therefore, Christianity's ultimate purpose is not to build the Kingdom of Christianity or the world of Christianity. Its most important mission is to prepare to become a bride qualified to receive the bridegroom.

Despite the significance of their mission, the Israelites could not carry it out and pass on this tradition because of the crucifixion of Jesus. Therefore, the Israelites, although called by God as the first Israel, flew away. Christianity, called as the second Israel, arose to carry out the mission in their place. God led the 6,000-year providence centered on this one purpose, so Christianity became the bride prepared to receive the bridegroom. We are now in the final stage of that providence.

Then, what is the core of the Messianic thought? It is a thought to save the world. It is the teaching that can unify the world and build an ideal family, and its main purpose is to restore the position of the True Parents that was lost by the fall of the human ancestors.

By looking into the teaching of the Old and New Testaments, one can understand that the Messiah comes with the authority of the father, meets a substantial bride, who represents the power of the Holy Spirit, and restores the position of the True Parents. Therefore, Christianity is in the position of a bride to the coming Messiah. The bride and bridegroom in the "marriage supper of the lamb" prophesied in the Book of Revelation refer to the stage of becoming the True Parents by first becoming a true husband and wife.

Jesus came with this mission. However, when he lost his people and nation, due to their faithlessness, he offered his life for the sake of the world and the Kingdom that God wished to build. The path of Jesus' suffering on the cross was the same as the path of tribulations that God Himself walked. In such a situation of trial and tribulation, Jesus desperately prayed, "Please forgive them for they know not what they do." Even in the place of death, he forgave Rome and the group of people who opposed him, waiting for victory in the future. Therefore, the life of Jesus did not end at the age of 33. With God's help, Christianity inherited his spirit and became one of the four great worldwide religions of human history.

The Flow of Civilization

Ladies and gentlemen: currently, America is recognized as the supreme power of the world, but unless it stands straight on the providential line of God, it will not continue to prosper. Let us look at the history of civilization. Ancient civilizations were born mainly in the tropics and subtropics. Examples include the civilizations of the Mayas, Incas, Egypt, Mesopotamia, India and China.

Yet the sphere of civilization moves from place to place. Had we not fallen, civilization would have begun in the warm zone, corresponding to spring, and moved to the cool zone, corresponding to autumn. The civilization centered today on the free world, the western civilization, is in the cool zone. In general, when viewing the equator as the center, nations such as America, England, Germany and so forth, linked around the latitude of 23 degrees north, are the developed countries of the west.

With the end of the cool zone civilization of autumn, the cold zone civilization of winter comes for a short time. This is the appearance of communism. Many intellectuals may think that the cold war system disappeared after the dissolution of the Soviet Union, but materialism and atheism still prevail throughout the world. They manifest in two major ideologies, democracy and communism, both of which are gradually losing power.

God's ideal of creation should have begun in the warm zone of spring, but due to the fall of the first human ancestors, the fallen world started as the tropical zone civilization. Now, the civilization of the true spring that we have been seeking from time immemorial will appear, overcoming the crisis of the tropical zone civilization and the threats of the cold zone civilization. Who will be able to melt the block of ice frozen in the heart of God? And how will he do it? It is impossible with power, money, science or knowledge.

We can see from the movement of civilization centering on rivers and coastlines that the center of civilization is not fixed but is always moving to different parts of the globe. Human civilization began to develop around the Tigris and Euphrates and the Nile Rivers. The center of human civilization then shifted to the Mediterranean, especially focusing upon Greece, Rome, Spain and Portugal. The center of human civilization then moved to the Atlantic, focusing upon Britain and the United States. Ultimately it has born fruit in the Pacific Ocean civilization of the United States, Japan and Korea. Thus, as viewed in this way, from the perspective of the history of cultures, the Korean Peninsula occupies a very important position. To the north of Korea lie the ultimate points of the cold region civilization that link Russia and China. To the south lie the ultimate points of the cool region civilization that link the United States and Japan.

Thus, it is consistent with the providential viewpoint that Korea give rise to a warm region civilization representing the spring season of world history and having the capability to digest both the cold and cool region civilizations. In this respect, the fact that Rev. Moon, who has dedicated his life to solving the North-South problem and the East-West problem, comes from Korea can only be described as the summation of God's providence.

My Role in History

In fact, throughout my life I have transcended race, ideology and national boundaries to pursue a movement for one world under God. It is because of God's providence that I have traveled this path. This is the principle of providential history, not a theory that I specially devised. I was enlightened regarding the will of Heaven, and rather than letting it remain as an idea alone, I have worked to bring God's concept into reality. Externally, there is no place in any region of the world where I have not been active. I have inspired evangelical and business activities in Alaska, in Antarctica, in the countries of the former Soviet Union, in the 33 countries of South and Central America and throughout Asia and Africa. We are making preparations to solve problems that humanity will face over the coming millennium, such as environmental pollution, hunger and disease. In recent years, I have worked in the Pantanal and Amazon regions of Brazil to lay a substantive foundation to protect the Earth's environment.

On the other hand as regards the internal aspects, I have worked through the International Holy Blessing and the pure love movement. Some 430 million couples around the world have participated, adding further impetus to the building of the Kingdom of God on Earth that God has longed to see for such a long time.

Ladies and gentlemen: up until now, countries possessing superior power politically, militarily and economically have controlled the world. However, no country can exist eternally unless it is in line with God's providence. The fall of the once glorious Greek and Roman civilizations are good examples of this. The United States, which today stands tall as a super power, is in the same position as Rome was in the past. The fall of Rome occurred more as a result of the internal cause of moral corruption than from any external invasions. Moral corruption caused Rome to lose the support of heavenly fortune.

In recent history, political forces favoring dialectical materialism and the materialistic view of history went as far as to take control of over one third of the world's population and two thirds of its land area, including the former Soviet Union and China. That expansion, however, could not stand forever.

The time will come when religious leaders who speak for the Will of God will rise to prominence. Religious leaders are prophets. They must stand in the place God wills, declare God's will, and point the way that humanity must go. However, the splintering of denominations and the struggles among religious groups that we see today serve no purpose other than to hinder God's providence. That is why I have for years devoted 90 percent of our church's budget to activities that reach out to other denominations and other religions for the purpose of resolving inter-religious conflict.

I also founded the Inter-Religious Federation for World Peace for the three purposes: to facilitate harmony and unity among religious groups, to contribute to conflict resolution in many areas of the world, and to help bring about world peace. Most recently, I founded the Inter-religious and International Federation for World Peace, and this body has held seven international *Hoon Dok Hae* conferences.

Recover God's Heart

All people should go beyond racial and religious differences, understand God's providence to bring His ideal world of creation into reality, and ultimately unite with God's heart. It is heart that will bring faith, hope and love—which humankind have been pursuing—to their ultimate conclusion. We must recover the heartistic relationship with God that we lost as a result of the human fall, and recover the positions of parent and child as God originally envisioned them to be. Thus, the Last Day that God has promised to us is the day when True Parents come. In other words, it is the day when the multitudes of people in the world, who lost their Parent as a result of the fall, will again be able to meet their original Parent. Thus, the True Parents are the final fruit of the desires and hopes of all humankind. They are the final fruit of the victories wrought throughout human history.

The Unification Church has worked to disseminate this tradition throughout the world through the International Holy Blessing Ceremony. The fact that black people, white people and yellow people are able to come together as brothers and sisters beyond the differences of ethnicity, race or skin color to form loving married couples is among the most significant factor in accomplishing God's Will. Today, through beginning to realize the blessed family tradition, humankind is beginning to recover the relationships of brother and sister, husband and wife, and parent and child as originally envisioned by God. Ultimately, we must go as far as to liberate God, who has been in the depths of sorrow ever since He lost His children. It is only then that the path to true happiness will be opened.

Until now, democracy has called for "human freedom" and "human liberation." In contrast, we must call for "God's freedom" and "the liberation of God." When we succeed in relieving God's sorrow, human liberation and the recovery of human freedom will follow automatically. Each of you should realize that you were born to liberate God and to liberate the world.

The Roots of America

Ladies and gentlemen: there is profound significance in the fact that I am discussing God's providence today in Washington, D.C., the capital of the United States. In many ways, the United States is a country prepared by God's blessing. The forefathers who built this country were the Pilgrim Fathers, who risked their lives for the sake of the freedom of religion and came to America seeking a land of freedom. For the sake of their search for true religious freedom, these people left behind their parents, brothers and sisters and homeland. They were even prepared to cut their ties to their home country as they crossed the Atlantic Ocean at the risk of their lives.

When the Mayflower arrived in New England in November 1620, it was already late autumn. While they endured their first winter, more than half of the 102 people who first arrived died of the cold and hunger. What was particularly remarkable about them was that many died refusing to eat the precious seeds reserved for planting the next spring. The Puritans strongly believed in serving the will of God in every aspect of their lives. After taking in their first harvest, they offered thanks to God. They first built a church and a school, and it was only after that that they set about to build houses where they themselves would live.

In the course of their pioneering, the Pilgrims began every activity with prayer. This was true whether it was plowing a field or fighting a war. When George Washington was at Valley Forge during the War of Independence, he must have prayed with great desperation. In a battle fought for the sake of God's will, God sided with America. In England, the king and the people were united in fighting that war, yet in America, it was fought by God and His beloved sons and daughters. Isn't this how the United States came into existence as a country advocating freedom of faith?

Even now, the United States Congress opens with a prayer. When the President is sworn into office, he places his hand on the Bible as he takes the oath of office, and a member of the clergy blesses him. America even prints the words "In God we trust" on its money. America is unique in the world in the level of importance it attaches to God. This is how the United States has come to occupy a unique position as a mainly Protestant country with worldwide influence.

Who Really Loves America?

What about America today, though? Prayer in public schools is officially banned. The theory of evolution is given preference to the theory of creation in education. The divorce rate of around 50 percent is completely obliterating the sanctity of the family.

In 1971, I left my family and homeland to come to America because I heard the voice of God sharing His concern about the current state of affairs here. Upon arriving here, I cried out that I had come as a fireman to a house that was on fire and as a physician to cure America of disease. Even then, I discovered that God was leaving America. It should be possible to find God everywhere in America, but God was departing from the hearts of people, from the families and from the schools. It seems like only yesterday that I stood on Fifth Avenue in

Manhattan and wept openly as I held on to God to keep Him from leaving America. Unfortunately, America has persisted in going the way of moral deterioration, as I predicted.

Ladies and gentlemen: I would like to ask you this. Why do you suppose Rev. Moon continues to cry out to Americans in spite of all the opposition and suffering he endures? It is because I know better than anyone the blood, sweat and tears that God shed in the course of establishing this country. During the past thirty years in America, I have not spent so much as a single day in comfort.

Who is the master of America? It is neither white Americans nor black Americans. The true master of America is the person who loves America as God does. Also, I continue to plead with you because God has chosen America as the first son, the nation representing the elder son realm in building the Kingdom of God on Earth. Even now, Jesus is spiritually present mainly in America, and is offering earnest prayers that his purpose will be accomplished in America.

In 1982, in accordance with the will of God, I founded *The Washington Times* here in Washington, D.C. Ever since then, this newspaper has led American public opinion as a conservative news medium showing the path for America to follow. Also, I have pursued a strong movement for national and world salvation through the true family values movement and the pure love movement for young people. I have invested in America in expectation that this country would stand upright before God's providence.

When I visited America in 1965, I blessed an area near the White House as a holy ground, and even today many people gather there and pray for America through the night. I hope each of you will open your hearts so that you will be able to hear the earnest desires of the Pilgrim Fathers and the many patriots who have lived in America's history.

America and True Parents

Ladies and gentlemen: the new millennium that has just begun is the time period in which God's six-thousand-year salvation providence is brought to an end and God's ideal of creation is realized throughout the cosmos. This is also the time when the lamentations of creation, which lost its true masters as a result of the fall, are finally brought to an end. This is the time when the Parent and children who have been long-separated meet again. The new Earth and the new Heaven, where there are no tears, are to be established. It is an age when there is free communication between the spirit world and the physical world, and when God's Kingdom is established in Heaven and on Earth.

The transition moment of the start of the new millennium marks the completion of the New Testament Age, the point at which all the promises of the Old Testament and New Testament are fulfilled. The future will be a time when God's realm of direct dominion will become apparent through His omnipresence and omniscience. It is an age when the East and West will come together centering on the Parents of Heaven and Earth as "one universe under God" so that a grand family of humankind is formed on Earth. This means the perfection of the Completed Testament Age, in which the promises of the Old Testament and New Testament will be fulfilled.

The time has come. The time has come for America to awaken once again. It is time for the country as a whole to create a new movement to build true parents, true families, a true country and a true world centered on God. In this way, America will keep God from leaving, and again become a society that attends Him. God worked a thousand years to establish America. If He leaves America, where can He go?

If America attends God properly, all America's problems—the family problems, moral problems, youth problems and racial problems—will be solved naturally. When America becomes a place where people of all races can live together in harmony, it will be a model for the Kingdom of Heaven on Earth. It is time for us to unite together and open the path for humankind to travel. It is time for America, as the elder son nation, to take the lead in attending God and to complete its mission as the helmsman that brings the nations of the world to God. I ask you to stand with me in accomplishing this historic task.

Again, I would like to express my sincere gratitude to you distinguished guests for your presence here. I would like to conclude by expressing my hope for the beginning of a new millennial Kingdom overflowing with peace, freedom and justice in Heaven and on Earth.

May God's blessing be with you and your families.

Thank you.

Renewing the United Nations to Build Lasting Peace

Reverend Sun Myung Moon, Founder, Interreligious and International Federation for World Peace, August 18, 2000, The United Nations, New York

Distinguished leaders, honored guests, ladies and gentlemen:

Today, in this beautiful and solemn building where the United Nations General Assembly meets, I greet you with deep gratitude for the opportunity to express my passionate concerns and views about the future direction of the world and the United Nations.

The sole purpose of all my undertakings in many areas over the past forty years has been the realization of a peaceful world that is the desire of God and humanity. This longing for a peaceful world has also been the core reason I have dedicated myself to the promotion of interreligious harmony and cooperation.

In the twentieth century, humanity has experienced many severe conflicts and unspeakable acts of violence, especially through the horrors of the two world wars, and through the seventy years of the Cold War and communism. When the Cold War ended, the world had a brief moment of celebration, as if peace had arrived. But, then, very soon humanity realized that the end of the Cold War did not automatically mean the advent of an age of peace. Even at this moment, fierce wars and brutal massacres are going on in numerous places around the globe.

Conflicts arise for many reasons. But one of the primary factors contributing to their emergence is the deep-rooted disharmony that exists among the world's religions. Therefore, when we witness the many global tragedies occurring around us, we should recognize how critically important it is that the religions come together, dialogue with one another, and learn to embrace one another.

In the modern age, in most nations, religious ideals have come to hold a place wholly separate from the centers of secular political power, and most people have come to accept this reality as the way things ought to be. I believe, however, that it is time that international organizations whose purpose is to support the ideal of world peace reconsider their relationship with the great religious traditions of the world.

On this point, the United Nations, more than any other international organization, can set a good example and lead the way. The world has great expectations for the United Nations as an organization embodying humanity's aspiration for peace. In the United Nations, the representatives of all nations work in concert to promote peace and human prosperity.

Of course, the conscientious efforts to establish peace, undertaken by these national representatives at the United Nations, often meet stubborn resistance. The accomplishments and achievements attained through the United Nations have been significant. However, there is much room for improvement. I believe there is an urgent need today, within the United Nations and through its many activities, to encourage mutual respect and increased cooperation between the world's political and religious leaders.

The original ideal for human beings is that we live with our mind and body united in resonance with God's true love. It is because human beings resemble God as His sons and daughters that the mind and body of each individual can truly unite without struggling against each other. Within God there is no disharmony between internal and external characteristics. This is so because the absolute God has no contradiction or conflict within Himself.

The human ideal to achieve oneness of mind and body can be realized only when people completely possess God's true love. The biblical verse, "Blessed are the peacemakers, for they will be called children of God," illustrates this point. Peacemakers are persons whose mind and body are in unity centering on the true love of God.

As a result of the fall, human beings lost the standard by which our minds and bodies could be brought into oneness and harmony, and humanity has lived in internal strife and self-contradiction. The clashes of the mind and body within the individual have expanded and now manifest themselves in the family, society, nation and the world. For example, this unresolved struggle between mind and body is what precipitated the elder brother Cain's murder of his younger brother Abel.

All the conflicts and wars in history have been essentially battles between a Cain camp, relatively tending towards evil, and an Abel camp, relatively tending toward goodness. Humanity must end these struggles between Cain and Abel camps and restore the original state of harmony and love. To do this, each of us must end the conflict between our mind and body, and bring them into harmonious union.

The principle that mind and body must be united should be applied and practiced not only by individuals, but it should be applied on the worldwide level. For this purpose, I founded a number of organizations to achieve world peace. For example, I established a number of interreligious initiatives, such as the Inter-Religious Federation for World Peace, to promote cooperation among religions, which represent the internal world of the mind. Also, to address the external management of human affairs, representing the body, I have worked to promote harmony among nations through the activities of the Federation for World Peace, the Federation of Island Nations for World Peace, the Federation of Peninsula Nations for World Peace, and the Federation of Continental Nations for World Peace. Most recently, signifying the emergence of an era when mind and body, or religion and rational governance, can work together cooperatively, I founded the Interreligious and International Federation for World Peace.

At their root, human problems are not entirely social or political, and so social and political approaches will always be of limited effectiveness. Although secular authorities rule most human societies, religion lies at the heart of most national and cultural identities. In fact, religious faith and devotion have far greater importance in most peoples' hearts than do political loyalties.

The time has come for religion to renew itself and manifest true leadership in the world. People of faith should feel responsibility for the plight, suffering and injustices experienced by the world's peoples. Religious people have not been good examples in the practice of love and living for the sake of others, and for this reason should engage in deep self-reflection. It is time for religious people to repent for their preoccupation with individual salvation and narrow denominational interests. Such practices have prevented religious bodies from giving their utmost to the cause of world salvation. Our age more than any other demands that we go beyond our faiths, and the interests of particular religions, and put our love and ideals into practice for the sake of the world.

In particular, God calls upon us leaders, especially religious leaders, in hope that we will stand against the injustices and evils of the world, and bestow His true love upon the world. Hence, all people of faith must become one in heart in order to give full expression, both in words and actions, to God's passionate desire for humanity's restoration and peace.

World peace can be fully accomplished only when the wisdom and efforts of the world's religious leaders, who represent the internal concerns of the mind and conscience, work cooperatively and respectfully with national leaders who have much practical wisdom and worldly experience about the external reality or "body." In this light, it is time for us to give serious consideration even to the prospect of restructuring the United Nations. For example, perhaps it is possible to envision the United Nations as a bicameral institution.

The existing United Nations structure, composed of national representatives, may be regarded as a congress where the interests of each member nation are represented. However, I submit that serious consideration should be given to forming a religious assembly, or council of religious representatives within the structure of the United Nations. This assembly or council would consist of respected spiritual leaders in fields such as religion, culture and education. Of course, the members of this interreligious assembly will need to have demonstrated an ability to transcend the limited interests of individual nations and to speak for the concerns of the entire world and humanity at large.

The two chambers, working together in mutual respect and cooperation, will be able to make great advances in ushering in a world of peace. The wisdom and vision of great religious leaders will substantially supplement the political insight, experience and skill of the world's political leaders.

Even at this moment, more and more conflicts are breaking out across the world over disputed borders. As a result, the world is sustaining substantial loss of human life. In addition, the money poured into war-making and peacekeeping runs into the billions of dollars. So many resources and efforts are being wasted. Yet, comprehensive solutions have not been fully achieved with respect to any given conflict.

To solve this problem, I would like to make some proposals for your consideration:

Peace Zones

I propose today that the United Nations and religious leaders join their hearts and work to create peace zones in areas of conflict. Whether the disputed borders pass through rivers, mountains, fields or the sea, we can create buffer zones or peace zones along these borders.

These zones would be governed directly by the United Nations. People from around the world dedicated to the establishment of peace would be allowed to settle in these zones. The United Nations would be responsible to provide guidance to those living in these areas so that they come to embody the founding ideals of the United Nations and comply with its declarations for peace. These peace zones would be havens that exist for the sake of peace, prosperity and reconciliation. They would be free of racial and sexual discrimination, human rights violations and war. These areas would also be ecological and environmental havens for the entire natural world.

To create such zones of peace, freedom and ecological harmony, the concerned nations would have to be willing to provide the necessary land. This is not a simple matter, for there will be resistance to the surrender of land, even for a peace zone. I have dedicated much effort toward finding solutions to this problem, particularly as it applies to my native land, Korea.

I have taught that there is a providential significance to Korea's having been a victim of the Cold War. As you know, both the division of Korea and the war that followed are outgrowths of the Cold War. The Korean War, in which the youth of sixteen countries shed their blood under the United Nations flag to protect freedom, was a righteous war unprecedented in history. I remain ever grateful to the United Nations and those sixteen nations. And yet, the peaceful unification of Korea still remains to be accomplished. For this reason I have continually pondered about the United Nations' solemn mission for building a world of peace and how this relates to God's providence.

I sincerely hope that the current mood of reconciliation and cooperation between South and North Korea, which began last June, will continue. I hope the entire demilitarized zone along the 155-mile military demarcation line that crosses the Korean Peninsula can be turned into a peace zone under U.N. jurisdiction. I believe the United Nations will take the lead in this effort and build exhibition halls, museums, educational sites and peace parks in this zone in order to teach visitors important lessons regarding peace.

I am purchasing almost 1.2 million hectares of fertile land in South America's MERCOSUR countries to help compensate countries for any land they may lose as a result of the establishment of U.N. peace zones. I have already notified leaders of North and South Korea that I am prepared to turn over to them portions of that land in South America for their use.

As I make this proposal public, it is my fervent hope that world leaders of good will can understand this purpose and join with me. In particular, I hope that they will join me in willingly donating their land and money for use in creating U.N. supervised peace zones. These zones, under U.N. leadership, will give rise to ideal moral societies where nature and people live in harmony.

Already in December 1998, I proposed the founding of an International Peace Fund in an address I gave to religious leaders gathered for an international conference that had as its theme, *"Realizing the Interfaith Ideal: Beyond Dialogue into Practice."* All the leaders who participated in that conference resolved to initiate a movement in which the world's religious people would lead the way in making donations for world peace. I proposed that donations be given in amounts related to the number seven. Because various individuals and countries face differing economic realities, one person might find it difficult to give even seven dollars, whereas someone else might be able to give even $7 million. I believe that if all religious people on earth become one in heart, they will actively participate in this fundraising effort. The funds thus created would be used to establish peace zones and to teach the ideals of peace and the methods to achieve it. In addition to religious people, the United Nations too could encourage all nations and their peoples to make annual contributions to this fund. These funds might be donated under the name of the "White Cross Fund."

Wealthy philanthropists, business leaders and industrialists, and leaders in other fields, along with individuals, and organizations, would be encouraged to actively participate in the construction of U.N. peace zones. In this way, they could lead the way in creating an atmosphere of peace and in raising the necessary funds.

An Interreligious Council at the United Nations

Furthermore, one of the reasons I founded the Interreligious and International Federation of World Peace was to help create an interreligious assembly to serve as a senate or council within the United Nations. To implement this plan, I propose that each nation, in addition to its current ambassador, send a religious ambassador to the United Nations to serve as a member of the religious assembly, or U.N. senate.

The mission of the representatives to this U.N. senate would require that they have a genuinely ecumenical or interreligious consciousness and that they have the training and ability to teach a universal, transnational ideal of peace. The nature of their purpose and mission would prohibit their promoting the narrow interests of a particular country. Rather, they would carry out their duties for the ideal of peace in the world and for the sake of all humanity in accordance with God's Will.

The interreligious ambassador appointed as a member of the United Nations senate or council should have a global consciousness and take responsibility to represent the United Nations' global vision and agenda. In this sense, these persons could be thought of as global ambassadors from the United Nations. Wherever they go in the world, these ambassadors would promote movements dedicated to the realization of peace and social welfare. Moreover, in all nations, they would serve as conscientious guardians of lofty ideals such as justice, security and peace.

This will provide hope to the citizens of the world, and especially the youth. People will then have the opportunity to see with their own eyes the emergence of young people around the world seeking true love and lasting peace. Those selected as ecumenical and transnational ambassadors will also be able to help guide and supervise various U.N.-sponsored projects in health, education, welfare and other fields.

Commemorating Ideals of True Love,
True Parents and True Families

I have worked through many groups and organizations to educate people around the world about the meaning and value of true love and true families, transcending religious denominations and nationalities. By use of the term "true," I mean centered on God's original will and purpose. My continuous investment in this area and ongoing efforts for dialogue and reconciliation over the last decades have demonstrated beyond any doubt that the strongest foundation for the unity of humanity is the universal and essential love generated through the ideal of the true family.

Based on these considerations, I urge all the organizations connected to the United Nations to uphold and promote the ideals of true love and true families. For this reason, I would like to make another proposal, that the senior decision makers at the United Nations proclaim, in accordance with existing procedures and regulations, a special day to be commemorated worldwide. I understand that the United Nations has made proclamations such as the International Year of the Family, and that it has declared various ten-year objectives such as the "Decade to End Poverty." Along these lines, I propose that the United Nations establish an official commemorative day to uphold the ideal of the family, so that the world can remember and celebrate this day every year.

Specifically, I propose that True Parents' Day be established as a day of global celebration. I have already initiated such a day that has been signed into law by the United States Congress. Each year, in America, model parents and families from throughout the nation are honored. By celebrating such a day each year, transcending barriers of race, religion and cultural differences, and loving and cherishing each other, we will be able to fully experience our true and common human roots, and understand the preciousness of true families. This day will be a special day of truly global commemoration, and a beginning of the celebration of the oneness of the world as one global family, leading us beyond all confrontation and strife.

Respected world leaders, let us join our hands and hearts to improve our institutions and organizations so that the precious wisdom of religion, along with that of scholars, statesmen, and people of insight and knowledge, can be mobilized to solve the serious and urgent crises of the world.

I believe solutions to world problems can come about if we establish the proposed council composed of religious leaders, in cooperation with the political leaders and diplomats of the current United Nations. The Interreligious and International Federation for World Peace will promote this ideal, for religion can offer great service in providing guidance in matters concerning the Absolute Being, the world of transcendence, our eternal life and the spirit world. For this purpose, the IIFWP will make devoted and sacrificial efforts to attain the goal of world peace. It will strive to establish the Kingdom of Heaven of eternal love and harmony, and the fatherland of God, where the United Nations' efforts for peace are honored, and where all humanity forms one universal family as brothers and sisters under God, the Parent.

I believe that the world leaders and officers of the United Nations, who possess knowledge, experience and wisdom, can offer many recommendations for implementing the proposals I've presented to you today. If we work together and make continuous efforts, peace and happiness will surely be realized on Earth.

I pray that God's blessing be with your families and your endeavors. Thank you.

Breaking Down Boundaries and Practicing True Love

Reverend Dr. Sun Myung Moon, Founder, Interreligious and International Foundation for World Peace, August 18, 2000, The United Nations, New York

Honorable and distinguished guests, ladies and gentlemen!

I would like to express my heartfelt appreciation for the Universal Peace Award my wife and I have received here at the United Nations, this historical landmark of world peace. Let me use this opportunity to speak briefly on the theme, "Breaking Down Boundaries and Practicing True Love."

Ladies and gentlemen, if we could break down all the boundaries in this world, world peace would come necessarily. But the thing we have to remember is that God is not the lord of boundaries. Satan, the Devil, first made them. Satan and his followers are dwelling wherever there are boundaries. Satan sits on the boundary between Oriental and Western civilizations, for example.

No Concept of Boundaries in God

God did not create boundaries among the various different cultures, traditions, races, etc. God desires one unified world, a world without boundaries.

God does not have even the concept of boundaries. Therefore, He does not tell us to take revenge on our enemies; if He did, it would imply that He had such a concept. By loving our enemies and bringing oneness among us, boundaries will naturally come down.

Thus, God's strategy and tactic is to have us love our enemies. That is a great strategy. It is unfortunate that throughout all human history until the present, people have not understood the value of the words, "Love your enemies." Unification Church members, as representatives of human history, have come to understand this strategy and are practicing it in reality. By exemplifying these words, they have become leading lights who can bring peace to the world.

What do you think? When our hearts are not happy, when our bodies are not comfortable, when we are dissatisfied with our actions, when we speak angry words, don't these create boundaries? Therefore, unless we unite our mind and body through the five senses, all kinds of boundaries will come into existence. For this reason, we need to reflect upon how many boundaries we are living with in our daily life.

When we say, "Go beyond having enemies. Stop building boundaries," some might think we should pull out our eyes. Actually, there are two kinds of eyes. If without differentiating

---

231

evil from goodness, our eyes welcome anything we see simply as good, then enormous boundaries will be built. The same is the case with hearing. If we rejoice over hearing the words of goodness or truth and at the same time listen to all the evil words of this world and support them, then boundaries will be built also in our ears.

Members of the Unification Church are not prohibited from singing popular secular songs, while some Christian denominations have rules against it. The question is not whether we sing popular songs or classical songs, but rather how we can digest the lyrics of those songs. Does singing the song create a boundary, or does it break down a boundary? If by singing a certain song or by speaking rough language a person is able to break down a boundary and thereby create a wider and less restricted world, certainly that will please God.

In sum, wherever we live with boundaries, whether through our senses or in our environment, we belong to Satan's side. On the other hand, if we can live without boundaries anywhere, we stand on God's side. Satan is the champion at building boundaries. On the other hand, God is the master of breaking down boundaries. God, the King of kings, does not like boundaries at all. He hates boundaries the most.

The Task of Removing Boundaries

Ladies and gentlemen, look at Korea. Do you think God appreciates a Korean who says that the 38th parallel that divides the peninsula is a good thing? Of course not! Hence, if someone works hard to remove it, that person will become God's favorite champion. If all seventy million Koreans have the determination to die for the cause of removing the 38th parallel, then the reunification of North and South Korea will come without doubt. That task, however, will never be easy. We must understand that those who want the 38th parallel to continue to exist in the Korean peninsula are on the side of Satan, the Devil. Satan is the master of the 38th parallel, and God is the master of whatever efforts are being made to remove it. That is why Unification Church members have been leading the movement to tear down the 38th parallel.

Ladies and gentlemen, when the day comes that people everywhere want their children to marry their enemies, desiring to have sons- and daughters-in-law from among their enemies, the entire world will be automatically united. This is the gift that I would like to offer to you tonight. Where boundaries exist, certainly Satan and his followers reside; but God and His people, born of His lineage, dwell where love and harmony abound, without boundaries.

Today, Unification Church members are very much interested in developing the leisure industry, which encourages people to travel all over the world and live anywhere in the world that they desire. This foresees a future international federation based on the United Nations, established someday in whatever location and name. When it is established, we should all come together under the name of this international federation. For this purpose, Rev. Moon suggested to Unification Church members that they gather a special fund, called the Total Living Offering Fund. In the future, we will use this fund to facilitate the development of this international federation of the United Nations.

In the Old Testament, animals representing all of creation were sacrificed on behalf of humans. They were divided into two, which represented two parties struggling against each other, the right side in the position of God and the left side in the position of Satan. However, as a result of the failures of some of the central figures in the Old Testament Age, God and Satan came to struggle over Jesus—who, as the Son of God, had a value far above that of the creation. As a result, when Jesus, the eldest Son of God, came to earth, he shed his blood, with his body taken by Satan and his spirit belonging to God. Because Jesus must yet recover his physical body, he proclaimed that he would return.

Ever since Jesus, the Son of God, was divided into the two realms, problems likewise have continued to plague the spirit world and the physical world. Further, men and women were divided, and the mind and the body were divided, remaining in continual conflict and struggle. Therefore, Jesus, who went to the spirit world to restore God's dominion over that world, must still return to earth in order to restore God's ownership of the physical world and bring oneness between the two worlds. What, then, would he do when he returns to earth? He would marry and establish his own family. Nevertheless, Satan took Jesus' body and the physical world with it, while God could claim the spirit world as His.

In the spirit world, Jesus has been toiling for two thousand years to bring the hearts of people on earth to one direction and lead God's dispensation centered on Christianity. However, Christianity also divided into two: Catholicism and Protestantism. They became enemies to each other and fought each other just as Cain, the elder son, had fought his younger brother Abel. Thus human history has developed, constantly creating more boundaries, multiplying struggles. We, therefore, have to liberate ourselves from this attitude of erecting boundaries and struggles.

Breaking Down Boundaries through Marriage

And so when the Lord returns, he will unify the heavenly world. Then, to bring oneness between heaven and earth, he will conduct many marriage ceremonies, bringing together men and women from tribes and nations that have been divided for thousands of years. He will conduct this providence centered on the Unification realm, which is in the same position as the chosen people of Israel in Jesus' day. This is the very Marriage of the Lamb prophesied in the Bible.

There was a wonderful opportunity immediately after World War II when heaven and earth could have been united centered on Christianity. At that time the Christian cultural sphere was united and leading the world. With Jesus playing the leading role in the spirit world, a united Christian cultural sphere was prevailing all over the earth. That would have been a perfect chance for Jesus and the Holy Spirit to come to the earth and substantially marry as husband and wife. They could have started laying the foundation to resolve all of the existing problems resulting from the separation and division between mind and body and between man and woman, and built the veritable Kingdom of Peace on earth.

I am not talking about something vague and unclear. Who should have married first from the perspective of God's ideal of creation? It was Adam and Eve. But due to their fall, they created the first human boundary—and the source of all subsequent boundaries. Now, in order to break down that barrier, all men and women should be restored to the state prior to the fall and then should marry. Then, not only our ancestors, but God also, will rejoice with dancing. When such a world arrives, it will be the Kingdom of Heaven on earth.

However, such a day has never existed in human history. Instead, people have been grieving and struggling in pain, entangled by countless boundaries. Accordingly, the starting-point of peace in the world requires that humankind find the way to break down this primary boundary. Yet the people of the world have not understood. This is why Rev. and Mrs. Moon have come into this world in the position of True Parents, giving God's Blessing to the men and women of the world and showing the world, for the first time in human history, the way to resolve the most fundamental human problems.

Knowing God

Even if there are a million boundaries, I am certain I can break them down. How can I do it? True love is what makes it possible. To get rid of these barriers, we have to know true love as God knows true love, otherwise we cannot do it. This means that we must know God one hundred percent.

Ladies and gentlemen, the spirit world consists of heaven and hell: heaven is likened to a world of daylight, and hell can be likened to the nighttime. But someone who is unable to tell the difference between day and night, how can he possibly take control of the boundary between the realms of heaven and hell? It is impossible. Only a person who knows them in reality can have dominion over the two worlds. That person can eliminate the darkness, because he clearly knows the substance of hell.

God, who is omnipotent and omniscient, can eliminate the darkness. But first we must know God. Can you say that you know God? How well do you know Him? Is it your understanding that God is pleased with wealth, power or knowledge? Such a God could never bring liberation to humanity. You must fully know God in order to expel Satan completely and resolve the fundamental problems of this world. Moreover, even if you fully know God, do you also know what it is about God that is useful in bringing down all the boundaries erected over thousands of years? This is the important thing.

God is the master of the universe. Then shouldn't there be an environment where God can dwell—a neighborhood and a nation where God can dwell? In order for us to know God, we must restore His nation as a realm that is objective to His governance. Still, the earthly environment remains blocked by numerous boundaries. By taking them down, we should build a world with which God can be happy. Wouldn't all creation like to be governed by God? Indeed, all creation is anxious to be liberated from its groaning—from pain and persecution caused by the control of Satan, and from the many borders that divide it.

Ladies and gentlemen, more than anything else, we need to understand God clearly, and we need to understand clearly the way to build the Kingdom of God. Then, wherever we go, and in whatever situation we are in, we will automatically receive answers about how to deal with difficulties among the world's diverse cultures and traditions.

Surely, God exists in heaven. However, today's world is blocked by countless boundaries. How did this happen? It happened because there are hardly any people who know God, His Kingdom, and the tradition in His Kingdom. Once people clearly know these, liberation will take place in both the spirit world and physical world. We will even be able to call out, "Hey, Satan!" and he will obey. Then we will come to know the way to live in unity with God's heart and with His Kingdom, in a culture with heavenly tradition and values.

Live for the Sake of Others

People who know God are the ones who live with love for the sake of others. Therefore, instead of seeking love for our own sake, we should seek to love others for their sakes, making them masters of love and letting them dance with love. Thus, we can become God's heirs, people who know God and beautify and protect His Kingdom. Satan will have no way to interfere with the heirs of God.

If you love your enemies, transcending anger and hatred even in situations where they kill the ones you love, you will come to have dominion over the world of enemies, and Satan will retreat. Eventually, the world of your enemies will show respect to you. If you live for the sake of others to the extent that you love your neighbors more than your own parents, then Satan will run away. Whatever you have given, God will reward you thousands of times more.

Again, what is the secret of knowing God, His Kingdom and His thought, which will enable us to chase out Satan from everywhere? It is to live for the sake of others, die for the sake of others and practice love for the sake of others. When we do that, Satan will certainly run away. And he will not just run away without doing anything. Before he leaves, he will break down all the boundaries that he had erected around us.

What will happen next? Once Satan is gone, the people who had been headed for hell will all be able to rise up and enter heaven, by practicing these principles of eternal life. Eternal life will finally become a reality. People who call on God, the Source of love, as their Father will earnestly desire to practice God's tradition of living for others and will continue to do so for tens of thousands of years. This is how individuals can become the people of eternal life, practicing the tradition of eternal life and endowed with God's eternal lineage.

Eternal life is essentially an attribute of love. Even God, when He created the universe, adhered to the standards of absolute faith, absolute love and absolute obedience. God lives this way, always desiring to invest more love for the world, even though everything in the world is transient. For this reason, there is no being that cannot help but attend Him as the absolute, unique, unchanging and eternal Lord.

We humans, created as God's children, should likewise be able to completely invest our own love absolutely and eternally. If we do so, then the Kingdom of God will become our kingdom, and God will belong to us.

In short, our life-style should be the same as that of God, the Master of the heavenly tradition. Then we shall surely become God's sons and daughters, and eternal life and immortality will necessarily be ours. That is why the Bible verse, "For whoever wants to save his life will lose it, but whoever loses his life for me will find it," is so true, although it may sound paradoxical.

God's Unrealized Love

Ladies and gentlemen, God is great, but has He ever really become the Lord of love?

True love is something you cannot experience alone. You cannot create love by yourself. For a man to experience love, he absolutely needs a woman. Having a woman whom he can love is the necessary qualification for the man to be the subject partner of love. This is a surprising fact. No matter how great a man he may be, without a woman, his situation is like that of a widower. What does it mean to be a widower? A widower is a father who lives alone. It is a pitiful life. Living alone, a widower cannot accomplish true love, no matter how rich or famous he may be.

God has true love, true life and true lineage. He also has true conscience—a mind that is even, not bumpy. It may seem that God has everything. Yet without a partner of love, how would He express all His values? By Himself He cannot express them, not for eternity.

Why is that so? A man is only half a person. No matter how great he may be—even a prime minister or a president—and no matter how big he may talk, as a man he cannot escape from being only half a person. Likewise, a woman is only half a person.

Why is a man only half a person? He has the convex part, but not the concave. For complete love, both the concave and the convex are necessary. A woman is the other half who supplies the concave, which a man does not have. Thus, a man accomplishes perfect true love only with a woman.

The Fall and Our Loss of God's Lineage

We understand that at the fall of the first human ancestors, their bodies and minds could not unite with the lineage of God, but instead formed a connection with the lineage of Satan. As a result, God could not see His grandchildren, who should have become His third generation. Through the providence of salvation, God has sought after His third generation and tried to connect them with His lineage.

God's sons and daughters who multiplied over the earth were supposed to become, without fail, the good seeds that God and Adam wanted. Wherever they were sown, they were supposed to be the children of original creation who would be breast-fed by their parents and who would follow them instinctively to enter the Kingdom of Heaven. But due to the fall, the lineage of Satan came to slither about within our bodies. Therefore, we should be ready to die, to cut our vein and bleed out our blood ten or twelve times over, if that is what it takes to be reborn.

It is an unalterable fact that our lineage is contaminated. This is a serious matter. Did you ever realize that your body was in such a state? Think about it! It is frightening that the blood of your enemy envelops your bones and courses through your flesh, as it has done for hundreds of millions of generations. It is alarming that you have not recognized how miserable is the condition of your self, in which your body dominates and tramples your mind.

The fall can be likened to connecting with a line running east-west when we should have connected with the line running north-south. Being so, our problem is how to correctly reconnect with the north-south line instead of continuing to mistakenly connect with the east-west line. The way of cure by disconnecting and re-connecting is the Blessing of the Unification Church, namely, the International Marriage Blessing, which reconnects us with the original lineage.

If in the beginning Adam and Eve had not fallen, they definitely would have become our external parents, bequeathing to us the lineage of God's love. United with Heavenly Father as our internal Parent, and sharing God's absolute true love, Adam and Eve would have become the spiritual and physical ancestors of humankind. The moment when they would have stood at the central focal point, able to unite with that love, was to have been their wedding day. Experiencing their first love on their first night together, they would have become one body centering on God.

But due to the fall, all that was lost. God wanted to sow conjugal love into humankind from His standpoint, but He could not get hold of a place to do so. Instead, God became a God of failure.

Can God love by Himself? Even a beautiful and talented woman needs a man, and even an ugly man can fulfill her need. A woman has love, life, lineage and conscience in her mind, but until a counterpart in the shape of a man appears they are not set in motion. Love is not activated. A life of loving is not activated. Lineage is not developed. Conscience is not objectified. Likewise for a man, only through the appearance of an object partner, namely, a woman, are his love, life and lineage all actualized.

If Adam and Eve had waited until age 18, they would have received God's blessing and authorization to become husband and wife and the true ancestors of humankind. But they fell at 16 by playing with love as children play with fire.

Ladies and gentlemen, is anyone born as a woman because she desired to be born that way? Is anyone born as a man because he desired to be so? Many men are arrogant and boastful, disregarding and belittling women. Such men cannot avoid going to hell.

Preparing a Place for the Lord of Love

Ladies and gentlemen, do you know why God became a miserable God? God is the great King of true love, but He lost the position where he could love as he truly wanted to love—by dwelling as one body with the first human ancestors. God can be compared to a widow or a widower, alone by Himself and unable to feel the true love He adores. Having lost the object partner of His heart's true love, God became a sorrowful God.

By becoming object partners in God's family, Adam and Eve were supposed to establish the seat for the Lord of true love, and thus to liberate God. They could not fulfill this responsibility; nevertheless, their lifelong desire was to let God occupy the seat of the Lord of true love.

Therefore, the first condition to receive the Blessing of the Unification Church is to live the tradition of truly loving in the position of God's bride and bridegroom. Although that tradition was lost, the true, unchanging love of God remains. As long as we as husbands and wives never ever deny that love for all eternity, we will definitely be joined to the lineage of God's sons and daughters.

Who will prepare the seat for the Lord of true love, the place where God establishes His lineal relationship and can truly love a man and a woman? Only that man and that woman can do it. In other words, Adam and Eve must restore through indemnity the position of counterparts to the Lord of true love by becoming God's bride and bridegroom.

Out of the divine polarity God gave birth to a son and daughter; they were born from these dual aspects of His nature. We have to know, therefore, that the son and daughter have equal value.

Restoring God's Third Generation

As a husband and wife with equal value, we can restore the true love of husband and wife that God desired. Also, because God could not love babies in the womb, we through our babies born in our family can restore for God the position of the Lord of true love for sons and daughters, which He could not enjoy. From this point, we can restore for God the

Lordship of siblings, the Lordship of adolescents, the Lordship of husband and wife and the Lordship of parents. In this way, our children can become God's long-sought grandchildren.

God is the first generation, and Adam and Eve constituted the second generation. But God's grandchildren, the third generation, were taken away by the Devil. When we deal with all this through our sons and daughters, we can restore through indemnity the position of the Lord of true love on behalf of God. At that point, God recognizes you as the second original parents, standing in the position to possess the love that was meant for Adam and Eve.

Only after thus passing through three generations can God as the Grandfather and we as parents truly love God's grandchildren and raise them as the perfect seed for tens of thousands of generations of their descendants. When grandchildren receive true love from the first two generations together, the grandfather is the representative of the spirit world and Adam as the second generation is the representative of the kingship in the physical world. The lineage of true love substantiates the two worlds in this way.

Grandchildren who are born into this lineage will have the value of the fruits of the Kingdom of Heaven in the future, representing both the spirit world and earthly kingship. This will be the third generation that is qualified to rule the Kingdom of Heaven on earth. From that generation onward, the fruits of the Kingdom will spread outward. Thenceforth, children will grow to mature character and true love only by their parents' instruction, without the need for religion. They will all become fit for Heaven. All people will realize the original model of the eight stages of true love, fulfilling God's ideal of creation.

When we restore this, we will become a unified tribe transcending the twelve pearly gates of spirit world and all the barriers in the physical world. This will open the gate to the liberated world of heaven and earth, the unified palace of the Kingdom of Heaven on earth and in heaven.

Eight Stages of True Love

There are eight stages of true love: in the womb, infancy, childhood, adolescence, marriage, parent, grandparent, and king or queen. Until today, God could not have a firm foundation of tradition to substantiate these eight stages of love on the earth. God could not become the Lord of true love of these eight stages. They remained entirely vacant. How, then, can we solve God's shame and resentment? The True Parents fill the emptiness of the eight stages and perfect them by uncovering and teaching all the secrets of the satanic world and the Kingdom of Heaven. They reveal this gate of lineage—the only way humankind can go to the Kingdom of Heaven. Every man is supposed to become a perfected Adam; every woman a perfected Eve. If God is her Lord of true love while she is in the womb and as an infant, and if she makes God her Lord of true love as a child, an adolescent, in her marriage, and through the stages of mother, grandmother, and queen as well, she will possess the real partnership of true love and perfect herself.

A family on earth, with its visible relationships, is only half a family. To become whole it must unite with God's invisible partnership. This means establishing unity of spirit and body. Such families will inherit the lineage and the tradition of true love. When our families do this, we will automatically participate in the unified realm of heaven and earth, and we cannot help but become heavenly people and a heavenly family. This means that we will enjoy the freedom of God's sons and daughters and become lords in the Kingdom of Heaven.

Becoming Citizens of the Kingdom of Heaven

Every person, man and woman, is the external substantiation of God and God's beloved partner. The invisible internal God and we His visible external substantiations have been waiting for this re-connection of lineage. This work is to be accomplished centered on mothers and wives. Once we are connected to God's lineage, we should live being proud that we are external substantiations of God.

The wife plays a key role in connecting her family to this lineage and tradition. The children also play a role. Ultimately, tribes and nations, even the whole cosmos, should be connected to God's lineage. Lineage is so important.

Why do we marry? It is so that a man who is half a person, and a woman who is the other half, may meet each other to become a couple experiencing perfect true love. God doesn't want to dwell with only a half. When a man and a woman meet each other to become perfectly one, God too unites His internal character and external form in a relationship of true love, establishing the vertical tradition of true love.

We have to respect our ancestors. We have to truly love people. We have to build unity by establishing true leadership. A king who lives well while ignoring his people is a swindler and heir of the Devil. He is making boundaries.

Today, humanity must undergo an internal revolution. We have to receive the heavenly fortune of true love from Heaven, establish it in the family, and let God stand as the absolute Lord of true love. Through this great revolution we, as resultant beings, come to serve and follow God, our cause, with absolute faith, absolute love and absolute obedience. Only this way can we attain a state of perfection, with no boundaries. Whenever a being deviates from this ideal, an opposing subject appears and a destructive barrier is raised.

From now, therefore, you should not gamble by creating boundaries in your path of love. Any woman who thinks, "My husband should love me. My children should love only me and should not love their father," etc., should give up that attitude. A woman has to embrace her children and receive the love of their father. If she raises her children together with her husband and returns her love for his love, she belongs to God.

Because of a woman, the gate of love to God's eight stages was destroyed. Hence, women have to show their utmost devotion to recreate their husbands and sons and daughters, perfecting in front of God the position of the Lord of true love of His eight stages in their blessed families.

Having elevated our families in this way, we can go on to prepare the kingship of true love in which we can love and thrive from the individual level to the family, tribal, national, worldwide and cosmic levels. Then we will be free to travel anywhere, even through the gate of the Kingdom of Heaven on earth and the twelve gates of the Kingdom of Heaven in the spirit world. We have to know clearly that unless we become qualified sons and daughters in the lineage of God, we cannot become the citizens of the Kingdom of Heaven in heaven and on earth. I cannot emphasize this too much. It is the key to removing boundaries.

The task of removing boundaries includes the lowering of national boundaries through the work of the United Nations, getting rid of religious boundaries, tearing down ethnic and racial boundaries, and ultimately destroying the boundary between heaven and hell. Yet, since all these boundaries stem ultimately from Adam and Eve, the false parents, no one other than True Parents can break them down. God alone cannot do it, and certainly Satan cannot do it—he is the one who has been creating them. Who can stop the conflict between God and Satan? Only True Parents can resolve that war, since the false parents started it.

Ladies and gentlemen, I hope you will leave this place this evening with determination to go out and destroy every boundary, bringing this message of liberation to all humankind.

Thank you very much.